D0710866

THE
GAMESMAN

MICHAEL MACCOBY

BANTAM BOOKS · LONDON · TORONTO · NEW YORK

THE GAMESMAN

*A Bantam Book / published by arrangement with
Simon and Schuster, Inc.*

PRINTING HISTORY

Simon and Schuster edition published November 1976

2nd printing ...... January 1977	5th printing .... March 1977
3rd printing ...... January 1977	6th printing .... April 1977
4th printing ...... February 1977	7th printing .... April 1977

Literary Guild edition published January 1977
Book-of-the-Month Club edition published July 1977
Fortune Book Club edition published July 1977
Bantam edition / February 1978
2nd printing
3rd printing

Bantam Books are published by Bantam Books, Inc. Its trademark, consisting of the words "Bantam Books" and the portrayal of a bantam, is registered in the United States Patent Office and in other countries. Marca Registrada. Bantam Books, Inc., 666 Fifth Avenue, New York, New York 10019.

PRINTED IN THE UNITED STATES OF AMERICA

ACKNOWLEDGMENTS

THIS STUDY was initiated in 1969 on my return to the U.S. after eight years in Mexico. There I had completed psychoanalytic training under Erich Fromm at the Mexican Institute of Psychoanalysis, and with him studied the work and character of villagers, in the process learning his theory and methods of socio-psychoanalytic research.* The village study also provided a perspective on how new technology has changed a culture and the character types most adaptive to it. In rural Mexico, the products and methods created by American corporations—farm machineries, chemicals, marketing techniques, TV—were undermining the traditional conservative society run by small landholders and propelling new entrepreneurs with a different social agenda into positions of leadership. In Mexico City, my clinical practice provided another perspective: the attitudes and dreams of a whole society were being transformed by the products and work methods created in American corporations.

Back in the U.S., I talked about my experiences with Professor David Riesman, who had first introduced me to the study of work and character at the University of Chicago in 1955–56, when I was his apprentice at teaching. In 1960, at Harvard, we had co-authored a paper which suggested that the organization of work was essential to developing a more idealistic national policy.† Riesman was enthusiastic about my idea of

---

*Erich Fromm and Michael Maccoby, *Social Character in a Mexican Village* (Englewood Cliffs, N.J.: Prentice-Hall, 1970).
†David Riesman and Michael Maccoby, "The American

studying the people who create new technology in leading corporations, and recommended me to Emmanuel Mesthene, then Director of the Harvard Program on Technology and Society, who agreed to fund a study of work and character in high-technology corporations. After 1972, the Project on Technology, Work, and Character was sponsored by the Seminar on Science, Technology, and Public Policy under the direction of Professor Harvey Brooks, then Dean of the School of Engineering and Applied Physics, and Professor Don Price, Dean of the Kennedy School of Government. (The project was also aided by a fellowship to the Center for Advanced Study in the Behavioral Sciences and a grant from the Andrew W. Mellon Foundation, and I am grateful to Dr. Nathan M. Pusey for his sympathetic support.) Under the auspices of the seminar and with the help and encouragement of Professor Brooks, the Project on Technology, Work, and Character has developed from its beginnings as an academic study to its present role of also initiating practical experiments to change work. The Bolivar Project mentioned in Chapter 9 has been supported by the National Commission on Productivity, The Ford Foundation, Harman International Industries, the United Automobile Workers International, the Sloan Foundation, the W. E. Upjohn Institute, EDA, and the National Center for the Quality of Working Life. Robert and Margaret M. Duckles have been the project members working on-site.

After the first stage of interviewing, a group of students helped with interviewing and took part in a weekly seminar at the Institute for Policy Studies in Washington, D.C., to discuss the findings. Dr. Douglass Carmichael and Dr. Rolando Weissmann, both students of psychoanalysis and social research, were the first to join me in traveling to corporations in dif-

---

Crisis: Political Idealism and the Cold War," *Commentary*, Vol. 29, No. 6, June, 1960, pp. 461–472; reprinted in *The Liberal Papers*, James Roosevelt, ed. (New York: Quadrangle Books and Doubleday Anchor Books, 1962).

ferent parts of the country. They contributed valuable observations and insights as participant observers and interviewers and I am grateful for their help. Dr. Carmichael contributed especially to understanding work relations in laboratories where small instruments were developed, since his background in both psychology and physics equipped him to educate the rest of us about technology. Later, Mac Greene made valuable contributions in a number of areas, including interviewing. His perceptive and lively notes on a project meeting are reported in Chapter 6. He also took charge of compiling the survey-type data and preparing the tables, helped by Jerry Hellman and Dave Lipsey, then students at New College. Kathy Terzi and Cynthia Elliott also participated and made significant contributions to the project by interviewing wives, children, secretaries of executives, and a group of women engineers and managers. Ms. Elliott helped especially in the analyses of managers' family relations, and I am grateful to her and Kathy Terzi for preparing the manuscript of this book and in the process suggesting that I clarify many points. During a two-year period, Dr. Alejandro Córdova joined the seminar, and for a time, Dr. Hilda Díaz, Jody Palmour, Edith Kropp, and Tony Wagner also participated. From time to time, Dr. Ignacio Millán, who was directing a parallel study of Mexican corporate managers, met with us, and I am grateful to him for permission to quote some of his material.

I am grateful to Erich Fromm and David Riesman for their encouragement and clarifying comments starting at the beginning of the project; to Ivan Illich for conversations about technology and society; to Richard Barnet, who shared his insights on corporations; to Marcus Raskin for helpful advice about organizing the project; to Sandylee Maccoby, who contributed valuable criticisms and support throughout the project; to Steve Roday and Mike Wolff for their help; and to Alice Mayhew, who in the final stages provided very helpful editorial criticism.

I am grateful to all those who have helped, and especially to the many executives, managers, and engineers we interviewed. Without their participation and interest, the study would not have been possible, and I hope this book will be helpful to them.

Contents

Introduction

THIS BOOK IS a study based on interviews with 250 managers from twelve major companies in different parts of the country. I started out with the point of view that any strategy for social change must take account of these people whose work so influences the quality of work and life for others throughout the world. What mix of motives—ambition, greed, fascination with technology, scientific interest, security-seeking, or idealism—determined their actions? What was the quality of their own lives? Were they concerned about the human effects of what they produced? Were they moved to do anything about pollution, war, militarism, bureaucracy, and poverty? How would they respond to pressures to set limits on industry and create democratic organizations?

In a way, the companies I studied most extensively selected themselves. In 1969, my entry into the first corporation resulted from a talk I gave on "fear and war versus love between the sexes" to a couples' study group that met regularly to discuss religious and social issues. Among the group members I met that evening was a manager at "Rutherford Instruments," a fictitious name for a large multinational company specializing in electronics. I described the idea of studying corporate managers to him, to discover how their emotional attitudes influenced their work and how the work itself molded their outlook and motives. Did he think the managers at RI would be interested? He thought many managers would probably want to participate but he was too low in the hierarchy to invite me in. He offered to raise the question with his own manager, who, in turn, was intrigued enough to introduce me to the corporate vice-president for industrial relations. (No one below corporate vice-president or division president ever took responsibility for letting me interview.) The vice-president was an old-timer who had started with the company when there were fewer than one hundred employees; now there are more than thirty thousand. The study interested him, but a divisional president would have to give permission and allot time for interviewing and he sent me to talk with the one he thought the brightest.

This executive and I were the same age, thirty-seven, and we liked each other. The project gave him a chance to test his intuitions about what motivated good managers. He said he hadn't learned much from the psychologists who had given questionnaires at RI, but a psychoanalyst might have more to offer. Since understanding people was the core of his work, he would help me if it also helped him and others to learn about themselves. He then proceeded to test me by letting me start by studying him. As we began, it became apparent that I knew little about corporations, marketing, development projects, etc., so I didn't know what questions to ask about the complex work. He and a few of his top managers agreed to help me design a questionnaire, and they suggested questions I should ask. For example: Did the individual's work involve creating an organizational and motivational climate? What were the criteria by which his work was evaluated? Which of those criteria were more important to him? They helped me design checklists of traits important to work (e.g., cooperativeness, satisfaction in power over others, coolness under stress).

They also described the industry and differences in managerial philosophies in different companies, and the divisional president introduced me to other top executives inside and outside RI.

The managers at RI maintained that I'd find all other companies less humanistic and less concerned with the individual. The divisional president believed that the typical RI manager was an individualist, an entrepreneur who could leave any time he felt like starting his own business. In fact, he wanted to believe that he was independent and didn't need the company. When we tried to track down those managers who had left to start their own businesses, there were no more than four or five and some of these had ended up in other large companies. But if RI was really so different, it seemed worthwhile that I tour the country and visit the leading companies in advanced technology, including some in chemicals and plastics as well as in electronics. Only that way could general conclusions be drawn about the kinds of people who manage large high-technology corporations. In all, I interviewed managers at twelve major companies, first by myself and later with the help of students.*

When the interviewing was about ended, a friend invited me to Bohemian Grove, a summer encampment north of San Francisco where corporate presidents meet Cabinet secretaries, senators, generals, university presidents, and a few movie stars. He believed a weekend there would supplement my experience of top executives at work and at home, showing them at play with the ruling elite. He thought I was seeing these executives only where they were trying to make good impressions, and that I would find they said what they really believed after they'd had a few drinks. And in fact, the chief executive officer of Rutherford Instruments and some of the others I'd met were at Bohemian Grove when I was.

It was a totally male society (even the meals were served by men) and the adolescent *macho* quality was emphasized by the fact that you were encouraged to urinate against the nearest redwood. Every

---

*In 1970, Dr. Douglass Carmichael and Dr. Rolando Weissmann joined the project, and a year later Mac Greene, Katherine Terzi, and Cynthia Elliott also took part in the interviewing and the case seminars.

year a play is put on in which men take women's roles. The play I saw was full of antifeminine digs and humor that expressed the executive's estrangement from home and family. Example: The president of "Amalgamated Consolidated, Incorporated" calls in his son, who has done poorly as vice-president for public relations. The president tells him he is no good. "I'm glad," he says, "that your mother isn't alive to see your failure." "But, Dad," the son answers, "she is alive; I saw her this morning." "Is that so?" says the president. "Well, I can't be expected to know every little thing that happens around here." Loud laughter.

All this may be a hangover from a vanishing society. My impression was that some executives were discomfited, even embarrassed, by the mildly *macho* antics, and were more interested in meeting one another and relaxing. It would surprise me if the locker-room culture of Bohemian Grove holds out long against the impact of the women's movement. What seemed more significant was the presence of Federal and military officials, mostly to influence the business executives, informally and through daily lakeside talks. An astronaut and a Pentagon scientist gave show-and-tell accounts of the space adventure, of the new knowledge and technology developed therefrom, and its importance for national prestige and military R & D. On another day, a top State Department official reported on the U.S. South Pacific Trust, describing the growing discontent of the Micronesian islanders who want independence. "If we examine our effects on the island culture, we see they have a real case," the official admitted. "Before the U.S. arrived, the natives were self-sufficient, picked their food off the trees or fished. Now, since we have them hooked on consumer goods, they'd starve without a can opener. Some of the radical independence leaders want to reverse this and develop the old self-sufficiency. We can't blame them. However, we can't leave. We need our military bases there. We have no choice. As some of my friends in Washington say, you've got to grab them by the balls, their minds and hearts will follow."

The message to the business executives was to rally 'round the flag, for glory and national security. But the president of RI later complained to me that State and Defense were too ideological and kept him from developing a healthy trade with China and Eastern Europe. And if U.S. industry didn't sell them the technology, we would lose out to the Japanese or the Germans.

After surveying corporations in all parts of the country, we concentrated on two multinational giants, RI and a company called "Business Data Corporation" (BDC), interviewing a large sample of managers and in a few cases their wives and children. Although company principles make some differences in corporate cultures, the similarities appeared to outweigh the differences. Besides studying a few people at many companies, we needed a sample of people at different levels of the same company in order to understand relationships between character type and work roles: Do some types of people stay at a certain level and fail if they rise higher? What type of person reaches the top?

RI and BDC are among the most dynamic and successful billion-dollar-a-year multinational corporations. Both have grown rapidly during the past twenty-five years. Although BDC is larger than RI (more than two hundred thousand employees to RI's thirty thousand), its management philosophy is similar to RI's. To the readers of *Fortune, Business Week,* and *The Wall Street Journal,* both are considered models of excellence in terms of management, the products they produce, and the value of their stock. The two companies compete with each other in some markets, but each company concentrates in a different product area, where it is considered the class of its field. Both practice (and have invented) managerial techniques and business strategies that others copy. Top managers from both companies speak out on major issues, are known publicly, and have held high government positions.

The reason for selecting these elite companies was the idea that by concentrating on the best, I would be studying not only the models for other companies, but also examining the attractions and the strengths as well as the limits of the American industrial system at its best. It is easy to describe the human problems caused by large aerospace companies that periodically lay off hundreds of employees, companies in which even engineers and managers suffer the insecurity and powerlessness of production workers. Someone can always say that these are the poorly managed or "immature" companies, that they should improve their management or be nationalized. It is common practice for muckrakers to report on the worst corporate examples, leaving the impression that these companies characterize the whole system. My strategy was to concentrate on companies no one has accused of trying to overthrow governments or of bribing officials or of begging the Federal Government to bail them out of their mistakes. Given the present view of things, one might say that they represent the ideal future from a corporate point of view, the cutting edge of excellence.

The managers we studied are not the victims of the system, but its beneficiaries, the most admired individuals within the best companies, the models for lesser companies. By interviewing the most effective and creative managers, we would discover the optimal human development the system allows. In contrast to psychoanalysts who study only those who suffer emotionally or can't adapt, we studied healthy people. In this way, if we discovered symptoms of stunted emotional development, this would be more illuminating about the system than if we had been studying less successful individuals in obviously dehumanizing organizations.

Executives of technology-creating corporations have

become leaders in the most highly industrialized societies. New technology is supposed to create markets, lower production costs, and solve problems of pollution, physical illness (cancer, heart disease), and neuroses of workers and consumers. While causing many of the problems, these corporations are expected to provide the solutions: unlimited energy, clean transportation, abundant food, new products, and humanized (if not automated) work. Some of these companies build weapons that can destroy the world, but many Americans hope that they will bring us peace by improving international communication and establishing joint space ventures with the Soviet Union. Their new automated machines put people out of work, but Federal policymakers hope they will solve unemployment by their innovations. Countries with fewer educated, highly paid workers can sell simpler products at a lower price than we can. Therefore in both the U.S. and Western Europe, economic strength depends more and more on high technology, in electronics, aerospace, chemicals, and agriculture.

Besides determining technology, modes of work, and the balance of payments, corporations like BDC and RI organize more human energy of higher intellectual quality than any other institutions in America. Each year, they hire and in part eventually shape the character of a large percentage of the most talented college graduates, reinforcing certain human potentials and not others. They create leaders with a very large say in determining society's definition of progress. They take the lead in finding new ways to motivate highly trained, ambitious professionals and the new breed of more educated, self-affirmative workers; they are the first to try out sensitivity training, organizational development, and job-enrichment programs. In the business of computerizing and automating factories, offices, supermarkets, and department stores, they cause the "future shock" but profit from a world in constant change.

It is well known that the high-technology corporations interact symbiotically with other power centers, that their top managers move in and out of the Pentagon and other executive agencies. To prosper, the corporations must be finely tuned to the main social currents; they respond to changing needs and attitudes in order to sell products and to keep attracting the best young employees. In turn, new educational methods and curricula—from the new math to encounter groups—are responsive to corporate requirements for employees of the future.

These companies were also the most receptive to being studied because they were so sure of themselves, were least threatened by visiting psychologists, and were most interested in what we might find, both in the sense of helping them become more efficient and because they saw themselves as progressive leaders with the responsibility of improving the organization of work and contributing to the education of society.

I had been introduced to BDC by an executive who wanted help in raising social and human questions in the company, which he felt had become exclusively oriented to goals of growth and profit. He thought the study's findings might help his cause. His enthusiasm and support secured interviews with divisional presidents. But this did not guarantee the cooperation of the managers below them. (Only those who volunteered were interviewed.) At one point, we seemed stalled at BDC. A manager of computer development who had been informed about the study by memo had no time to see me. When his manager, himself not enthusiastic about the project, called with the bad news, I asked whether they would at least give me a chance to sell the study to the managers in person. I figured correctly that since all projects at BDC had to be sold internally, and everyone liked the excitement of a sales presentation, they might be willing to treat this one the same way. The presentation became a seminar on work and character for a group of development managers, all of whom subsequently participated in the study.

Although corporate managers had come to me for psychotherapy, the roles of doctor and corporate anthropologist are very different. Sitting in your own office, you are the expert. It's a role that feeds a sense of superiority, and even if the psychotherapist does not feel humanly superior to the patient, the latter is the one asking for something. ("Why have you come to see me?") In contrast, the corporate managers didn't invite me. I had to sell them on the idea of being studied ("Why are you interested in us?") and risk being rejected and thrown out. It was good for the ego.

In some ways, entering a large corporation was like my experiences of walking into a Mexican village for the first time, stepping into a different culture. But villagers are among the most powerless and vulnerable people in the world, while corporate managers are among the most powerful and protected. To enter the corporate world, you travel to the outskirts of the city (sometimes to a building resembling a baronial manor of glass and concrete surrounded by woods and superhighways). In the waiting room, you are greeted by an aging uniformed security policeman and a pretty young receptionist. One of them tells you to write down your name, nationality, organization (no one ever comes without an organizational affiliation), and the person you are visiting. You are given a badge and you wait for your host or, more likely, his secretary to lead you through a maze of corridors (after a while you stop trying to remember the turns) to the proper office. Inside the shiny corridors, the well-scrubbed, totally clean smell is like nowhere else. Of course, there are differences among companies. The glass roof and hanging plants at the Bell Labs at Holmdel, New Jersey, look like those of a hothouse, but the plants are plastic, since real ones couldn't survive. An older corporation, Du Pont, still has labs that look like nineteenth-century university science buildings. Texas Instruments suggests futuristic ranch houses. The style and philosophy of the company make a difference in terms of whether the inner architecture is more open and informal or whether people are consigned to independent cubbyholes.

Once inside the office, the contrast with rural villagers becomes even greater. Villagers have an abundance of time and enjoy talking for hours on end. The corporate manager must fit the visitor into a carefully budgeted schedule and he must be convinced that he will get something more than a pleasant conversation out of the meeting.

The interview itself was structured around a questionnaire that was used both as stimulus for free discussion and as a survey instrument. Although we included the checklists of intellectual and character traits important in work, personal goals, sociopolitical priorities, and emotional and psychosomatic symptoms (anxiety, depression, frequent back pains, insomnia, etc.), most of the questionnaire was open-ended questions. (See Appendix for full questionnaire.) We wrote down what the individuals said verbatim, which limited our concentration, since we had to divide our attention between taking notes and observations. But we all preferred this to the alternative of using a tape recorder. Although the tape recorder leaves the interviewer's hands free, speeds up the interview, and provides an indisputable record, I believe that consciously or unconsciously people start playing to the cameras. Perhaps it is a conceit to think that people are going to be any more open or spontaneous talking to an interviewer they do not know well and who is taking notes, but it seems to me the quality of the relationship changes, and it is easier to trust another person, even with notes written down, than a tape that might end up in anyone's hands. I doubt that everyone would even have agreed to be interviewed if we had used tape recorders, although some would have. Those managers I've asked about this agree with me.

Individuals were interviewed for periods lasting from three hours to, in a few cases, more than twenty hours. In fifteen cases we also interviewed wives and secretaries of managers. The interview questionnaire was divided into five parts. Part I included information on the individual's background and education, and that of his parents and grandparents. Then there were questions having to do with work history and what he did at work. For those cases that we decided to study more fully, it was not enough to ask those questions; we also had to observe the person at work. This sometimes meant attending meetings or just hanging around the work site. It was not easy to describe what people do at work, and from the start we learned that most managers had never before tried to describe their jobs. We would ask a person, "What do you do at work?" and he'd say, "I manage such and such a project." But this didn't describe what he really *did*. Did he keep schedules and make sure proper materials were at hand? In fact, the paper work was usually a minor part of managing. The most important part might be getting people excited about the project or being a sounding board so they could work out their ideas, or sensing a problem before it becomes unmanageable, or resolving conflicts between people. The more we understood the manager's real work, the more we saw why aspects of his personality, such as his ability to understand and stimulate people, were so important to his work.

In talking about their work, managers spoke freely and with animation. Their work was what most interested them, and they appreciated a receptive and critical student. By starting with work, it became easier and more natural to ask about their feelings and personal life than if we had started off with psychological questions.

The second section began by exploring the relationship between work and psychological characteristics, starting out with the question "How would you describe your character in your own words?" We also asked the individual to describe the character of those people he worked with most closely. Which traits, both intellectual and emotional, had been developed by the work, which were necessary for the work, and which got in the way of the work? We also asked about dreams, both those having to do with work and any other recurrent dreams that might come to mind. And we asked about work goals and how the work might be improved.

Part III included questions about social and political issues. We wanted to find out whether social considerations played a role in the manager's choice of work, and whether he was concerned with the social implications of what he produced. How did he see the relationship between technology and the pressing human problems of our time? Did he consider that technology had any dehumanizing effects? We were interested also in his sociopolitical attitudes, how he thought the corporation and society in general should be run, how he viewed the role of experts versus democratic decision making. What did he feel was the responsibility of the corporation and how free should corporate managers be to advocate social and political positions? We also wondered whether these corporate managers in advanced technology fit the view of philosophers such as Jacques Ellul, who has maintained that those in the forefront of technology believe that anything that *can* be built *should* be built.* (We found that the majority did not agree. They were not in favor of building the SST so long as questions remained unanswered about its harmful environmental impact. Only in the field of weapons did many believe they

---

*Jacques Ellul, *The Technological Society* (New York: Knopf, 1964).

should build every new technological possibility, so as not to fall behind the Russians.) Furthermore, what issues did the managers consider most important to resolve in America today? How did they define progress for our country?

The fourth section included questions on values. Here we addressed some of the fundamental issues of the American character, such as the striving for individuality with the hope that one can still be co-operative and yet creative and self-expressive. What did the individual believe in? Who were the people he most admired? What were his views of marriage, friendship, and love? What were his religious beliefs or spiritual philosophy? What were his life goals? What was the source of the individual's deepest values? How much was he deeply attracted to what was alive and free versus a need to control life and, more pathological, to destroy or mechanize that which threatened him? How compassionate and caring was he toward himself and others versus an alienated attitude or narcissistic isolation, often rationalized in terms of independence? Was he generous versus stingy? Was he striving to develop independent creative thought or did he submerge himself in others or in the company?

Part V asked questions about the individual's family life, his relationship with his wife and children. We were interested in the spiritual basis of the marriage and how the children were brought up, according to what principles and with what goals in mind. How did he spend his leisure time? Was it active and creative or was it passive TV watching and consumership? Finally, we asked questions about childhood, relationships with mother and father, and what it was like growing up. To complete this full interview as it should have been done would have taken at least six hours. Most of our interviews were limited to three hours, although those cases studied in depth took fifteen to thirty hours of interviewing. In many instances, we could complete only parts of the questionnaire, but even though everyone did not answer every question, we explored every question with many managers.

The strategy of choosing a sample of managers to interview was to start with a person who was both interested enough and high up enough in the organization to support the study and ask him to introduce us to subordinates whom he considered effective managers. After we interviewed them, they in turn would select certain of their subordinates, until we had studied a "slice" of the technostructure. Sometimes, I also interviewed the chief executive officer of the company, but only after most of the interviewing was completed. That way I took less of a risk if for any reason the president disapproved of the study. Besides, it was more interesting to interview the president after learning about the company; he would speak more openly if I already knew something about the organization. In this regard, it is interesting to note that corporate presidents, vice-presidents, and those on the way to the top decided very quickly whether or not they were going to talk with me. Practically all of them did. They were remarkably unsuspicious and nondefensive and without hesitation answered all my questions about their personal lives.

I carried many academic prejudices into the corporations. One professor asked how I would be able to stand it, spending so much time with such dull and narrow-minded people; anyway, we knew all about them, so why go? Another warned me that corporate managers would be unwilling to say much, since they were trying to hide from themselves and construct an image that could only be threatened by a psychoanalyst's probing.

Given my antiwar, antimilitaristic views, would there be any common ground to discuss social and political issues with managers who built the military technology? In fact, I was surprised to discover in

1969 that many of the managers opposed the war in Vietnam and favored decreased military spending.

Hardly any managers rejected the invitation to look into themselves. Of the 250 corporate executives, managers, and project engineers whom my colleagues and I invited to take part in studying themselves, only two said no.

A manager who refused a Rorschach was brilliant, gifted but grandiose—one of the few who really needed professional help. But he said, "I don't want you to know more about me than I know about myself." A year later, he was in a psychiatric hospital. He was the exception. In practically every case, the individuals would have continued the analysis if I'd had more time for them. Even those who were at first skeptical about psychology became interested in what we could discover about them, fascinated especially by the Rorschach and dream symbolism that seemed so far from the engineer's world of measurements. Why were they so willing to invite a stranger inside their heads? A philosopher friend raised this question and, apologizing for the implied insult, suggested that we were seen like gypsy fortune-tellers, who might reveal secrets about them. Perhaps this crack expressed the superior humanist's double-barreled contempt for psychologists and businessmen. In fact, the managers were not looking for divinations, but pressed us to explain how we reasoned and frequently helped refine the conclusions we reached.

No one was forced to participate in the study, and, as I have said, there were different reasons for choosing to do so. Most people are naturally suspicious about someone who comes around asking questions. They want to know who sent you and what the information is going to be used for. The study was supported by Harvard, and this connection with legitimized wisdom got us through many doors. Most managers saw an opportunity to gain greater knowledge about themselves which they could use either to become more effective managers or to better their competitive chances, and they agreed to participate only if we promised to point out character "flaws" that they might fix. Corporate managers are people in motion, creating new products, using new methods. They can't be too defensive or conservative. Under constant scrutiny from those above and below them, they can't afford certain illusions about themselves and are grateful for whatever they learn that helps them work better. That is the main reason that the largest corporations spend so much on managerial training and behavioral-science consultants. In a few cases, narcissistic individuals felt flattered that a psychoanalyst was interested in them, and they took it as an occasion to expound their views. I believe that managers cooperated more fully because we did not hide our values. They knew we were searching to understand the human consequences of technology and work. When someone wanted to know more about what I thought, I was always willing to explain my values or views on any question that I had asked him. I was not then prepared to compare their work to some ideal, but rather to stimulate them to suggest alternatives. However, from the start, my evaluation of work organization was in terms of its development of the heart as well as the head, of compassion, respect, emotional truth, courage, and love of life as well as competence and ingenuity. Some individuals decided to participate because the study sparked hope that their working conditions might be improved to minimize needless competition, anxiety, and, as more than one put it, the pressures to become a "mean bastard." Some managers also believed that because of corporate life they had become failures as husbands and fathers, and they hoped to learn why. Clinical psychoanalysis demonstrates that in the context of hope, people are more willing to open up and examine their feelings and motives.

We promised that in writing up the study, we would identify neither individuals nor companies by name. Although most individuals described in this book will be from either RI or BDC, these companies will hardly be mentioned again, so as to minimize possible identification. In return for their participation, we offered to discuss our findings individually and/or in a seminar where we would present general findings.

In most instances, the chance to talk about themselves and perhaps air their complaints about work to an interested listener was enough, but about 10 percent of the individuals wanted to know as much about themselves as we could tell them.

This practice of communicating the results transformed the study into a dialogue, and helped refine, corroborate, or modify interpretations that were presented as hypotheses.

Of course, the interviewer's attitude is essential to this methodology. Unlike many social scientists, neither my colleagues nor I claimed to be "detached-objective" observers. But if we did not hide our own ideals, concerns, and antiwar views, we also did not try to force them on the managers. We were not interested in teaching them how to be better people or in proving a point, but rather in understanding them. We tried to be compassionate. Beyond all this, we knew we would not learn very much about another person unless we were genuinely interested in him. Otherwise, he would not want to be known, and what we learned would be closer to the results of an FBI investigation than to human understanding.

The sociopsychoanalytic interview also requires professional competence. You must be sensitive to the individual's anxiety and resistance, and stop a line of questioning if it is too threatening. However, you should not be so fearful and conventional that you hold back from asking embarrassing questions that a person is perfectly willing to grapple with. The clinical experience of a psychoanalyst helps to carry out these interviews more effectively. Although it is possible for a sensitive student without years of clinical experience to give a satisfactory interview, the dialogue about the findings requires much more skill and knowledge.

Although these educational dialogues were not psychoanalysis, psychoanalysts have asked how we handled "resistances." How can people accept interpretations of feelings or attitudes that they are not conscious of without going through the process of developing a relationship of trust (building a "positive transference"), slowly exploring layers of experience, etc.? To answer this question, we must distinguish between different types of resistance encountered in psychoanalysis. Some resistance can be termed rational self-defense against the psychoanalyst's confusing mystification or incorrect understanding. Off the mark and unrelated to the real experience of the individual even though they are based on some brilliant theoretical scheme, the analyst's "interpretations" may intensify rather than dissolve resistances. In this sense, knowledge of the individual's life, particularly his work, informs the understanding. There is less resistance if observations of more painful or embarrassing inner realities are made in the context of a full understanding of the individual's creative strivings. When I described a manager, I talked about his intellectual strengths (e.g., ability to integrate information, sensitivity to other's feelings) and cooperative tendencies (e.g., pleasure in helping others, teaching) as well as his repressed emotions and, in some cases, primitive attitudes.

The language used also makes a difference. To communicate about feelings, attitudes, and character, we must speak in language that describes experience, but it is hard to find the right words. George Orwell wrote, "Everyone who thinks at all has noticed that our language is practically useless for describing anything that goes on inside the brain."* Language works best with shared experience, least well with private worlds entered only partially by another person. Psychologists have a better excuse than most specialists for using bureaucratic jargon to talk with one another about inner lives. But such jargon will not penetrate anyone's resistance to being known; risking a metaphorical or symbolic description of inner reality is more likely to touch the truth.

To say that an individual has "aggressive tendencies" may just provoke a debate; while the observation that when humiliated he experiences cold rage may cause him to wake up to previously repressed feelings and critical thoughts. To take an example of a character trait, to call a person's attitude "exploitative" may be correct but too abstract and general to touch him. In contrast, to say that he squeezes the juice out of those under him and then throws them away like used orange skins may be both more penetrating and precise, thus stimulating the person to become aware of this attitude.

For different reasons, an individual also resists knowledge that exposes a contradiction between values, such as between love and power. Most managers were rather unconflicted and realistic about themselves. They had started out as conservative careerists and had been liberalized by corporate demands for cooperation and working with different kinds of people. Unlike many intellectual neurotics, their work life was not a series of betrayals of adolescent ideals rationalized in narcissistic terms. Nor were they trying to convince themselves and others that they wanted to get ahead in order to help others.

When character analyses were penetrating, even unflattering, the managers welcomed them as education that increased their knowledge about themselves and others. In some cases where I told them what I had learned from their dreams or Rorschach re-

Right or Left, 1940–1943 (New York: Harcourt, Brace & World, 1971), p. 3.

sponses, I was surprised how little resistance there
was to interpretations of feelings and attitudes that
most people would find threatening and that most
psychoanalysts would consider as requiring a long
period of analysis and the establishment of a positive
transference. I believe the reason for this was that
most managers were not neurotic, but rather underdeveloped. A neurotic person may repress competitive impulses such as pleasure in putting down others
or humiliating them because these feelings conflict
with other needs (e.g., for approval) and with his
self-image as a moral person. He then suffers the effects of this repression in symptoms, loss of energy,
lack of spontaneity. But an executive is not necessarily conflicted about putting down others to keep
them in place. He may consider such humiliation
kinder and more useful than more severe disciplinary
alternatives. While a more conflicted neurotic with
high ideals may be ashamed of these somewhat sadistic feelings, this kind of executive sees nothing
wrong in gloating over his triumphs unless he loses
control and makes a fool of himself. Furthermore, he
may believe that everyone would feel the same way:
the only difference is between winners who can afford to express it and losers who never have a chance
to experience victory.

In psychoanalysis, a neurotic individual most
strongly resists truths that threaten to dissolve illusions supporting a complicated and fragile solution
to life based on infantile attitudes. A neurotic whose
solution is extremely irrational and costly (e.g., remaining symbiotically tied to mother or mother substitutes and sacrificing changes for independence)
will fight off any challenging insight because he resists
giving up his unconscious passions and reexperienc-
ing the events that caused the repression. To inter-
pret such deeply repressed material in a way that
will be heard does require a carefully developed
psychoanalytic relationship between therapist and
patient. But the life solutions of most managers were

not based on repressed infantile attitudes, nor were they threatened by what we had to tell them. For the most part, they had weighed the costs and benefits of merging themselves with the corporation and nothing we could add seriously challenged their conclusion or suggested an alternative.

Thoughts and emotions may also be unconscious or only semiconscious for a very different reason, because a person has never been educated to pay attention to his emotional life and is "emotionally illiterate." Thoughts and experiences remain outside of awareness because they are not conventional, that is, no one the individual knows ever talks about love, humiliation, shame, guilt, or other strong emotions. The study created an atmosphere of emotional realism that allowed the managers to look at themselves in a new way. Some had flashes of insight of the profound emotional costs of corporate life, especially the loss of spirit in the pursuit of career. Back in the ordinary atmosphere of work, with its requirements to adapt and satisfy ambition, the same person might once again experience his emotional experiences as foreign, again needing to be repressed or rationalized. We noted often that although a gifted manager might develop awareness during the interview to see and feel ideas and emotions he had previously ignored, this experience usually faded away as he immersed himself in the ordinary routines. (After a seminar of four hours a week for six weeks on understanding the relationship between character and work, one executive said he had a "re-entry problem.") All this was evidence of the emotional potential of these gifted and brilliant men, and that their work was incompatible with developing deeper knowledge about themselves and others.

CHAPTER 1

Managers

The psychology of individual types of character has hardly begun even to be sketched as yet—our lectures may possibly serve as a crumb-like contribution to the structure. The first thing to bear in mind (especially if we ourselves belong to the clerico-academic-scientific type, the officially and conventionally "correct" type, "the deadly respectable" type, for which to ignore others is a besetting temptation) is that nothing can be more stupid than to bar out phenomena from our notice, merely because we are incapable of taking part in anything like them ourselves."*

—WILLIAM JAMES

It is the function of the social character to shape the energies of the members of society in such a way that their behavior is not left to conscious decisions whether or not to follow the social pattern but that people want to act as they have to act *and at the same time find gratification in acting according to the requirements of the culture. In other words, the social character has the function of molding human energy for the purpose of the functioning of a given society.*†

—ERICH FROMM

---

*William James, *The Varieties of Religious Experience* (New York: Longmans, Green, 1902), p. 109.

†Erich Fromm, "Psychoanalytic Characterology and Its Application to the Understanding of Culture," in S. Stansfeld Sargent and Marian W. Smith, eds., *Culture and Personality* (New York: Viking Fund, Wenner-Gren Foundation for Anthropological Research, 1949), p. 5.

A NEW TYPE of man is taking over leadership of the most technically advanced companies in America. In contrast to the jungle-fighter industrialists of the past, he is driven not to build or to preside over empires, but to organize winning teams. Unlike the security-seeking organization man, he is excited by the chance to cut deals and to gamble. Although more cooperative and less hardened than the autocratic empire builder and less dependent than the organization man, he is more detached and emotionally inaccessible than either. And he is troubled by it: the new industrial leader can recognize that his work develops his head but not his heart.

Since the 1950's the popular view of corporate man has been that of David Riesman and William H. Whyte, Jr.* In *The Lonely Crowd*, Riesman described a new "social character" emerging in the bureaucratic salaried classes that James Burnham and Peter Drucker had identified. In contrast to production-oriented, inner-directed entrepreneurs—both industrial barons and craftsmen—who relied on technical competence and determination to create and develop new companies, the people-oriented, other-directed managers greased bureaucratic machinery with human-relations techniques and manipulated the public through the arts of marketing. Although Riesman cautioned that key roles in big business and government still needed inner-directed managers, in general the new executive had to learn personality specialties and soft-pedal his old-style skills and attitudes.

Less willing than Riesman either to grant other-directed man any credit for his human sensitivity or to recognize the jungle fighter in the entrepreneur, Whyte worried over the disappearance of tough-

*See David Reisman, *The Lonely Crowd: A Study of the Changing American Character* (New Haven: Yale University Press, 1950); and William H. Whyte, Jr., *The Organization Man* (New York: Simon and Schuster, 1956).

minded individual initiative. He warned that the emergence of a corporate "social ethic" would eventually destroy individualism and transform American society into a collective of security-seekers. From Whyte's point of view, the problem lay not in social and technical changes requiring different kinds of people, but in the decline of the Protestant ethic and the unwillingness of most individuals to struggle against organizations. If there was any hero in *The Organization Man*, it was the exceptional executive conflicted about conforming who does so only to reach the top so that he can dominate and control his environment. Like Whyte, both C. Wright Mills and Erich Fromm were concerned about the organization man's weaknesses, but unlike him, they saw the problem of conformity as the outcome of a corporate-bureaucratic system that undermined the human spirit and alienated individuals from their powers of craftsmanship, reason, and decision making.*

Despite these significant differences in analysis, the overall impression left by all these books of the fifties was that a single type of other-directed, marketing, security-seeking, bureaucratic man would inevitably take over large businesses (and government agencies). Alan Harrington's *Life in the Crystal Palace*,† the most extreme corporate caricature of the period, summed up the social analysis of a decade of describing managerial life in a rich company like Standard Oil of New Jersey. No one ever failed, or was fired, but there was no innovation; everyone fol-

---

*Erich Fromm emphasized the loss of self of the corporate-bureaucratic marketing character who becomes a commodity in order to sell himself to the organization and loses the capacity for deep experience, spontaneity, and productiveness in love and work in *The Sane Society* (New York: Rinehart, 1955). Mills described the disappearance of self-employment and the loss of the economic basis for individualism and craftsmanship in *White Collar: The American Middle Classes* (New York: Oxford University Press, 1951).

†Alan Harrington, *Life in the Crystal Palace* (New York: Knopf, 1959).

lowed a safe and dull path. The best policy was to look good and not make waves. This passive and flaccid opulent image of corporate life fit the spirit of the Eisenhower years. Ike himself seemed to symbolize the cultural change from inner-directed nineteenth-century farm boy to other-directed twentieth-century bureaucrat whose smile and charm appeared to smooth all troubles away while the country slid into a recession.

As a description of corporate reality, the other-directed organization man is too narrow and time-bound. The modern technology-creating corporation needs more than one type of person, and those who reach the top in the seventies are more active and adventurous than the stereotype of the fifties. The election of John F. Kennedy introduced the new era with a policy of "get America moving" in space, missiles, electronic communications, and the computers needed to make the new systems work. In the 1960 Presidential campaign, Kennedy attacked the Republican missile gap (later proved nonexistent), and as President he teased, prodded, and exhorted the country to compete. Stimulated by massive Federal spending, companies developing the new technology grew most rapidly in the early sixties and became the leaders of industry, fully supported by first Kennedy and then Lyndon B. Johnson. Even in the fifties, as majority leader of the Senate, Johnson had championed aerospace development against the more cautious Eisenhower Administration.

But it was Kennedy who most embodied the new competitive, adventurous spirit and became the model for the corporate gamesman. The most dynamic corporations prospered both because of the military-aerospace demand and their own ability to create new markets for innovative products. Companies like Texas Instruments, IBM, Xerox, or Dow Chemical did not look like the slow-moving bureaucracies described in the fifties, such as U.S. Steel, which was falling behind foreign competition in production technology, or the automobile companies, which substituted styling changes for engineering innovation.

The new companies could not develop new products and market them against tough opponents if they were manned by benign organization men who never took any risks. The high-technology corporations that grew most rapidly in the early sixties were infused by the same spirit of intense international competition and the quest for glory, to be "number one," expressed by Kennedy. A new type of company man—the gamesman—rapidly emerged as the leader of corporate projects and eventually of American industry. It is his character that holds the key to understanding the modern corporation and its future.

On the average, the corporate managers we interviewed shared many attitudes, values, and behavior patterns, but there were also personality differences that determined managerial style and eventually how high the managers could rise in the hierarchy. We found that high technology corporations can be conceived as psychostructures which require different kinds of people at different levels.

Taking the interview material at face value, the typical manager interviewed was a man (only 4 percent were women).* The range of ages was early twenties to mid-fifties. The typical manager had three children, and he had never been divorced. It was significant that only 7 percent of the sample had been divorced, and almost all the successful managers re-

---

*At the company we call RI, we were also asked to study the question of why young women engineers were receiving low ratings from their supervisors. This report, based on interviews given by Cindy Elliott and Kathy Terzi, was written up by them. One of the main findings was that many of the women needed more encouragement from male supervisors who were overly shy about seeming too intimate with these young women. They were unable to pat them on the back in the spontaneous, supportive way they did with the young men they managed, and this reserve also limited their ability to give needed criticism.

ported closely knit families, a finding consistent with the Defense Department's "Hindsight"* study of key contributors to weapons development. Most likely, he held a degree in electrical engineering. The range of salaries was from $15,000 for young managers to more than $400,000 a year for corporate presidents. (Sixteen of the 250 individuals interviewed were corporate presidents or vice-presidents earning around $100,000 or more.) The average manager had worked for ten years at his present company (few of the elite managers move around), which he joined right after his military service (usually the Navy). Most executives had risen from the ranks of the company and had never worked anywhere else.

The typical manager grew up in a town or small city. About half went to little-known colleges and half studied at leading state universities or elite private institutions. (More of the top managers went to the leading state or private universities, especially to the graduate schools in business administration.) A middle-of-the-road, family-oriented person, he inherited traditional values of hard work, self-sufficiency, and thrift. His parents were middle class (American-born or Northern European); his father was either a manager, a white-collar worker, or a skilled worker in some technical or technically related work such as railroading, engineering, surveying, or technical sales. His grandfather was probably a farmer, although he might have been an independent professional or semi-professional, such as a craftsman, contractor, clergyman, lawyer, or elected official. His mother probably worked for a time as a bookkeeper, secretary, schoolteacher, or nurse.

The typical manager was father-oriented. He shared his father's values, even though he had outdistanced him economically, and tended to admire successful father figures in the company. His experiences in the corporation had revised his inherited

---

*Hindsight, Final Report, Department of Defense, 1969.

conservatism, and politically, he is likely to call himself an independent or "liberal Republican."

The typical manager we interviewed worked with advanced technology, either creating it, marketing it, or using it in new ways. He considered his work "extremely important" in his life and said he would rather do what he was doing than any job he could imagine. His work was central to his life, his view of himself, and his sense of fulfillment.

He reported working forty to forty-five hours a week, including a few hours at home. Although a few managers said they worked as many as fifty to sixty hours, among those who didn't exceed the normal week, some labeled the fifty-hour week as "overactivity" which lessens effectiveness, and they took pride in *not* working so much.

Outside of work, most preferred active sports to spectator sports or TV watching. Most (75 percent) played on high school teams and 64 percent played in college.

On the middle and lower levels, managers and engineers were nagged by thoughts of being merely part of a huge machine, of becoming technically obsolete, or of being by-passed for promotions. Most didn't feel they had much power to affect company policies and wanted more say in how work is organized and in how products are developed. If they had the choice, said more than half of the people interviewed, they would rather run a small company of their own than reach a high level in a large company; thus, the ideals of individualism persist even within the large organization.

The managers reported that their work had influenced their intellectual and emotional development. Although most gained a sense of competence and intellectual self-confidence, corporate life did not stimulate compassion or idealism. A majority admitted that competition and uncertainty made them constantly anxious.

To differentiate types and arrive at a deeper understanding of those we interviewed, our research group held regular weekly seminars to analyze interviews, Rorschach tests, and dreams in the context of observations about organization and work.

When we considered an individual case, material from the interview, Rorschach, dreams, and observation was analyzed in order to arrive at an analysis of the motives, traits, and values that form character. Conclusions were based on all we were able to discover about an individual. Although the information gained in a three-hour interview is minimal compared to the many hours of analytic work often required in order to understand character, in general it was sufficient for sociopsychoanalytic study. Erich Fromm and I have considered this problem in *Social Character in a Mexican Village*,* a study of the character and the work of *campesinos*, in which we used methods that have been further developed here. Certain points deserve emphasis. After a few hours of psychoanalysis, the psychoanalyst generally has enough information to describe the broad outlines of the patient's character, although not the developmental and genetic influences in its formation. Interpretation of social character requires even less time, since we are not studying any one individual in depth but rather describing the dominant traits that are shared by many people who belong to the same type. This is not to underestimate the difficulties in this process. The task of character diagnosis, like any other psychoanalytic formulation, requires knowledge of psychoanalytic theory, clinical psychoanalytic experience (including the experience of one's own analysis), and a vocation for this kind of work.

Besides all this, we must understand the culture of the individuals, their symbols, their ways of perceiving, thinking, and remembering (cognitive style),

---

*Erich Fromm and Michael Maccoby, *Social Character in a Mexican Village* (Englewood Cliffs, N.J.: Prentice-Hall, 1970).

and their religion and history. Usually, this is not a problem in psychoanalysis because the analyst and patients belong to the same culture. Where this is not the case, as in the culture of the corporation, the psychoanalyst or social-character analyst must become anthropologist as well as clinician. The psychoanalyst must learn about the culture and adapt his psychological knowledge to the new social context.

In some ways, the method used by Oscar Lewis in *The Children of Sánchez** might seem similar to ours since we both used the main anthropological method of participant observation (living with and getting to know people in their daily lives) and wide-ranging discussion. Aspects of the psychoanalyst's method are, of course, similar to that used by the anthropologist. Both psychoanalysis and anthropology study individuals and culture. In both, participant observation occupies a central role, although traditionally the psychoanalyst's direct observation has been limited to what he has seen and heard in his office. However, at least four elements of method are unique to psychoanalysis.

Unlike anthropology, the sociopsychoanalytic approach is directed by theory toward the illumination of areas of inner life. In the case of Oscar Lewis, as in that of other anthropologists whose study is not directed by a psychodynamic theory of character, the interview material is very difficult to understand, although easy to read. The material may be misleading in terms of character if opinions, repetition of culturally determined explanations, and folk sayings are taken as convictions, personal experience, and individual motivation. The psychoanalytic dialogue is not merely one in which the individual speaks and the interviewer records what he says. The psychoanalyst is sensitized by his theory to listen to contradic-

---

*Oscar Lewis, *The Children of Sánchez* (New York: Random House, 1961).

tions between what is said or what is communicated by body movements, facial expressions, etc. The interview is a constant process of clarification and of checking hypotheses, of asking questions in order to try to resolve doubts about the meaning of statements with motivational or emotional content. To give a simple example, an individual may express aggressive feelings toward someone else. The psychoanalyst wonders, "Where does this aggression come from? Is it rooted in a drive for power and domination over others, or is it in response to an attack, rooted in the need to maintain one's integrity, dignity, or self-respect?"

The second element is the process by which one becomes a psychoanalyst—a long period of self-study in which the psychoanalyst is the object and the instrument of analysis simultaneously. The psychoanalyst participates in a systematic self-exploration, different from any other specialization in the human sciences, where his goal is to develop himself as the instrument of investigation. A third is that, unlike other forms of science, in psychoanalysis the object of study, the patient, ideally becomes the co-investigator, and in the process of dialogue and discovery, he increases his capacity for understanding. A fourth difference between anthropological and psychoanalytic study is that above discovering new knowledge, the goal of psychoanalysis is to improve the life of the person being studied, and it is solely for that reason that the individual takes part.

There are, of course, many different ways of describing character, and no description of an individual is ever complete. Character includes qualities of both the head and the heart, creative strivings, courage and cowardice, values and moral principles, sense of identity, and cognitive style. Character is a person's psychic fingerprint, or as Heraclitus wrote more dynamically, it is what determines the fate of man. The study of character was further developed most no-

tably by Aristotle, who explored the relationship of character, virtue, and happiness in the *Ethics*, Thomas Aquinas in *Summa Theologica*, and Spinoza in his study of ethics. The psychoanalytic approach to character added a new dimension by systematically exploring the deeply rooted, often unconscious, relatively fixed emotional attitudes that determine what a person finds satisfying or dissatisfying, what motivates him in his relationships with himself and others at work, in love, and as a social and political being. Freud conceived of this emotional nucleus of character as the result of childhood psychosexual development. His first paper on character described how stinginess, orderliness, and obstinacy were a syndrome of traits formed in the child's struggle to renounce anal erotic interests on the one hand and on the other to resist the adult's attempt to break his will.*
While accepting Freud's clinical description of character types, such as the receptive orientation, the anal-hoarding orientation, the cannibalistic type, the narcissist, and so on, Fromm revised the psychoanalytic theory of character to integrate it with the philosophical tradition and to expand the latter with the clinical findings of psychoanalysis. Fromm describes character in terms of how individuals satisfy survival needs for food, shelter, and safety and existential needs for a frame of orientation and devotion, relatedness, unity, effectiveness, excitation and stimulation. These needs can be satisfied in different and characteristic ways that can contribute either to creative development and integrity or to psychic discord and psychopathology. In terms of Fromm's sociopsychoanalytic theory, the nucleus of character includes

---

*For example, "The cleanliness, orderliness and reliability give exactly the impression of a reaction-formation against an interest in things that are unclean and intrusive and ought not to be on the body." From "Character and Anal Eroticism" (1908), *Collected Papers*, Vol. II (London: Hogarth Press, 1924), p. 48.

the modes of satisfying these needs for things, other people, creative expression, and meaning.*

Neither a meaning system nor emotional strivings alone describe character. Both are necessary, but the individual is in trouble if the two do not mesh. Without a sense of meaning that fits reality sufficiently, the result is anomic paralysis and despair. But to satisfy the need for meaning, values and principles must be rooted in emotional attitudes. For example,

---

*See Fromm's other books on the theory of character: *Escape from Freedom, Man for Himself, The Sane Society, The Anatomy of Human Destructiveness.*

Fromm and I believe character traits are *relatively* fixed in childhood, formed by influences of culture, modes of work, environment as mediated through the family, and the child's constitution. In contrast, Freudian theory considers character as set in childhood and unlikely to change without psychoanalytic intervention. However, Freud did not consider sufficiently the role of social structures in the formation and maintenance of character.

> The importance of childhood experiences by no means excludes later changes in character. This is to say, while the character under the influence of early experience (plus constitution) is formed in the first years, the structure is normally flexible enough so that changes may occur at a later period. In principle, we would not even set an age limit to the possibilities of such changes, for the better or worse. However, there is a good reason why one might conceive a completely inflexible character. The character of the child, as we believe with Freud, develops as a result of dynamic adaptation to the family constellation. Since the family represents the spirit of the society into which the child enters, the same influences which have been the main determining influences from the beginning continue to mold the adolescent's and adult's character structure. Institutions of schooling, work, and leisure do not differ essentially from the way of life transmitted to the child in his family. Thus the character structure acquired in childhood is constantly reinforced in later life, provided the social circumstances do not change drastically. Since this is not normally the case, the impression arises that the character is definitely formed at the age of six and not subject to any later change.
> —Fromm and Maccoby, *op. cit.*, pp. 21–22.

This addition to Freud does not contradict the expectation that unconscious and deeply irrational attitudes formed in childhood resist change, even if social conditions are different.

the craftsman's individualism and pride in quality are felt values based on productive-hoarding emotions.

In practice, we found that the first fifty or sixty interviews required at least six hours of analysis to arrive at a satisfactory interpretation, and this sometimes took a lot longer. This preliminary analysis established the dominant social character types and made subsequent analysis much easier.

A word about typing people: The very mention of types embarrasses those with simplistic democratic and egalitarian values who want to believe that everyone is at once different from and equal to everyone else. Although we all should recognize that we share the same human rights, consciously or unconsciously, no one can avoid the cognitive necessity of typing people. We commonly classify people stereotypically according to differences in age (young, middle-aged, old), sex (male and female), and race (black, white, etc.).

Types based on a single trait are from a naturalistic point of view misleading and from a moral point of view dangerous. Any single trait may have a different meaning according to a total syndrome of psychological traits. For example, high IQ in a manipulator is different from the intelligence of a wise and responsible person. Typing according to single traits also lends itself to moralism, which thrives on simple dichotomies which can be labeled good and bad. Correspondingly, moralists tend to reduce complex alternatives to dichotomies or one dimensional continua which can be treated as good (high score) vs. bad (low score).

Bureaucracies tend to type people to fit the requirements of their hierarchies; teachers type students as bright, average, or retarded; police type criminals and law abiders; psychiatrists type normals, neurotics, and psychotics. Factory managers typically type workers and managers into categories of hardworking, lazy, incompetent, responsible, irresponsible, etc.

—all according to how well they serve the organization. In contrast, the types we developed cut across demographic classifications according to age, sex, and race, and they are based on emotional attitudes— frame of orientation shared by a large number of people.

A true social character type cannot be labeled simply as good or bad. It describes a syndrome of traits that are adaptive to the requirements of physical and psychic survival. If circumstances are favorable, such adaptation allows creative development, especially in gifted members of the type. When social conditions are no longer adaptive for a type, negative traits become stronger. For example, if farmers or craftsmen are forced into industrial hierarchies, their independent attitude tends to become negativism and obstinacy. Of course, the creative development of some types, like the jungle fighter, may be at the expense of others just as the prosperity of the lion is gained at the expense of the animals he hunts.

From a social point of view, by distinguishing types according to their *own* strivings and values, we are trying to develop knowledge that increases compassion, respect for differences but also understanding of what we like and dislike in ourselves and others and why. Such knowledge also illuminates the relationship between work, family life, and the formation of character.

But most important, the purpose of studying social character is to understand the real possibilities for progressive social change. Any new program or project must take into account social character types if it is to engage the support of the people affected. Otherwise even the most idealistic plans may conflict with emotional attitudes rather than being supported by them. In this sense, social character types are an approximation of the human reality that must be considered together with the economic, technical and social factors that determine work organizations.

But for all our efforts, no typology of character is

fully satisfying as a way of understanding any particular individual. The subject matter defies boundaries. Although he described character as "man's destiny," Heraclitus also wrote, "You could not in your going find the ends of the soul, though you traveled the whole way: so deep is its Law."* We recognize that although our typologies may increase understanding, they must be treated dialectically, as conceptual tools. While expanding our sense of reality, they also limit our capacity to experience the uniqueness of individuals. To resolve this dialectic, however, requires more than further conceptual development. To begin to know another person in his uniqueness, to explore his soul, is a function even more of heart than head.

Once we had scored all the interviews in terms of dynamic character traits, different types began to emerge as distinct from one another in terms of the individual member's overall orientation to work, values, and self-identity. We eventually came to name four main psychological types in the corporate technostructure: the craftsman, the jungle fighter, the company man, and the gamesman. These are "ideal types" in the sense that few people fit the type exactly and most are a mixture of types. But in practically every case, we were able to agree on which type best described a person, and the individual and his colleagues almost always agreed with our typing. In fact, our discussion of these different character types sometimes crystallized feelings about differences among people, feelings they had never been able to put into words. Once seen, interpersonal conflicts and problems of communication were better understood. In labeling these character types, I kept in mind the ancient observation that naming is a legislative act, and without putting the question to a vote, I tried to select names that corporate managers could identify

---

*Kathleen Freeman, *Ancilla to The Pre-Socratic Philosophers* (Oxford: Basil Blackwell, 1947), p. 27.

with. Within those companies where we have reported the results, these types are now used as tools to better understand human reality. When I described the craftsman, jungle fighter, company man, and gamesman in *Spectrum,* the journal of the IEEE (the Institute of Electronic and Electrical Engineers), many managers wrote to say they recognized themselves, and understood organizational problems better.

Since then, managers in other kinds of companies and elite bureaucracies ranging from the civil service to the Foreign Service to universities have found that these types fit their worlds of work.

Among those who found our analysis useful was an exceptionally creative and compassionate divisional president of BDC who became so interested in the project ("Understanding character is ninety percent of my work") that he eventually suggested I give an experimental six-week course to a group of top executives on the relationship between work and character. That experience was an opportunity to discuss the findings with a group of friendly critics who also found that the types increased their understanding.

The next chapters describe the types who man the technostructure of the advanced-technology corporation. Here are brief introductions to each type.

1. *The craftsman.* The craftsman holds the traditional values of the productive-hoarding character—the work ethic, respect for people, concern for quality and thrift. When he talks about his work, his interest is in the *process* of making something; he enjoys building. He sees others, co-workers as well as superiors, in terms of whether they help or hinder him in doing a craftsmanlike job. Most of the craftsmen whom we interviewed are quiet, sincere, modest, and practical, although there is a difference between those who are more receptive and democratic versus those who are more authoritarian and intolerant. Although his virtues are admired by everyone, his self-containment and perfectionism do not allow him to lead a

complex and changing organization. Rather than engaging and trying to master the system with the cooperation of others who share his values, he tends to do his own thing and go along, sometimes reluctantly, toward goals he does not share, enjoying whatever opportunities he finds for interesting work.

Some corporate scientists we interviewed are essentially craftsmen but there is a type of scientist who shares some of the craftsman's interest in knowledge and creating, but who is more of a prima donna, and is found exclusively in research labs. Although these scientists might be more at home in universities than in corporations, among them are some of the most independent contributors who work in corporations. Since so few are successful managers, and do not reach the top levels of the technostructure, the "corporate scientist" type will be sketched only in passing.

Some of the most creative and gifted scientists whom we have seen in the corporate world are included in this type, together with the most unhappy misfits, resentful failures whose gifts do not measure up to their ambition. What most distinguishes the "scientists" from the craftsmen is their narcissism, their idolatry of their own knowledge, talents, and technology and their hunger for admiration. They are the corporate intellectuals and many are fascinated by esoteric issues (e.g., outer space or eternal life) only tangentially related to either corporate goals or social needs. In exaggerating their own importance, some of the scientists we interviewed belittled those who were more down to earth. Yet beneath their narcissism we found a receptive and dependent attachment to those in power, both corporate and state leaders, the "decision makers" who could support them and make their ideas into reality. A grandiose scientist does not trust the public to understand him, and it doesn't occur to him that the reason may be that he does not create things that benefit the public. He invents what is demanded by those who pay him

—the corporation and the state. Both at home and at work, the grandiose scientist seeks a protected nest. He wants an admiring mother-wife to meet his needs in return for a chance to share in his glory, and he seeks patrons at work who will agree to similar symbiotic relationships.

2. *The jungle fighter.* The jungle fighter's goal is power. He experiences life and work as a jungle (not a game), where it is eat or be eaten, and the winners destroy the losers. A major part of his psychic resources is budgeted for his internal department of defense. Jungle fighters tend to see their peers in terms of accomplices or enemies and their subordinates as objects to be utilized. There are two subtypes of jungle fighters, lions and foxes. The lions are the conquerors who when successful may build an empire; the foxes make their nests in the corporate hierarchy and move ahead by stealth and politicking.

3. *The company man.* In the company man, we recognize the well-known organization man, or the functionary whose sense of identity is based on being part of the powerful, protective company. His strongest traits are his concern with the human side of the company, his interest in the feelings of the people around him and his commitment to maintain the organization's integrity. At his weakest, he is fearful and submissive, concerned with security even more than with success. The most creative company men sustain an atmosphere in their groups of cooperation, stimulation, and mutuality. The least creative find a little niche and satisfy themselves by feeling that somehow they share in the glory of the corporation.

4. *The gamesman.* The gamesman is the new man, and, really, the leading character in this study. His main interest is in challenge, competitive activity where he can prove himself a winner. Impatient with others who are slower and more cautious, he likes to take risks and to motivate others to push themselves beyond their normal pace. He responds to

work and life as a game. The contest hypes him up and he communicates his enthusiasm, thus energizing others. He enjoys new ideas, new techniques, fresh approaches and shortcuts. His talk and his thinking are terse, dynamic, sometimes playful and come in quick flashes. His main goal in life is to be a winner, and talking about himself invariably leads to discussion of his tactics and strategy in the corporate contest.

In the sixties, the gamesman went all out to win. In the seventies, both the country and the corporations are more skeptical about adventurism and glory-seeking. Some of the biggest companies have discovered that symbiosis with the military weakens their ability to compete in other markets. Watergate shamed those who flew the banner "Winning is not everything; it's the only thing," which in the sixties decorated corporate walls and desks. In the seventies, America no longer considers itself the land of unlimited abundance. Rising energy costs and international competition still call for competitive, risk-taking corporate gamesmen as leaders, but they have become more sober and realistic, more concerned with reducing costs than overwhelming the opposition with innovation.

The new corporate top executive combines many gamesman traits with aspects of the company man. He is a team player whose center is the corporation. He feels himself responsible for the functioning of a system, and in his mind, his career goals have merged with those of the corporation. Thus he thinks in terms of what is good for the company, hardly separating that from what is good for himself. He tends to be a worrier, constantly on the lookout for something that might go wrong. He is self-protective and sees people in terms of their use for the larger organization. He even uses himself in this way, fine tuning his sensitivity. He has succeeded in submerging his ego and gaining strength from this exercise in self-control.

To function, the corporations need craftsmen, scientists, and company men (many could do without jungle fighters), but their future depends most of all on the gamesmen's capacity for mature development.

CHAPTER 2

The Craftsman

Neither talent without instruction, nor instruction without talent can produce the perfect craftsman. He should be a man of letters, a skillful draughtsman, expert in geometry, not ignorant of optics, well grounded in arithmetic; he should know considerable history, have listened to the philosophers diligently, should be acquainted with music; he should not be ignorant of medicine, he should be learned in the findings of the legal experts and should be familiar with astrology and the laws of astronomy.*

—VITRUVIUS

I'm basically conservative. I'm amiable but I'm driving for myself, not that I necessarily expect people that work for me to be driving. I'm conscientious. My basic philosophy is that any job worth doing is worth doing well. I prefer to slip a schedule than doing something halfway. I don't believe in turning loose something half finished. Quality is more important than quantity.

I don't know how deep you want to get into. I'm basically a principled individual. Unless proven wrong, I believe in firmly abiding by those principles.

—SELF-DESCRIPTION OF A CORPORATE CRAFTSMAN

THE CRAFTSMAN, traditional builder, farmer, artisan, has a sense of self-worth based on knowledge, skill, discipline, and self-reliance. More than any other character type, he has a sense of limits—of materials, energy, knowledge, and the moral constraints—that

---

*From Vitruvius, *Architecture*, cited by Friedrich Klemm in *A History of Western Technology* (Cambridge, Mass.: MIT Press, 1964), p. 43.

must be respected to live a good life. Yet it is his work and inventiveness, the technology he has built, that have been used by jungle fighters, gamesmen, and other managers to expand and break through those limits.

In the eighteenth and early nineteenth centuries, American craftsmen were self-employed. Before the Civil War, some of them joined together in guildlike unions that maintained autonomy over work methods in their contracts with capitalists in newly developing industries such as iron, shoemaking, and coal mining.* But today, most independent craftsmen have been absorbed into large corporations and agribusinesses. Only the exceptional small businessman or farmer survives.

Throughout the industrialized world, the craftsmen complain about the loss of freedom that results from their own creations, and many yearn for a more traditional society with God-fearing virtues. In this sense, Alexander Solzhenitsyn, himself a prototypical, larger-than-life craftsman with a gargantuan appetite for work and a sustaining hatred of all bureaucratic managers, speaks for the traditional society that is forever lost to them. In *The First Circle*,† he described how a group of electrical and mechanical engineers in a prison camp was forced to develop new technology, in this case, a secret telephone for Stalin with a built-in coding device.

In contrast to the Soviet system, Harald T. Friis, a craftsman-inventor, described how the engineers in the Bell Labs were given a great deal of autonomy and support to develop new products.‡ But only so long as the project remained small. When organized

*David Montgomery, "Trade Union Practice and the Origins of Syndicalist Theory in the United States" (unpublished paper, Columbia University seminar on American civilization, 1972).

†Alexander Solzhenitsyn, *The First Circle* (New York: Harper & Row, 1968).

‡Harald T. Friis, *Seventy-Five Years in an Exciting World* (San Francisco: San Francisco Press, 1971).

into larger developmental projects, the American craftsman is motivated less by fear than by appeal to his greed and ambition. Zealous gamesmen play on the craftsmen's pride, coaxing them to share their knowledge with others, promising rewards, and by creating an exciting, competitive atmosphere, seduce them to speed up their work. (One might conclude that the secret of successful U.S. technology over Soviet technology is that of "motivating" and organizing rather than coercing the craftsmen.)

Of those we interviewed on the lower levels of the technostructure, the majority were craftsmen. And even on the higher levels, many high-technology managers maintain some craftsmanlike attitudes which may be expressed in their approach to developing new ideas or building an organization.

The social character of the craftsman is responsible —family- and work-oriented, productively hoarding, self-contained, self-affirmative, prudently conservative —and paternalistic. He grew up in a small town where he inherited traditional conservative values of hard work, self-sufficiency, and thrift. (The few blacks, Chinese, and East Indians we interviewed were all craftsmen from this type of background.) Unlike the company man, he does not idealize or worship the powerful organization, but he does defer to what he considers legitimate authority, at work and in government. He fits easily into a system of masters and apprentices.

Although the craftsman wants to do well and make money, he is motivated even more by the problem to be solved, the challenge of the work itself, and his satisfaction in creating something of quality. Rarely satisfied in a large organization, he feels more at home working in a small group or on a project with a defined and understandable structure. He wants to stay with the product from conception to completion. One craftsman remarked that for him "electrical engineering is a great hobby, but I wonder about it as a profession. I'm not strongly motivated by money; I turned down jobs three hundred to four hundred dollars more per month because I didn't like the work. I wanted a job like this, with the satisfaction of putting something together and seeing it work."

Craftsmen, more at home with themselves than are jungle fighters, company men, or gamesmen, reported many more dreams. Most of the dreams deal with solving problems, either those that are brought home from work or imaginary ones (e.g., "I had a weird dream of walking around on top of a microwave circuit trying to figure out what was wrong with it").*

Other dreams express childhood fears of a hostile natural environment, as though to say that the craftsman must conquer nature and his own inner nature in order to gain security. (One craftsman told us, "I used to have the recurrent dream of wading barefoot in a stream with a copperhead about every foot." Another dreams that bees are chasing him.)

Unlike the jungle fighter or the gamesman, the craftsman does not compete against other people as much as he does against nature, materials, and especially his own standards of quality. Craftsmen do not play or like to watch team sports. They hardly ever watch television. They enjoy inventing, tinkering with old cars, building their own house, hiking in the mountains, perhaps skiing. One sport that appeals to some is golf, since essentially you compete against yourself, to better your own score.

Together with work, the craftsman's main goal is to be a good provider, a good parent, and to create a secure home, an enclave away from work. A productive craftsman stated his goals in life: "To successfully raise my children. A happy marriage and

---

*Harald Friis writes: "The research worker should become obsessed with the job and it should haunt him day and night if he is the right man for the job. He may believe that scheduled hours of work limit his freedom of activity, but actually he has lost his freedom to the job itself. Excessive amounts of outside activity such as committee work and local affairs may indicate that the research worker is not in the right job." *Ibid.*, p. 49.

a stable home with the children, so that they have some relationship with their father. Second, to be successful in business, respected for my work. A by-product of that is to make money. Also to make some sort of contribution to mankind, to society. And to enjoy living."

Most craftsmen are more concerned with being good fathers than good husbands. They make it a point to spend time with their children. (Camping and backpacking, also teaching building and repairing are popular activities.) Furthermore, they stress the importance of the father's role as an example to his children as well as a teacher and disciplinarian. One stated, "A good father provides consistent disciplinary action on children promptly, the degree depending on the type of behavior. But there should always be a two-way discussion. The father must set the example by good, clean living." Another craftsman: "A child should respect his father, but the father should earn it as a teacher disciplinarian—understanding, open-minded, fair."

In fact, they are less likely than other corporate individuals to have problems with their children. In contrast to the ambitious, rebellious children of some executives, the children of craftsmen are as respectful as their parents.

Although managers complain that workers have lost the craftsmanlike work ethic and concern for quality, there are many Americans with the craftsman orientation, both men and women, particularly in areas of the country that have not lost their farming traditions, such as the South and the Middle West. In the Tennessee auto parts plant we studied and in the many high-technology labs through out the country, we found two varieties of craftsmen, the dutiful and the receptive. Both share the enjoyment of building quality products. Both respect competence and hard work. The difference is that the dutiful are more driven, compulsive, and hierarchical, while the receptive are more life-loving, tolerant, and democratic.* The dutiful craftsman is more likely to rise to foremanlike positions, in charge of production and scheduling, while the receptive craftsman is more likely to seek out a position where he can help others without having to boss them around.

Arthur Jansen is a dutiful craftsman in his late twenties whose grandparents were Scandinavian farmers and craftsmen who immigrated to the U.S., and whose father was an electrician who tried to run a small business and failed. His parents encouraged him to go into electronics because there was "the greatest opportunity," and he has reached the first management level in a development lab of a giant company. But his goal is still to own his own business and he works nights and weekends as a plumbing contractor.

Jansen's self-description was typical of dutiful craftsmen: "I'm probably an honest person, straightforward. Family-oriented. Probably, if I had to choose between time for my family or job, I'd choose my family. I'm conservative in most of my thinking. I have fairly strong religious beliefs. In some ways, I'm a perfectionist. I like to stand on my own two feet. I don't owe anyone. No credit cards. If I can't afford it, I don't buy. My wife doesn't always agree, but she has learned. I'm fairly ambitious, but probably security is important. I'm not willing to take too many chances that might affect the family. I'm kind of materialistic. I want to have a big house and a big car and I will someday."

Although Jansen is a no-nonsense manager, he is more good-humored and friendly in his large, bearish way than his responses suggest. The type of devel-

---

*In the factory, we asked workers to choose among various self-descriptions. The dutiful craftsmen checked "You are skilled and competent. You do your duty and work hard. You like strong people who do their job well and don't complain."

The receptive craftsmen checked "You enjoy skilled work and you also like socializing. You don't get too heated up by problems. You tend to believe in 'live and let live.' "

opmental engineer he wants under him is "a guy I can give a job to and he will get it done, not a constant complainer, a bitcher about insignificant things." His view is that as long as you must work for the large organization, you do your duty and make the best of it. He respects others who feel the same way.

Both his religious and political beliefs support Jansen's work attitudes and life goals: "Religiously, I am quite strict. I believe in God, the Ten Commandments and life after death, heaven and hell. You follow the way or you don't, there is no in-between." Asked if he had been influenced by any religious figure, he mentioned Billy Graham. "I've been to his meetings, three or four. Once I even went up."

"Did it change your life?" I asked him.

"No, I don't think I was sincere enough. I think it does change many people's lives and values," he answered.

"Is it that you feel you are still too materialistic?" I continued.

"Maybe that's what would change," he said.

Jansen described his political philosophy as "conservative" and he gave money to conservative candidates. He checked as national priorities strengthening the police and national defense, tightening the enforcement of antidrug laws, ending crime, ending big-government interference in local issues, and community control. (Yet he did not believe that citizens qualify to make decisions on the use of advanced technology. Experts should do it.) His goals for America were "conquering disease, increasing the life span, lessening of poverty, lessening of lawlessness, increasing productivity, and making able-bodied individuals who can work, work." He said that the computer he is helping to create should help lead to these goals by "freeing up people from laborious tasks they had before and solving problems not before solvable, especially in the field of health, where it may lead to a longer life span." But he does worry that the computer he builds may eliminate jobs.

While Jansen's perfectionistic, dutiful attitude has served him well in a foremanlike management position, and he is respected because he is himself willing to do all he asks of others, he is unlikely to rise to higher positions that require subtle sensitivity to different interests or the need to sell himself. (And can you imagine an executive without a credit card?)

In the corporations we studied, the most craftlike work is found on the lowest level of the R & D organization where the engineer has the maximum contact with the hardware and tools. But for the young engineer at the bottom of the large projects, such as computer development or aerospace, the work tends to become formatted, that is, he is just solving routine problems set by someone else, and there is no need for imagination. He feels that he is a kind of worker on an intellectual assembly line.

One craftsman told us, "Many nights I go home frustrated and work four to five hours on a car and accomplish something. I work for myself." Others moonlight as repairmen or cabinetmakers with the idea of eventually opening their own business.

If he wants to become more independent and inventive, the craftsman must be both original and able to sell his project to managers. If he fails to do this and wants to improve his status and salary, he must become a manager. Despite the fact that many craftsmen would prefer building to managing, they are moved to climb the ladder. They want the money, and, anyway, the lower-level work is not craftlike enough to hold them.

There are a few exceptions to the inevitable rise upward, usually among the receptive craftsmen. One was a fifteen-year veteran of a number of successful small-instrument projects who actively chose to stay at the bench where he could work out solutions to difficult problems, work that he deeply enjoyed. He became a troubleshooter throughout the lab of a hundred engineers where he worked on yet another small-instrument project. So while formally he remained at the lowest level, with no subordinates, each day he talked with a number of engineers on other projects, helping them with solutions to their technical problems. In the interview,* he hardly touched on this aspect of his work, but those around him consistently mentioned him as being the person in the lab of greatest help to them in their own work.

"If I had the opportunity to do anything I wanted, or to study for a new career," he said, "I'd choose the work I'm doing now. Even if I didn't have to work I'd still like to do what I'm doing now. I went into engineering because I liked Tinkertoys, Lincoln Logs, Erector sets. I played less with other children. For my tenth birthday my aunt gave me the *Radio Amateur's Handbook*."

Asked "What is your goal in life?" he replied, "I can say at least a few things, but not a thing. Contribute to the happiness of at least a few people. If I do a good job [at innovation] there will be nice paychecks for people in production. Develop some of the talents I have. Grow old gracefully. Not like I've seen many people grow old."

How did he maintain this attitude without feeling left behind, a loser? His job had real craft attributes, and he was not ambitious in terms of salary or status. He lived simply, supplementing his income by farming with his wife. They eat little meat and grow all their own vegetables. They each drive a VW with 130,000 and 180,000 miles on the speedometers. Furthermore, he gained the esteem of co-workers by being the informally recognized senior craftsman in the lab.

Needless to say, few corporate craftsmen find positions that meet these requirements.

A younger craftsman in his twenties hoped eventually to "be independent of any corporation. Ideally I'd like to be working as a craftsman in some creative

*Dr. Douglass Carmichael gave this interview and the following one.

capacity strictly on my own. If I stay, I'll still be in the same position; it suits me, from my point of view."

Although married, he had no children, and did not feel financial pressure to move up into management. He said that he actually saved half of his income of about $14,000 and invested it. His wife made her own clothes and enjoyed organic gardening. When asked what he liked to read, he said, "Books about clocks and watches, Zen Buddhism," and his political philosophy was "consistent with my way of looking at other things, the word 'acceptance' is the key word, laissez-faire. I'm an isolationist as an individual." Needless to say, this isolationist attitude would not serve for a manager who must motivate others to work interdependently and meet corporate project goals.

The majority of all engineers are not such purists. Although they have come to engineering with a basically craftlike orientation, they needed other qualities to succeed in college and masters' programs, and to impress the corporate interviewer who hired them. The competition and pressures to enter management strengthen these traits, since success in most companies requires that the young engineer develop them.

Nevertheless, those who preserve some of their interest in craft work and quality, even if that interest is frustrated at work, maintain values that keep them from being completely absorbed by corporate careerism. This interest also serves to keep a man awake and interested later in his career when the competition and the game, the struggle for promotions, have lost some or all of their interest for other corporate types.

THE GENTLE CRAFTSMAN

Bill Steward is the rare craftsman who has risen to a high middle-management position in a large corporation, with headquarters near Boston. He may have gone as high as a craftsman with some company man qualities can reach in a large company. For that reason, and to describe an individual within a social character category, we will explore him, his work, and his family life in greater depth. Steward started out as one of the most brilliant and innovative bench engineers in a lab (part of a huge multinational company) where groups of three, four, five, and sometimes up to eight craftsmen work cooperatively in developing fine electronic instruments used by the leading companies and university research labs. At the age of forty-five, he had become a lab director, supervising the work of five section managers and, overall, close to one hundred professionals.

His work required study, meetings, planning, and responsiveness to the needs and problems of those under him. Together with him, we summarized his work role requirements as follows:

1. Corporate integration and policy. He meets with those on his level (marketing, manufacturing, microelectronics) and with the division president to plan the division policy. He needs to have a detailed sense of instrument design management, and to see the relation of his lab's work to the business strategy of the division. He then transmits the division product strategy to the section managers, in a style that attempts to decentralize authority.

2. Administration. He keeps figures and charts on inventory, projected costs, and actual monies spent in their relation to lab objectives in the form of thirty specific projects. Daily he monitors such figures in the form of computer outputs, and spends 30 to 40 percent of his time in direct discussions with lab personnel to assure that there are no problems. He advises section managers on personnel issues, including staffing groups with compatible people.

3. Motivation. He tries to create an atmosphere where craftsmen work well, yet are responsive to strategic changes in work assignments; and to see that there is a friendly atmosphere within each project so

that each worker relates meaningfully to the over-all project strategy. He responds to personnel problems and tries to find a just solution. He evaluates the work of subordinates, giving praise where it is due and trying to help correct weaknesses. (He has never fired anyone.) However, when it becomes necessary to push a group, Steward's superior, a gamesman, may step in.

4. Coordination.

A. He coordinates lab projects with marketing and manufacturing counterparts, involving project leaders in this communication.

B. He oversees communication within the lab and arbitrates disagreements between groups. He holds a monthly meeting with each lab section. While section leaders oversee communication within the projects, he keeps aware of what each individual is doing on an assignment basis (what each person is working on for about six months).

5. Learning new skills and attitudes.

A. He must keep aware of competition—the whole field of instrument systems—and he studies the competitors' products in terms of technical development and price.

B. He must keep aware of new technology opportunities for use in instrument design. He must keep up with the state of the art.

C. He learns new methods of quantitative management.

D. He takes part in management courses that analyze managerial attitudes.

6. Technical work. He doesn't work on the hardware, but he must judge the time, cost, manufacturability, reliability, and effect on the company image of the technical solutions proposed by individual projects.

The man who fits this role so well is tall with close-cut dark hair. He is shy, but friendly and forthcoming once he gets to know you, with a warm smile. Yet there is an elusive quality about him, as though part of him is far away in himself even when he is listening closely.

Here's how he described himself: "I think I'm a pretty sensitive person; I'm sensitive to other people and a sensitive type myself." (When we get to know him, this seems to mean also that he respects others and expects to be respected.) "I consider myself to be very responsible and take a good deal of pride in following through. I can be counted on to follow through and to be prompt.

"I like such things as hiking and sailing. I'm a physical type more than an intellectual. I prefer doing rather than contemplating a lot." At home, Steward likes to build cabinets and play with electronics.

"I miss involvement with hardware which is because I like to work with my hands as well as my head. I like going to the trade shows so I can demonstrate the equipment." In contrast, he is uncomfortable making the speeches required by his role and spends hours memorizing them. "I'd like the opportunity to make the equipment, but it's hard to get time to do my own project."

Finishing his self-description, Steward said, "I am not as naturally socially conscious as a lot of people are these days. My wife is more interested in politics, but it doesn't seem natural for me. I'm a pretty simple type of person in terms of needs and as far as saving and investment as opposed to buying objects and goods."

Although Steward described himself as a person who enjoys building, he modestly left out that he also enjoys helping others at work. He said that what he most likes about the work, what motivates him, is "the technical involvement, the learning about new things. The natural stimulation for me is my interest in the work; the competition seems to me unnatural. For others it might be different." What he likes least is "when we do have disagreements. I like to see everyone happy."

Steward presented himself as neither ambitious nor

particularly competitive. He said, "I would not like to go any higher because my natural interest is in technical involvement. I'm happy with what I'm doing."

I asked whether he might not be secretly or unconsciously ambitious. "I don't think I would agree. I never had the need to be the leader in the group, I never felt that." Even in high school, he never held any office more exalted than secretary of his fraternity, and the only team sport he played was basketball in the church league.

The how did he get so high up? "Things under me have gotten done well," he said. "I've gotten on well with the people under me. The people over me see this as something that works. Then they try another step. I'm not sure I understand why."

Recently he took a managerial mini-course that described four managerial types: the analytic, amiable, driving, and expressive. Bill described himself as analytic (industrious, persistent, serious) and amiable (responsive and supportive, also complying and retiring) but not driving in the dominating sense nor expressive in either the exciting or the promotional sense.

"I'm a collector and synthesizer of good ideas," he said. "People like to work under me. The best seems to come out of them. I have organizational ability in laying out the work that needs to be done. I help and serve the people under me as much as possible."

How do others see Steward? When I asked the president of the company, he answered simply, "Bill is a very gentle soul." The top managers, the gamesmen, consider him a good man, technically and humanly right for his job, but too mild and cautious to move into the upper realms of dynamic corporate risk-taking, and Bill agrees with them.

A peer described him as "intelligent, tenacious, open-minded, fair, good perspective, good judgment, good imagination, a low-key, effective leader, he delegates responsibility well."

A young gamesman on the way up: "He's a great

guy. Every time I meet him, I discover something new. Thoughtful. When he says something, he really means it. Doesn't get excited under any condition. Very cool. When he says something, he sticks to his word. He gives me the idea of something very stable."

One of the older craftsmen: "Interesting person, I worked with him a number of years ago. A very cool type person. Nothing upsets him. I don't think he manages just to be a manager; he does it for the company. He's very technically competent. I used to sail with him."

Another craftsman: "A very warm, personable, friendly person who can create an atmosphere where people feel free to express themselves, and like to work. . . . He is the stable pole to the division president's dynamism."

The lab's most creative engineer: "I have definitely enjoyed working for him, very happy with that. He's a fair guy, an excellent sense of humor. A sharp fellow. He's beginning to lose touch with technical things. Once upon a time, before managing, he could do my job, but not now. He's losing touch, losing some skills."

His secretary: "A super person. He's a really good boss, kind, considerate, even-tempered. I've never seen him mad. He has the respect of everyone who has ever worked with him."

His wife Betty's view of him complemented the others.* She said, "He's a very nice man, a very gentle man. He rarely loses his temper; once a year, and then he becomes reticent, not critical. He bends over backwards. A few times he hurt me; after a party, he didn't approve of my gossiping about someone.

"He's very active physically. He backpacks, skis, and sails. Reads quite a bit more than most people, less than I do. He likes to jump up and do things. He does not sit at length.

"He's been easy to live with for twenty years. We re-

---

*Kathy Terzi interviewed Betty Steward.

spect each other. We're able to be nice and not remind each other of our faults. He wishes I'd stop smoking. I'm critical at times. I have strong opinions on politics, and we argue. Eventually, he comes over, like three years later on Vietnam. I'm strong on child care, and I think women should get into office. He votes for the man.

"He's a very good father. I'm pleased he's the father. They are too. He takes them camping, sailing, skiing. They wouldn't have learned it without him. The kids have all these skills from the father. I've been the disciplinarian all the years."

Asked about his weakest points, she answered, "Reticence, I think. He is not forward enough. He could be a little more aggressive." Asked what she meant by this, Betty said, "He does not stand up and disagree."

What are Bill's goals and ideals? "That's a tough one," he answered. "To be happy, to live up to my responsibilities with my family and children." He did not mention work here, but he had said before that work and family should be fifty-fifty. The area of freedom and independence for Bill seems to lie outside of work. "I want to enjoy life and travel," he stated. "And I feel a conflict in coming to work each day. I worry I'll get too old to enjoy things."

Bill enjoys his life, including good food, wine, the outdoors, and reading detective stories for relaxation. But part of him yearns for the life of the explorer, adventurer, or inventor—man against nature, like Sir Francis Chichester, who went around the world in a small boat. Organizational work does not satisfy that yearning. Does that faraway look mean that he is far away in the ocean or on a tropical island? I asked him. "No." He laughed. "I don't daydream at work."

Although he was brought up a Presbyterian, he said he does not believe in God and has no religious affiliation. He believes above all in honesty and respect for others. "I think that what a person should do is be good to his fellow man, that that is satisfactory. If later it turns out there is a God, that will get you through. I can't imagine a God pleased with devotion." His philosophical views were influenced by reading Bertrand Russell and also by the central influence in his life, his father.

Although his political views have become more liberal in recent years, especially due to Betty's influence, he stated that "social and community problems have little weight with me. I appreciate them, but there is no strong personal concern."

He checked as the main issues facing the country: pollution, the need for guaranteed jobs, overpopulation, and overinvestment in the military. His idea of progress for America would be "making the country a better place to live for more people in two ways: (1) Ecology, air and noise pollution. (2) The minority and poor people who get a pretty low share of the things that we have."

Steward said he worries that unscrupulous leaders may take advantage of social problems to expand their power. He was attracted to John F. Kennedy as a "great character with ability to lead people in the right direction." He did not share my criticism of Kennedy's adventurism and support of militarism.

Nor did Bill express criticism of his corporation's role in society, although he is uneasy about the fact that 10 percent of the products are sold directly to the military and 30 to 40 percent indirectly. He said he is "quite satisfied that the application of our products is in the field of better communication." What are socially harmful products? "Some military, it depends on the situation. Drugs that are not used for medical purposes. Products that contribute more to pollution, things like that." Like the SST? "Not exactly," Steward said. "The SST was too costly but not polluting. We should have bigger, cheaper planes, not faster ones, but the ecological reasons seemed to me false."

Bill said he accepts the competitive, mechanized

world as a given and worries only about extreme totalitarianism. Both Betty and Bill's secretary were more critical of technology and his work.

"Take the moon program," Betty said. "It causes people to place more emphasis on things than on the human beings and needs on earth. We should put more resources toward social problems versus cars, washing machines, the space program, planned obsolescence. People, not gadgety things, are what count. But they just seem to blast ahead, like the SST, without concern for the noise and pollution. They insist we have the capability without thinking about the cost in money and quality of life. Car companies make cars go a hundred and twenty miles per hour. They should show some restraint and make them go less fast. This is an area where Bill and I argue. He feels I'm being sentimental and idealistic."

Betty also felt that many corporate managers prefer things to people, and she stays away from their gatherings. She said, "I don't really approve of the engineer types. It's a good company from the employee point of view, in terms of pensions, stock sharing. I suppose I believe them when they say only three to four percent of what they produce goes to the military, but I was on the side of the students throwing paint at the building. I try not to think about it. It's a very important company and part of the Establishment. It's benevolent, though, and they'd like their people to become involved, to wield power."

Bill's secretary, responding to the question "How would you define progress for America?" answered, "To some people it's great—more building cement, bombs, airplanes to pollute, more crime because more people are replaced by machines and out of work. I don't see where technology has been all that positive. More and more psychologists and screwed-up people."

For her, real progress would mean "a better environment in terms of more emphasis on human development and not machines. People need an opportunity to learn and grow. They need a constructive feeling of accomplishment at work."

Family is at least as important to Bill as work, and his is one of the most successful marriages we have seen, based on respect, considerateness, and responsibility. The implicit marriage contract seems to establish a comfortable, friendly, and responsible life together, where neither restricts the other's freedom to develop in his or her way, or makes unreasonable demands. It is not a passionate relationship or even a deeply intimate one. Although Bill and Betty enjoy being together and to a point know and understand each other, there is a sense of limits and distance, as if too much passion or intimacy would upset a delicate balance and unleash feelings that would be difficult to manage.

This was expressed in their answers to the questions "What is love?" and "What is a happy marriage?" His view of love was "a genuine liking for another person, you enjoy being with them." A happy marriage is "good companionship, being comfortable with each other, enjoying being with each other." Her view of love: "There are probably two distinct meanings. Sexual infatuation, maybe that isn't love, but I guess it is though. That's passion. Then there is a warm, protective feeling toward someone. You probably have it for your children and husband as you grow older. I don't know, maybe a few lucky people could keep the absolute joy of the first time. Personally, it's hard to sustain for twenty years. I don't like the word 'love.' I prefer 'respect,' 'joy,' 'liking.'" A happy marriage is "where you have mutual respect, you know. Love's a hard word. I'm not sure what love is. Joy of life covers it for me. You enjoy things together. Sex wanes; as Hitchcock said, 'after the first few years, food replaces sex.' Bill and I were talking. You have to be realistic, respecting each other's rights and feelings. . . . He's worn well over the years. I feel comfortable with him, I enjoy being with him, I feel he's my best friend. I really am satisfied with him."

Betty grew up fearful, rebellious, but seeking approval from an authoritarian, moody, and temperamental father who worked all the time, and when he came home, terrorized the household as much by his silences as by his anger. Her childhood wish was that he would leave, and she vowed to marry a completely different kind of man.

Betty remembered her mother as a comfortable, warm, and accepting type of person, and in many ways, Bill also has these qualities; she believes she takes after her father. "I tend to shut things up, tend not to discuss things. I'm not manic-depressive as he was, but I won't touch things that are uncomfortable."

Growing up, she felt worthless and powerless. Her goal was to be just like her mother, "go to college because most kids in my economic range went and marry a man who went to college and then have kids. No career. I look back on it with horror. My father had the theory that a woman who worked was bad news. It implied her husband couldn't support her." Betty used to have nightmares of total powerlessness. Only in recent years, through her job as a departmental secretary in a university and the stimulation of the women's movement, has she begun to feel a greater sense of self-affirmation and self-respect. She belongs to NOW, "and I like Betty Friedan. I recently took a course in anthropology. No men were allowed. It was called 'Institutionalized Inequality.' We studied other societies and primates. There were a lot of not straight women in the class." Betty explained that housewives and mothers have lost their importance and much of their social function. "They're not needed in this day of appliances, dryers, TV dinners, and permanent-press clothes. Some say they like to bake bread. It seems artificial if I can buy bread. It seems more reasonable to have some bakers bake it instead of some woman, although it's not very good in the grocery. It was important for a woman to have children, now it's a liability. A woman who doesn't limit her family isn't socially responsible. What do you want to do with your life? You can't say be a mother. You have to say something else."

When asked to describe her husband's responsibilities to her, she answered, "You're talking to a feminist. It's not to support us—that should be half and half. Children are a fifty-fifty proposition. We should pool our money. I don't believe in alimony at all. It's her responsibility to work unless she's crippled. He's got a responsibility to help around the house. We all take turns cooking. The oldest boy thinks if he cooks bad, we'll stop asking. I still do the grocery shopping. After twenty years it's unfair to the husband to hand him a totally new marriage contract. He's been very understanding and cooperative."

Bolstered by her new sense of self, Betty seemed to be struggling to move out of herself, to be less controlling and more concerned about others. Like Bill, she left organized religion and no longer believes in God. She said, "Ethically I believe in respecting other people's rights. It takes in an enormous area. You don't kill, you don't rob. The Golden Rule, treating other people the way you want to be treated . . ." She stopped to think. "That's a negative, egoistic way of looking at it. It should be a feeling of responsibility to others less fortunate . . . and not less fortunate. The Golden Rule means responsibility to your fellow man."

The family members—Bill, Betty, and two teenagers—respect one another. Neither Bill nor Betty liked squealing infants; the more the kids can do for themselves, the better they like them. Now they take trips together and ski (Betty learned at forty); Bill sometimes takes the children camping, leaving Betty at home; she dislikes camping and would rather go to a restaurant than cook out. Bill also tells the children stories, as his father did, stories about his own childhood, mystery and ghost stories. But the kids go to Betty for advice about their problems. They emphasize that she has always been the disciplinarian, the strict one, while Bill is the parent who never gets angry. (Is it that he is so understanding? Is he detached? Or is it that he doesn't hear anything that might make him angry?)

The children, in turn, like their parents and try to live up to the family values of respect and self-reliance. They feel the home atmosphere is stimulating, active, and democratic. At the table, they talk about politics or school life.

George, the seventeen-year-old son, named three people he most admired: "Thoreau, he wrote *Walden*, went away after he was taxed unfairly and lived off the land. Neil Armstrong, the first person to walk on the moon. I don't think too much of him, but I wouldn't mind being first on the moon, to do what he did. My father, because he does a lot, he's a talented person."

He said his goal in life is "to live it to its fullest, to have a good time the whole time, have a party. I want a job I like, to do things I like, and be with people I like." What kind of people? "They must be able to decide for themselves, that's very important. At least you have friends who help you, who know you well enough to help. You must be willing to work, but that's easy, because you get bored." Why do you get bored? "I hate it being bored. That's putting your attention on yourself, like someone's talking and you don't listen." He remarked that many young people he knew were bored and looked for excitement in drugs and alcohol. George tried marijuana but he gave it up by himself because it slowed him down. He said, "Biologically, your body is very closely knit. A drug throws it off balance. It's not good. Anyway, I can get high traveling." It is interesting to note that George worked this out himself. Bill, who feels deeply that drugs are destructive, neither gave advice nor did he become angry when George told him about it afterward.

George said his ideal is a world without money, where people are given the necessities of life and where they work because they don't want to sit around bored. "It's a communist point of view," he said, "but it would be a great way to do it."

Bill Steward is more or less an open book. Others see him as he is and can count on him. His responses to the Rorschach and what we know of his life history fill in the picture and were consistent with what we learned from his self-description.

Rorschach's ingenious ink-blot test was a main instrument we used to explore the inner life and style of thought. Making sense out of the ink blots requires active thought, and allows imagination and playfulness. There is no way to fake the right answer, which reassured some executives who feared that "others" would just try to give nice-sounding answers to our interview questions. Most managers saw the Rorschach as an intriguing challenge and did not hesitate to respond if I agreed to tell them how I interpreted their responses. In a number of cases, my ability to tell them about themselves from the Rorschach was what convinced them that the exploration was worth the effort.

There are ten ink blots mounted on 6¾-by-9½-inch white cardboard. Some of the blots (I, IV, V, VI, and VII) are in tones of black and white. Cards II and III include blotches of red also, and Cards VIII, IX, and X are multicolored.

In accordance with standard practice (the object of which is not to undermine the clinical usefulness of the cards by making them too familiar to the general public), the Rorschach ink blots are reproduced here at about one-sixth their original size. (See insert between pages 146 and 147).

I told each individual: "Here are ten ink blots. I am going to show them to you one at a time. Tell me what they look like. Look at them any way you wish. Take as much time as you want. I will write down everything you say. When you are finished, hand the card back."

The exact wording of instructions doesn't seem to matter so long as it is made clear that the person is free to see as much or as little as he likes, holding the card right side up, upside down, or sideways. (Many Rorschach investigators just ask what the blots look like, giving no further instructions, and then treating further questions from the individual as material for interpretation.) After the person has given his responses, it is customary to review them to find out what aspects of the blot were taken into account in what was seen.

Interpreting the responses well requires experience and training both in relation to the "formal" attributes of a response (use of space, color, shading, etc.) and in the meaning of symbols.* For example, whether a person sees something in the whole blot versus a small detail may indicate how he approaches new information. Is he able to integrate a set of information into a dynamic whole (systems mind) or does he make collections of unrelated data? Does he stick to tiny, well-defined details and avoid the big picture? How accurately does he perceive complex reality? Do his needs distort his perception so that he sees things that make no sense to anyone else? If he does see reality accurately, is this achieved at the expense of ignoring emotional stimuli (represented by colors and shadings)?

Can he integrate thought and feeling into more vivid perceptions? Or do reds suggest passions that break through his controls and upset his intellectual effectiveness? Does he interject movement, and life into what he sees? Does the movement show active identification with human activity? Is the movement a projection of animal strivings, not fully inte-

---

*Some basic books in Rorschach interpretation include:

Hermann Rorschach, *Psychodiagnostics: A Diagnostic Test Based on Perception* (Berne: Hans Huber, 1942).

Ernest Schachtel, *Experiential Foundations of Rorschach's Test* (New York: Basic Books, 1966).

Roy Schafer, *Psychoanalytic Interpretation in Rorschach Testing* (New York: Grune & Stratton, 1954).

Bruno Klopfer and others, *Developments in the Rorschach Technique: Technique and Theory* (New York: World, 1954).

grated with conscious values? Does he feel comfortable with spontaneous impulses? Or does the movement express natural forces experienced as totally beyond control? Is his world constricted? Is the content of his responses conventional and careful? Is he afraid to see anything different from others or does he have the imagination and daring to perceive originally?

The content of the responses—the symbolic themes —expresses the individual's interests, needs, fears, and mode of relatedness, which may be conscious or unconscious. The sequence of responses may indicate the way in which a forbidden desire provokes fear and guilt or the way a habitual attitude (e.g., submission or servility) stimulates anxiety or, more unconsciously, fury and rage. The possibilities for response are limitless; no two sets of responses are ever alike, although there are particular responses (populars) that are frequently given and types of responses that inevitably suggest certain meanings.

The symbolic content of responses is in part determined by the shapes and colors of the different blots, which tend to suggest different themes.

Card I generally suggests a common winged creature like a butterfly or a bat, but it may stimulate expressions of inner conflicts (the side figures struggling) or central problems (having to do with the central figure).

Card II suggests two figures touching, with common themes of intimacy, passion (the red), play, or lively celebration. In managers, it sometimes stimulated themes of performing for others with repressed negativism and feelings of humiliation and anger.

Card III presents two figures in some type of relation to each other and to objects. It often stimulated themes in the managers about work or structured play relationships (picking up things, bowling, waiters, etc.).

Card IV presents a bulky figure that is often seen like a child's view of a looming authority figure. Responses may indicate how one handles authority—

directly, by going around it, etc. In both this card and Card VI, the shading suggests texture and may stimulate attitudes toward affection.

Card V is another winglike figure. In Mexico, it often suggested images of the mother, either protective or predatory. In managers, there was no general theme, but, rather, many possibilities.

Card VI, with its phallic, totemic top and furry shading below, stimulates symbols of sexuality and potency (with some engineers, the phallic image is mechanical and metallic).

Card VII has a cloudy, soft, and fluffy texture and often evokes the individual's attitude to women, femininity, the mother (e.g., graceful dancers versus stuffed toys versus pet dogs versus old gossipy women). Some who are threatened by softness turn the figures into rocks.

Card VIII, with its many colors, seems to stimulate themes of self-image, in part due to the two animallike figures on the sides. (Craftsmen often see these figures as beavers, while jungle fighters see them as tigers, wolves, or other predators.)

Card IX, with its misty colors, presents a certain sense of the spiritual or supernatural, which produces total rejection from some people and from others a stimulus to express their deepest values and purposes, their frame of orientation and devotion or sense of ultimate meaning. For some managers, it is the corporation itself, but for others it is the possibility of human unfolding or caring for others.

Card X, with its many small, colorful figures, evokes in some symbols of undisciplined appetite, underdeveloped emotions, or an intellectual challenge to integrate seeming unrelated events.

Bill Steward's Rorschach responses are those of a highly intelligent person with a systems mind that creatively integrates details into meaningful wholes; he ignores small details peripheral to the task and doesn't undertake more than he can handle. He knows his limits and respects them.

He does not waste energy, nor does he try to show off by giving many responses. He takes the unstructured ink blots as a problem to be solved precisely and elegantly.

The responses also expressed respect for people, identification with them in joyful activity, and a deep sense of responsibility. Bill is able to accept his feminine as well as masculine side with easy grace, which explains why he is happy to share the housework with Betty. When we asked whether women should have the same rights as men, his response was "You just have to put yourself in their place. I know how I'd feel." I asked if he ever felt threatened by expressing a nurturing attitude that might be considered feminine. "I help my wife with the housework," he answered. "Women's lib doesn't bother me."

His responses to the Rorschach expressed little passion or intimacy. He sees the colors as muted, and figures are either distant from each other or barely touching their palms together (as in the case of two bears seen on Card II).

His response on Card IX (which often expresses deep existential goals) gave a clue to his childhood development. First, he saw an anatomical response, the inside of the body, which suggests narcissistic preoccupation with one's inner condition, possibly hypochondriasis. Then he developed a new percept: "A tree trunk and foliage with a couple of birds under it," a symbol of strength, rootedness, and protection. Bill was a sickly child who worried a great deal about his health, and was worried over by his protective parents. The Rorschach responses suggest that he has overcome this tendency to narcissistic introversion by sheltering others, and in this sense his managerial work probably reinforces the productive, caring side of his character.

The Rorschach responses also touched on Bill's lack of aggressiveness, what Betty described as his failure to "stand up and disagree." The male authority image was seen on Card IV "like a person flat on his back."

Bill told me that he feels he has a problem giving in too easily. I asked to whom he gave in? "To the more expressive types who come after me strongly. Very, very often they are people over me. I do it to avoid conflicts."

In giving in to authority, Bill may also be taking after the father he admired, an immigrant from Scotland who, with only a high-school education, became chief engineering manager in a paternalistic company in Vermont, where he worked for fifty years. As Bill described it, the relationship between Mr. Steward and the aristocratic general manager of the plant had a feudal quality. He recalled that "my father would go over to see the boss every Christmas morning. He would take me and give him a present." Bill also remembered that his father kept opinions to himself, while his mother, like Betty, was more outspoken; for example, she was opposed to war. We might speculate that Bill modeled himself not only after his father's supportive craftsmanlike qualities ("He always gave me the impression he was standing behind me, he gave me a sense of security"), but also his submissive, admiring service to authorities he considered superior.

Yet this is not the whole story. In another Rorschach response (to Card VI, the phallic blot), Bill saw a rocket taking off with smoke coming out the back. For a person with such a controlled, even repressed, impulse life, this is a significant response. The nonhuman movement implies an impulse that is felt as alien, that takes over the person despite himself. It might express a strong impulse to become erect, to assert himself, but if so, this impulse is experienced as aggressive and threatening (the smoke indicates diffuse feeling, anxiety) and it is not integrated into Bill's conscious value scheme. Both his marriage and work have stimulated cooperative and responsible qualities in Bill, but not a critical, penetrating attitude.

It is fair to ask whether Bill's not standing up to authority has helped him to move up in the company.

By avoiding sharp criticism of the "expressive, controlling" types directly above him and genuinely admiring the baronial top management, Bill has avoided what he can't handle and has exercised his productively nurturing and craftsmanlike qualities. Both he and his superiors agree he does not have the competitive, aggressive drive to go higher. But we don't really know the form his aggressiveness would take if it were stimulated to develop.

I asked Bill if he could imagine a situation in which he would take a strong stand against those in power. He answered, "If things got very totalitarian." This was right after Watergate, and I asked if he had followed the testimony. "I watched it with fascination; I'm not sure why." Didn't he feel that the Nixon gang was moving toward totalitarianism? "You better believe it," Bill said with uncharacteristic passion. "That's just the thought that passed through my mind. The methods they used. I recently saw the movie *State of Siege*. That's the direction. If things were moving there, I could see myself moved."

Bill's last remark to me at the end of our conversation was "You know, engineers feel things are more predictable than people. But it's not true. People are predictable if you understand them."

Like some of the most receptive and humanly productive craftsmen, Bill has not developed a deep understanding of himself or others. Nothing in his education has prepared him to explore inner reality. Nor has he concerned himself with the social implications of what he makes. In fact, no one we interviewed ever stopped working on something because it was socially harmful.

The craftsman's priority values of quality, problem-solving, and a satisfying family life allow Bill to serve the company's needs without questioning whether these are also the needs of humanity. Within the corporate world, the craftsman is on the defensive, trying to preserve his integrity from the exploitative demands of more aggressive managerial types. Inside his protective shell, he does not let difficult issues penetrate, and he is unable to reach out to others who might share a new point of view.

CHAPTER 3

The Jungle Fighter

HISTORICALLY, the jungle fighter has been an entrepreneur and empire builder. In the Mexican village we studied, Fromm and I found that a small group of bold and innovative jungle fighters was the first to break away from the traditional practices; these villagers were the first to buy tractors, which they also rented out to others, the first to try out new farming methods with chemical fertilizers, and were the most likely to become middlemen.

Some of the most successful also operated by means of force, blackmail, and bribes to gain wealth and political influence. The sadistic attitude symbolically expressed in their Rorschach records of predatory animals, blood, and stone idols was behaviorally acted out in their ruthless suppression of opponents and castrating domination of subordinates by their own force or aided by *pistoleros*.

In the "developing" village society, such jungle-fighter entrepreneurs were the new men and were known as the "progressives." They were the ones who opposed traditional fiestas as a waste of money and a temptation to drunkenness. They argued that the money would be better spent for new roads useful for their agribusinesses, and for schools, which gave their children a chance to prepare for university careers. When the small landowners or artisan-craftsmen spoke for the traditional ways, the entrepreneurs accused them of opposing progress. Their wealth, new values of material accumulation, and modern methods deepened class divisions in the village and destroyed

73

traditional limits and protections against envy. Eventually, the entrepreneurs succeeded in dominating the village economically, politically, culturally, and ideologically. Yet, despite their material success, the jungle fighters seemed to enjoy life less than others in the village. They distrusted the people they controlled and feared revenge from those whose land they had gobbled up. They had no comrades, only accomplices and servants. They did not like the fiestas, and were uninterested in the welfare of the poor, condemning the landless day laborers they exploited as lazy and stupid. Most of these men had destructive effects on their wives, children, and others in the village.

The robber barons of post-Civil War America were also jungle fighters who rationalized their exploitation of people and resources under the ideology of social Darwinism and progress—new technology, railroads, industry, open lands, immigration, education. An example of one of the most intelligent, subtle, and complex of these entrepreneurial jungle fighters was Andrew Carnegie. His father was an unaggressive receptive craftsman who failed at a small business. His mother, as is so often the case with jungle fighters, seems to have been a protective, self-sacrificing tigress whose ambition for her son may have terrorized him to succeed;* the alternative of failure meant facing her ferocious contempt. She remained his jealous

---

*Once a well-meaning friend suggested that young Carnegie might take a job as a salesman. Carnegie remembered, "My mother was sewing at the moment but she sprang to her feet with outstretched hands and shook them in his face. 'What! My son a peddler and go among rough men upon the wharves! I would rather throw him into the Allegheny River. Leave me!' she cried, pointing to the door . . . we were taught idleness was disgraceful; but the suggested occupation was somewhat vagrant in character and not entirely respectable in her eyes. Better death!" From *Andrew Carnegie* by Joseph Frazier Wall (New York: Oxford University Press, 1970), p. 86. I am grateful to Jody Palmour for his research on Carnegie's character and for his helpful suggestions.

confidante and shrewd business adviser throughout her life.*

Carnegie was always open to new industrial, technological, and financial techniques that would increase profits. But his relations with business associates are a story of seduction, manipulation, and betrayal. He hired subordinates who fed his insatiable narcissism, and kept them as dependent as possible. He was ungrateful to those who had helped him, once he no longer needed them. It was practically inevitable that he and his partner Frick, two deadly jungle fighters, would finally turn on each other.†

Like many jungle fighters I have met, Carnegie liked to believe that he was a good man, concerned about progress and the well-being of the workers. He even thought of himself as a radical. As a young man, he was a Jacksonian Democrat and a religious skeptic. Later, as an industrialist, he wrote tracts in support of the working man's rights to organize and to negotiate contracts. But his own industrial goals were power and profit, to be gained by the new technology and by large-scale production, which cut costs, and by new management techniques which cut wages. Led by Carnegie, steel was the advanced industry of its era, the model for other industries in crushing unions of independent craftsmen and instituting the Tayloristic management methods that

---

*When Carnegie was first getting to know Henry Clay Frick, he asked him to have dinner with him and his mother and several guests. Toward the end of the meal, Carnegie called for a toast to the new Frick-Carnegie partnership that had not yet been discussed explicitly. "The sudden silence at the table was broken by the brusque query of Margaret Carnegie," Wall writes. " 'Ah, Andra, that's a very good thing for Mr. Frick, but what do we get out of it?' " *Ibid.*, p. 484.

†Years later, when Carnegie had turned to philanthropic concerns, he sent a messenger down the street in New York City to Frick's house, saying that since they were now old, he would like to meet Frick one last time and forget the past. Frick's reply is a classic: "Tell Mr. Carnegie I'll meet him in Hell." *Ibid.*, p. 764.

stripped workers of their dignity and restructured jobs so they could be filled by unskilled and semi-skilled labor. The craftsmen who struggled against industrial "progress" at Homestead in 1892 were beaten up, wounded, and killed by police and soldiers, despite Carnegie's assurances and public support of unions. Once management had gained control over the production process and the union was destroyed, Carnegie offered shorter hours and other benefits which would pacify workers.*

During his later years, Carnegie wrote and lectured that American democracy was the wave of the future, in large part because it allowed the exceptional individual like himself to emerge, the poor boy who rises to lead society (as he did), the " 'wild flower . . . found in the woods all by itself, needing no help from society.' "† (Jungle fighters never like to believe that anyone has freely helped them; from their point of view, the other person has been manipulated.)

His philanthropy, aimed especially at providing educational opportunities for the ambitious poor, was an attempt to rationalize his life in terms of his early ideals. This activity may have soothed his conscience and gained him admiration, but it does not seem to have made him happy. Thirteen years after his retirement he admitted that life outside the business jungle was boring. " 'It is the *pursuit* of wealth that enlivens life,' " he said, " 'the dead game, the fish caught, become offensive in an hour.' "‡

In Carnegie's day, industrial opportunities for the brilliant entrepreneurial jungle fighter were wide open. Today, the jungle fighters may succeed in highly competitive industries, like auto parts or clothing, where cost-cutting, risk-taking, and sharp sales practices can determine survival. But these entrepreneurs

---

*He used to quote Richelieu's advice: "First, all means to conciliate; failing that, all means to crush." *Ibid.*, p. 658.
†*Ibid.*, p. 394.
‡*Ibid.*, p. 827.

are no longer the progressives. They are now the re-
actionaries for whom government interference, in terms
of minimum wages and health and safety legislation,
adds costs which may cripple their ability to compete
with giant corporations. Like the old-style entrepreneurs, they still tend to be ideologists, who now defend their cannibalism in terms of "individualism" or
anti-Communism. But the successful corporate jungle fighter, like the patriarch in *The Godfather*, is
fast becoming a figure of the past.

In advanced-technology corporations, the jungle
fighter may have his triumphs. He may seem to be
an effective leader, developing group cohesion by
making other parts of the organization appear to be
the enemy. But in the long run, he becomes a liability
to the company because he foments hostility and
undermines the community. Sometimes a talented
and brilliant jungle fighter will be brought into a
corporation in trouble and given the task of reorganizing the company and getting rid of the "deadwood." The other types—craftsmen, gamesmen, and
company men—deeply dislike having to fire anyone,
while the jungle fighter takes pride in being feared,
but rationalizes this by claiming that such fear stimulates better work. In some companies, especially during periods of recession when they have to cut back,
the jungle fighter may rise to a high level, though he
is likely eventually to fail in all companies where economic success depends on teamwork.

Too suspicious and sadistic, he is unable to cooperate with strong peers in highly interdependent
teams. (Can you imagine Bobby Fischer on a basketball team?) The craftsmen feel that he wants to
emasculate them and retaliate by withholding information or acting stupid. Those whom he has betrayed, but not destroyed, patiently wait their chance
for revenge.

There are two kinds of jungle fighters—the foxes
and the lions. Foxes operate by seduction, manipulation, and betrayal. The lions are also wily, but like

Charles de Gaulle, they dominate through their superior ideas, courage, and strength; others follow them because they are feared and revered, and they may reward the loyalty of worshipful subordinates.

We interviewed only eleven jungle fighters. Most of them were essentially foxes, cunning and secretive, with strong exploitative, narcissistic, and sadistic-authoritarian tendencies. They wanted to dominate other people and be admired as superior beings. About half had enough of the gamesman's traits to allow them to function as team players, and these were the most successful. In two giant multinational companies, we met brilliant young jungle-fighter managers who were considered on their way up; both crashed soon after.

Similarities between the two cases are remarkable. Both were from working-class backgrounds, the father of one was a craftsman and the other a longshoreman. Both had degrees from leading universities and were known as brilliant theoreticians. Both had a grandiose idea for revolutionizing the industry (and as it turned out, they shared the same unrealistic idea). Both were secretive and conspiratorial, but at the same time childlike, enthusiastic and eager to bring the stranger-researcher into the group. (For all their suspiciousness, they wanted an audience.) Both had put together teams that included brilliant, erratic misfits who required constant mothering to produce. Both developed sadomasochistic relationships with some of their subordinates. Both ended up leaving the corporation to become entrepreneurs.

There were also differences, mainly in the degree of emotional maturity. One of the jungle fighters was smoother and more self-confident than the other. For example, both wanted to control their wives, but while one was able to dominate, the other was more like a spoiled child who had to compete with his sons for the wife-mother's total attention.

The more self-confident jungle fighter, whom we'll call Phil Bass, illustrates the fact that sheer brilliance, energy, and subtlety is not enough to reach the top in a major technology-creating corporation.

On my first day of interviewing at a high-technology company in Southern California, I started by explaining the study to a corporate vice-president. He was helping by trying to select people who fit the types we were looking for—those on their way up, brilliant innovators, managers who were best at developing people, people who had been successful in the past and had dried up, and so on. At one point, I was describing the concept of the "systems mind" (one that integrates disparate facts into a creative whole, a person who asks questions in order to test a hypothetical model in his head rather than making a list to later analyze and make sense of). I had observed this type of mind in the most creative innovators and top managers in other companies, and the vice-president remarked that they had a prime example there, a brilliant young man who might go all the way, Phil Bass, age thirty-two.

An appointment was made for the next day and I met Bass in his elegantly carpeted and decorated office, with awards on the wall and trophies representing successful projects on the walnut bookshelf. He was short and blond, with faded blue eyes. First, he told me about his work, how he had organized his own entrepreneurial group within the division, thus circumventing the chain of command. He also described his background, education and career in the company. The son of a longshoreman in San Francisco, he had won a scholarship to Stanford in physics. As a fledgling manager, he had taken advantage of a lucky chance by reorganizing a military project in trouble, and as he moved up, he consolidated his position by knowing when to leave projects that he figured would eventually fail. His career had also been boosted by working as assistant to and becoming a protégé of one of the toughest, most feared executives in the company.

Feeling Bass's impatience and curiosity about what

I wanted, I suggested that he respond to the Ror-schach ink blots, as a way of discovering his intellectual style and emotional attitudes. He agreed readily but only if I would tell him about himself.

His approach to the blots was bold and impressionistic, but, with one exception, colorless. His main emotion was primitive, anxious, greedy lust, although he controlled himself by a certain amount of gamesmanlike self-ridicule and playfulness. (Everyone is to some degree a mix of character types.) The main symbolic themes he expressed were the struggle for and worship of power, combined with enjoyment of work. He came across as brilliant and original, but moved by primitive irrational strivings.

The Rorschach was an X ray of Bass's soul. It exposed the world view and grandiose strivings that eventually led to his downfall, and on Card VIII, the animal expressing his self-image was in fact a fox.

Bass's first response to Card I was "I see a group of witches around some kind of altar. It's not clear what they're doing. Don't ask me why." A complex systems percept, symbolizing a world where conspirators gain power through worship of evil. Later, when I asked him whether he experienced the corporation in this way, he made it into a narcissistic joke. "Whenever I see a group in the corner," he said, "I feel they are conspiring to help me in some way."

Responses to Card III, with two equal figures facing each other, often symbolize one's attitude to cooperative or competitive projects. Many craftsmen see two people lifting something or otherwise working together. Bass seemed anxious as he picked up the card. "The trouble is they are all so damn symmetrical . . . Gee, I guess I have a dirty mind. It looks like a gang bang is about to occur. A couple of guys are spread-eagling on a broad. But don't claim *I* have a dirty mind; you drew the pictures!" I've given the Rorschach hundreds of times, but this is the first time I'd heard the response of men joining together in a conspiracy to rape.

Later, when he asked me what I'd learned about him, I suggested that he probably didn't trust anybody, and Bass said he trusted only his wife. "She is easy to live with and totally receptive to me. She wants to do things my way. She doesn't even want to do things on her own. For example, I pick her clothes and she likes my taste better than hers. She never presses me in terms of an emotional tie, and she never uses the emotional relationship in any destructive way. She never translates her anger into belittling me in any way. She never uses ridicule. She holds me in very high regard and considers me a genius." Since we did not interview Bass's wife we cannot say whether or not this view of her is wishful thinking. Nor do we know whether or not he is able to express more playful and generous feelings when he feels loved and is able to trust.

Card IX often suggests interpretations symbolizing the individual's spiritual center, his strivings for individuation and self-realization. Steward described a leafy tree, protecting birds in its branches. Bass said, "That's one that's dynamic! It's a fight, rather a violent one . . . but not a primitive fight, but organized, harmless. It's not a mortal combat of any kind. And there are spectators, who seem to be applauding. It reminds you of phony wrestling, but not phony, a legitimate athletic event." Bass first described violence, but then denied it. Was he trying to contain his primitive impulses within the rules? The response also suggested showmanship and duplicity (phony wrestling), even though he insisted that the contest was legitimate.

His next response developed a wishful theme of magical power and showmanship allied with technical genius. "Unrelated to that area," he continued, "seems to be a Merlin-type magician with some apparatus. Or even a Leonardo da Vinci. This individual is quite different from his contemporaries. He has a device in front of him which he is testing or demonstrating. I can't tell which. It's a complicated linkage of gears and what have you." I suggested this was his view of corporate life, a struggle in which those on top combined showmanship, magic, and technical knowledge. He agreed.

Later he told me he wanted to create the system of the future, and he believed he could achieve whatever he set out to do, if he wanted to enough. Yet he also told me a recurrent dream of "ultimate frustration," where he was turning something over and trying to pick it up, but it was an overwhelming mass of inertia and he could never succeed. I suggested to him that his ambition was endless and could never be satisfied, and that he was not living in the real world. He laughed. "Wait and see," he said.

More than a year later, I returned to see him. He had just been moved to a smaller, uncarpeted office in a new building. While we were getting coffee at the machine, a couple of men said to him, "We really enjoyed screwing you, Phil." They were the people who had assigned the space.

Despite his comedown, Bass remained cheerful and optimistic. Although he complained that the company's leadership was too cautious and conservative, he still hoped that his ideas would prevail, and he had been working with others to present a radically new concept for the future, one that could launch him into the power center of the corporation if it was accepted. I asked if I might interview people who worked for him, both to see how their characters meshed and what they thought of him as a manager. He agreed and suggested I interview two managers directly under him, one of whom was very angry with him because he had cut out his program. The other had also lost a program, but as it turned out, this man was a rather loyal and servile lieutenant (his Rorschach responses included poodles, an earthworm, and dissected testicles) who admired Bass and was willing to be his hatchet man. Yet he joked that Phil "likes to play things loose and avoid commitments. Both sides of the conflict feel they have his support, their best interests at heart. I'm under the impression that I have his support, but the other guy asked why I'm so happy, since I didn't have Phil's support."

The other manager, the one Bass said was angry, was a craftsman. He became more and more heated as he described his boss. "I don't know how he *feels*. I can only hear the words. He never commits himself. He's a cat that walks alone." He went on to say that you need technical trust to solve difficult problems and develop new projects. There needs to be a dialogue in which you find the solution together, not a battle where one person's view prevails.

He continued. "Phil prefers the approach that politically allows him to do it himself without having to cooperate with others. His henchmen denigrate their rivals, talk in the corridors, and write letters. Phil is a more subtle version of the same. He has led people on and betrayed them after promising to work jointly. In other words, he worked with others until he didn't need them. He has left a trail of corpses that smells. The others will wait to get you with a knife. It's a competitive group looking for revenge."

A year later, I met an executive who told me that Phil Bass was no longer an important person in the company. Soon after, he left for a key job with a small, up-and-coming competitor.

Brilliant jungle fighters may succeed in crisis situations or in roles that do not require trust and interdependency. However, the modern technology-creating corporation needs leaders who are competitive but not destructive, as the jungle fighter is. What about the company man?

CHAPTER 4

The Company Man

They are not the workers, nor are they the white-collar people in the usual, clerk sense of the word. These people only work for The Organization. The ones I am talking about belong to it as well. They are the ones of our middle class who have left home, spiritually as well as physically, to take the vows of organization life, and it is they who are the mind and soul of our great self-perpetuating institutions. Only a few are top managers or ever will be. In a system that makes such hazy terminology as "junior executive" psychologically necessary, they are the staff as much as the line, and most are destined to live poised in a middle area that still awaits a satisfactory euphemism. But they are the dominant members of our society nonetheless. They have not joined together into a recognizable elite— our country does not stand still long enough for that— but it is from their ranks that are coming most of the first and second echelons of our leadership, and it is their values which will set the American temper.＊*
—WILLIAM H. WHYTE, JR.*

SURVEYING the corporate landscape of the fifties, Whyte recognized the company man as the emerging type. He could not predict that changing technology and markets would call forth a type of organizational leader who combined technical and business skills and was more oriented to risk-taking. Even so, the company man Whyte described is still the type most frequently found among the middle managers of the companies we studied.

＊William H. Whyte, Jr., *The Organization Man* (New York: Simon and Schuster, 1956), p. 3.

On the whole, these managers accepted the categorization of company men but resented the overwhelmingly negative implications. Aware of their weaknesses, they also wanted credit for their contribution to the organization.

The idea that one is not an individualist touches a very sore spot in the American psyche.

Company man or not, we Americans still like to think of ourselves as an independent people, self-reliant, individualistic, and to a degree anarchistic. Compared to Europe, these traits still exist in the American character, but they were developed and reinforced by modes of work that have almost disappeared. The Republic was founded by farmers, craftsmen, proprietors, professionals, and entrepreneurs, and our form of democracy was rooted in the belief that there were enough independent Americans to stand up against demagogues and would-be dictators.

Of course, this view has always been exaggerated and romanticized. The slaves were not free, and the independence of many other Americans was antisocial. As with any other character trait, the meanings of "independence" vary according to the total character structure. For the crusty farmer or backwoodsman who rallied to the banner "Don't Tread on Me," independence meant stubbornness, suspiciousness, and uncooperativeness, as well as self-reliance. For the jungle fighters and hustlers, it meant being a lone wolf, free to exploit the suckers. As David Riesman pointed out in *The Lonely Crowd,* many nineteenth-century Americans appeared independent because they obeyed the internalized dictates of idealized parents, and were rigidly authoritarian and emotionally childish; their independence was bought at the expense of compulsive submission to the past.

The humanistic concept of independence implies following the dictates of conscience, as Ralph Waldo Emerson wrote, rather than submitting to either inner or external idols. But such creative independence needs roots in one's whole practice of life and usually in one's way of making a living. The traditional material basis of independence in America has been self-employment, ownership of property, or salable skills. The farmer, small shopkeeper, or craftsman could speak his mind, hold his ground, and even choose dignity over profit because he had no boss to worry about.* So attractive is the ideal of self-employment as a basis for independence that many corporate managers and engineers cling to the belief that the hardworking individual, with a little capital and a new idea, can make a go of it in business by himself, despite the evidence that this is seldom achieved. In the early nineteenth century, some 80 percent of all Americans were self-employed. By 1950, only 18 percent of all employed persons were self-employed, and this figure shrank to 14 percent in 1960 and 9 percent in 1970.† Furthermore, for every successful new business opened each year, eight or nine fail. The prevalent belief among corporate managers —that if one feels locked into an organization, it is due to lack of get up and go—has soothed the consciences of those who see no need to improve the quality of work. This same belief has in the past tranquilized workers who accept unfulfilling work because they hope someday to set up their own shops.

We should be learning how to establish the rights

---

*Many small shopkeepers seek profit as the first priority, but this may in part be due to the extreme competition from chain stores, so that the small businessman must struggle to stay solvent. In less industrialized countries, such as Mexico, where there is less of such pressure, small shopkeepers sometimes take pleasure in refusing to sell their goods to rude or overbearing clients. Sometimes this attitude is abused, by its justification of racial discrimination. However, it contrasts sharply with that of the employee of a large chain—such as Sears or Safeway—who is paid to maximize profit, not to exercise his sense of dignity.

†See Michael Maccoby and Katherine A. Terzi, "Character and Work in America," in Philip Brenner and others, eds., *Exploring Contradictions: Political Economy in the Corporate State* (New York: David McKay, 1974).

of managers and workers so as to develop a new basis of cooperative independence in the corporations based on mutual respect, equity, and democratic participation. Instead, we indulge in unreal daydreams of romantic independence, and they tend to support narcissistic fantasies, jungle-fighting careerism, and game-playing. (For some people, independence means "I pursue my career without asking from or giving to others.") We even distort reality into this romantic mold. In an attempt to assimilate the heroic astronaut into the traditional image, schoolteachers compare him to earlier explorers, such as Columbus and Magellan. Although both twentieth-century astronaut and fifteenth-century seafarer share traits of competence and bravery, and faced the risks of sudden death, structurally they are poles apart. The early explorers were individualistic jungle fighters who overcame superstition, setting out in largely untested craft, with a fearful crew that needed to be kept in line, to confront unforeseen weather conditions and unknown cultures. There was no Mission Control back in Madrid. There was no backup system when Cortés burned his boats. In contrast, the astronauts were fine-tuned parts of a highly technological, intricate, and centrally controlled machine. The fewer the unknowns and the fewer decisions they had to make, the more successful the project for the team as a whole. They were in many ways similar to high-technology managers, and some, like Frank Borman, now president of Eastern Airlines, have gone on to lead corporations.

Company men are essential to the functioning of large corporations. They equate their personal interest with the corporation's long-term development and success. Company men believe they will benefit most if the company prospers, but their belief in the company may transcend self-interest. In the elite companies we studied, company men care about the corporation and its future development. As much as they are motivated by hope of success, they are also driven by fear and worry, for the corporate projects and the interpersonal relations around them, as well as their own careers. Separate from the corporation, company men feel insignificant and lost. As part of the organization, they have their spot at (or on) the cutting edge.

To rise to the top of the elite companies we studied requires many company-man qualities, though that is not enough. The typical company man—the functionary—can rise to middle management or a high-level staff position. But he lacks the risk-taking ability, toughness, detachment, confidence, self-control, and energy to reach the very top. (The managers told us that energy is extremely important for reaching the top. This is largely genetically determined, but not completely; energy is also generated by the fit between character and work, and conversely, internal conflict blocks energy.)

On the positive side, the belief of company men in something beyond themselves (the organization) may provide them with a sense of belonging, modesty, responsibility, and loyalty. On the negative side are their feelings of little self-worth and the persistent fear that they will lose their place. They are worriers. How are they doing? Are they falling behind? Do they understand what is going on? Can they believe the gamesmen who seem so sure of themselves? Will they be overtaken by brighter competitors?

Once I presented a seminar to a group of eight corporate company men of upper middle management and asked how many had anxiety dreams of arriving at an examination unprepared. (Failing the test for promotions.) Three hands went up. How many had dreams of being chased? (The competition catching up.) Five hands. How many had dreams of falling? (Losing one's position, failure.) Everyone's hand went up. Many company men told us dreams like this: "I dream I'm trying to run from something and not being able to move. Ending up at the end of a long, dark tunnel feeling totally insignificant." (Note that the speaker stops using the first person singular, I, and just uses gerunds, "not being," "ending," "feeling." The disappearing "I," the lost subject, is a common linguistic symptom of the centerless person.)

The typical company man is a functionary who accepts a bureaucratic role and expects to go no higher than middle management. He is likely to come from a large family (and an Irish-Catholic background), and he adapts to the corporation as if it were a new family where he must mediate among conflicting fraternal and paternal demands for the good of all. Self-sacrifice feels right to him and he describes love in terms of giving up self, submerging oneself in the other. (For example, "Love is the complete acceptance of the thought of another person and a desire to completely subject your wishes or desires in order to achieve the well-being of the other person or thing.") He enjoys serving others as the way to serve himself. (A typical company-man symbol expressed on the Rorschach—usually Card IX—is a coffeepot.)

In general, company men tend to be inside men who feel in an inhospitable environment outside the corporate culture. Although this makes them dependent on the corporation, it also heightens their sensitivity to the feelings, the emotional ups and downs, of the people around them, and to the politics of their bounded world. Corporate power centers are to them as baronies with territorial rights, and they are acutely aware of who belongs to whom and how far they can go before crossing a border. Because of this understanding, they contribute to forging alliances and making the treaties and compromises that are necessary to develop complex projects. Company men are suspicious of the craftsmen whose desire for perfection is uneconomical, and of the overzealous and tricky gamesmen who use people up and who in wanting so much to win shift position so easily and threaten the integrity and good name of the organization. In turn, craftsmen speak derisively of functionaries as "technical incompetents who are politically ambitious," and gamesmen call them "boy scouts" and often complain that if they would put as much effort into project success as they did into internal politics, everyone would be better off.

In bureaucracies less dynamic than high-technology corporations, many company men gain their sense of autonomy in a negative way, by sticking to the rules and resisting change.* This attitude may block progress but it also protects the organization against the gamesman's tendency to cut corners or the unprincipled manipulations of the jungle fighters who were unchecked in the Nixon Administration. *The Wall Street Journal,* in an editorial, commented that a few individuals emerged from the Watergate episode with their integrity intact; the *Journal* had a point when it argued that "the explanation seems to be that these officials had an unshakeable determination to defend their institutional interests, therefore they couldn't be persuaded to join in the Watergate circus. It's fashionable to ridicule the limited loyalties exhibited by organization men and bureaucratic institutions, and to disparage their preoccupation with minor improvements rather than sweeping reform. Yet while such institutional inhibitions may be frustrating, they are also likely to be prudent."†

Company men function particularly well in the middle management of whatever size group they're in: project, division, or corporate level. They maintain the organization rather than setting the goals or doing the creative design work. As they move up to positions of direct line responsibility, they are often seen as trustworthy but unexciting leaders. Being trustworthy and responsible are their key terms (although they are more often conscientious than truly responsive to people). In normal times they negotiate between conflicting claims. It is they the organization

---

*See Michel Crozier, *The Bureaucratic Phenomenon* (Chicago: University of Chicago Press, 1964).

†*The Wall Street Journal,* April 4, 1974, p. 18.

turns to when it is a time for caution and retrench-
ment. But when strategic risks must be taken, or
when it is necessary to spark the team to higher performance, they are replaced by tougher, less cautious
types (like the gamesman). The same qualities that
help company men to stabilize the corporate atmosphere also limit their rise.

Company men exemplify what Fromm has called
the "marketing character." When they describe themselves, they seem to be trying to give the right impression, to sell themselves to the interviewer. It is
as though they are constantly working on themselves
in order to have the right kind of personality to fit
the job. There is a movement in leading companies,
General Electric a notable example, to develop careful assessment techniques in order to reward competence and not merely the right image. Yet this attempt at a rational and fair procedure sometimes has
the contrary result of putting more pressure on people to stay within the boundaries and not risk a bad
evaluation. Company men's self-descriptions often
sound as though they are trying to satisfy everyone's
view of what they should be with the result that there
is hardly any self to describe. A manager of a development project: "I'm just a little bit introverted,
just a teeny bit. I've been accused of not bending
my principles enough. Not that there is a definite
company code. What's fair and so forth is the company code. You have to be aggressive. And sort out
what's right and stick to it. You can't blow from side
to side. The guys make me stay fair. The job requires real consideration. You have to consider the
guys as well as the project." What started as a self-
description ended up as a job description. He went on
to say that the kind of people he most disliked working with are "those who have no concern for others,
and are just concerned with themselves [the games-
men] or the technology [the craftsmen]." His goal is
to develop the project and protect the interests of
his people. The winners and those overly concerned

with technology and perfection are going to upset things if they are allowed to follow their egocentric paths. He added that the ideal manager is one who sacrifices his individual career for the company's needs.

In a similar way, another company man described himself in contrast to tougher, gamier managers as "humble, more reserved, more of the quiet thinker, wanting to analyze thoroughly before speaking or coming out with anything. Speaking my mind only when I know I'm right. I want to be a nice guy. It's difficult for me to take a hard-nosed attitude. Gradually becoming more hardnosed, but it's frustrating, my wanting to be a nice guy. It's an internal conflict. I'm a straight arrow as opposed to a wheeler-dealer. Dependable. Always follow through. Sometimes get focused on too many details. Sometimes have to force myself to stand back and look at the big picture, allowing subordinates to carry through the details. Really enjoy working with people, particularly the co-ordination of several groups on a common project. One of my strengths is more on organization, stabilizing controls and order in a chaotic situation. Many of my subordinates seem to thrive on chaotic situations, it's part of their being wheeler-dealers, they really enjoy dynamic situations."

This self-description gives one the feeling of constant self-comparison, self-monitoring, self-criticism, and analysis of interpersonal situations. Through their work, company men develop their sensitivity to people and organizational politics, but as Joseph Heller illustrates in his novel of an oversexed functionary, *Something Happened,** this development may be one-sidedly careerist, at the expense of deeper personal development and relatedness. The quality of relations at work, while extensive and varied, is generally restricted to organizational roles without the regard

---

*Joseph Heller, *Something Happened* (New York: Alfred A. Knopf, 1974).

and interest in each other that characterize a friendship which grows only gradually and bears fruit in real trust and mutual understanding. Company men, in general, tend rather to develop the routine graciousness and courteousness that allow them to avoid deeper encounters with themselves and others. Their careerist goals, their anxiety to constantly move ahead so as not to fall behind, leave little room for self-development or concern beyond what is necessary for performance.

They may agree that work satisfaction and the quality of life are worthwhile goals, but this receptivity rarely develops into a serious commitment to restructure the organization in order to stimulate the fullest possible human development of all workers and managers. Yet, if such a program were to be initiated from the top down, many company men would welcome it. And if they do not concern themselves with social conditions inside the company that directly affect their well-being, even less do they worry about the corporation's influence on the larger world.

Furthermore, company men overvalue the company in relationship to their family life, where, paradoxical as it may seem, they are less at home than the craftsmen. While craftsmen like Steward take outings with the family or organize family projects to build something, functionaries tend to go home looking for rest, peace, and quiet. For the craftsmen, family is equal to or more important than work, and they sometimes mention being a good husband and father as goals in life even before work; company men always mention work goals before family goals.

Although the company man's work tends to reinforce a responsible attitude to the organization and the project, it may also strengthen a negative syndrome of dependency: submissive surrender to the organization and to authority, sentimental idealization of those in power, a tendency to betray the self in order to gain security, comfort, and luxury.

Many functionaries have given in: they have surrendered and been swallowed by the company. In extreme cases, this total submission becomes masochism, in the sense described by Fromm in *Escape from Freedom*.* The masochistic individual actually is satisfied to be humiliated. That is the only way he experiences a sense of belonging, feeling that while the dominant person (or in this case the representative of the powerful organization) is treating him the way he should be treated, the way he deserves, he is also accepted unconditionally.

Although submissiveness and idealization of the company turn out to be adaptive for the functionary, more extreme masochistic tendencies cripple the modern corporate manager at work as well as in his personal life.

A manager in a computer company sought psychotherapy because, at age forty, he was failing at both his work and his marriage. He had been unsuccessful in achieving three goals: to be a vice-president, to have a good relationship with his wife, and to become a warm human being. In fact, his work was falling to pieces because he was desperately trying to please all the people above him rather than understanding the business problems and resolving them. He was alternately bored and frightened by his beautiful wife, who, he said, didn't respect him because he wasn't a big success. In one dream, he saw her looking at him with contempt because he was taking orders from a black man. The black man was actually an employee whom he wanted to help, but he "knew" that his wife would consider him a worm because he put himself out for a black.

Beneath the self-hatred and fear, this man seemed to me to be a sensitive and receptive individual. As a young man he had been interested in religion and philosophy. He rejected an academic career or the

---

*Erich Fromm, *Escape from Freedom* (New York: Rinehart & Co., 1941).

church because he wanted to be rich and part of a glamorous elite company. He felt that he had sold himself to the devil, that he was damned. "I am afraid I feel nothing," he told me, "I am a hollow man," and his Rorschach responses described a world in which all impulses toward life and joy had been crushed by greed, decay, and evil.

This is an example of failure. What do the most successful company men feel about themselves?

Ron Goodwin, one of the most gifted and idealistic men we interviewed, reached a high executive position in a large company but he faltered near the top because he did not understand the game well enough.

Goodwin was in his middle fifties, courtly, elegant, good-humored, receptive, and helpful. If he had not seemed a little too soft, he would have looked the part of a company president. In his forties, he thought he would at least become a corporate vice-president. At that time, he had risen rapidly through sales and marketing to become a general manager of a division, and he had successfully organized one of the company's overseas operations.

His success had been due to a combination of three factors. Goodwin understood how the product sold and why people bought it. He knew how to give the product glamour, and how to provide service. He could take a system and make you believe that your business life would become classier if you bought it, even though the price was much higher than that of other systems that less elegantly performed the same technical functions.

Second, Goodwin's attitude of courtly deference to superiors and idealization of those in power flattered the corporate rulers and served him in the struggle for position.

Third, his sincere concern for peers and subordinates gained him their respect and affection.

Goodwin's goal was to combine Christian principles with corporate growth and profit, and "to have an effect on the world to promote understanding and more satisfaction and happiness by changing the company." He felt there was little he could do to change the world by himself, but by improving the company, he would better the world. How did Goodwin think the company could improve the world? It would not produce products before it was known whether or not they were good for humanity. The motto would be: If you can't foresee the results, don't build it. The company would also take a humanistic position on improving the quality of work and women's rights, and ending pollution, war, and racial injustice. How would the company determine these positions? By all the employees having a say.

Goodwin's managerial philosophy was that "responsibility and authority must be shared." He told me, "I believe in democracy with a strong recognition of its need for leadership and honest communication that can be understood by everyone."

But how would such a philosophy be put into effect within a giant multinational corporation? Goodwin was no one to organize or take part in a corporate revolution. His style was to flatter and persuade those in power. And they were not receptive to his idealistic views.

One of Goodwin's Rorschach responses expressed the contradiction and the lack of grounding for his goals. He saw fish, which he associated with the Christian faith, tied to a couple of court jesters teetering on the top of two docking spaceships. This symbolized his approach to corporate policy, an unstable combination of Christianity and the politics of the impotent courtier resting on technology in outer space. (The court fool tells the truth, but he is powerless.) He also expressed the contradiction between the principles of religion and power in the two historical figures he most admired: "Alexander the Great, he affected the future and was a great leader, but understood people and how to bring them together. And Jesus, he changed man without force, showed the power of working with people."

Goodwin wasn't tough enough to deal with the real challenges at the top. Nor was he radical enough either to organize an internal battle or leave the company. Instead, he was moved out of the mainstream. He was liked by the top executives, who appreciated his past marketing contributions, praised his humanism, but eased him out. In the meantime, he developed psychosomatic symptoms: depression, anxiety, restlessness, obsessive doubt, back troubles, and finally serious gastrointestinal difficulties.

Looking back at the top executives, now that he has left the company, Goodwin sees them as "people who don't like people—compassion is missing." In his own case, he told me, the traits that got in the way of success were his openness and spontaneity, idealism, generosity, and his critical, questioning attitude to authority. He also felt that he lacked sufficient aggressiveness, tenacity, decisiveness, and energy to reach the top. He was not quite the right type.

CHAPTER 5

The Gamesman

*The whole life of an American is passed like a game of chance, a revolutionary crisis, or a battle. As the same causes are continually in operation throughout the country, they ultimately impart an irresistible impulse to the national character.**

—ALEXIS DE TOCQUEVILLE

STUDYING AMERICANS in the 1830's, Tocqueville questioned why the American shipping industry was able to navigate at a lower rate than those of the Europeans. The reason was not that they had cheaper ships or paid less for labor. American ships cost almost as much to build as European vessels, and pay for the American sailor was higher. "How does it happen, then, that the Americans sail their vessels at a cheaper rate than we can ours?" Tocqueville asked. "I am of the opinion that the true cause of their superiority must not be sought for in physical advantages, but that it is wholly attributable to moral and intellectual qualities."†

Tocqueville went on to focus on those aspects of the American character that impelled crews to take greater risks and try new methods in order to triumph over competitors, and he saw the American spirit

---

*Alexis de Tocqueville, *Democracy in America* (New York: Vintage Books, 1958), p. 443.
†*Ibid.*, p. 441.

infused by the spirit of a game. Inventiveness, flexibility, and the love of novelty gave America its advantage in an industry where success depended on technology, interdependence, and competitiveness.*

During the late nineteenth and early twentieth centuries, although the gamesman streak was never absent from the American character, the gamesman took a minor role in large organizations, which were run by autocratic jungle fighters like Carnegie and Frick. In the organizational world of the 1950's, the gamesman was too independent and irreverent to reach the top of the largest corporations.

But increasingly this trait in the American character has proved adaptive to the changing markets and technology. The modern gamesman fits the leadership needs of organizations based on:

(1) Competition—internal, national, international.
(2) Innovation—continual creation of new products or projects to gain an advantage over the competition.
(3) Interdependent teams—experts who must discover, develop, and market the product.
(4) Fast-moving flexibility—the need to meet chang-

---

*Francis J. Grund, a German visitor around the same time, was also impressed by the spirit of American business:

There is, probably, no people on earth with whom business constitutes pleasure, and industry amusement, in an equal degree with the inhabitants of the United States of America. Active occupation is not only the principal source of their happiness, and the foundation of their national greatness, but they are absolutely wretched without it, and instead of the *"dolce far niente,"* know but the *horrors* of idleness. Business is the very soul of an American: he pursues it, not as a means of procuring for himself and his family the necessary comforts of life, but as the fountain of all human felicity; and shows as much enthusiastic ardor in his application to it as any crusader ever evinced for the conquest of the Holy Land, or the followers of Mohammed for the spreading of the Koran.
    —Francis J. Grund, *The Americans in Their Moral, Social, and Political Relations* (Boston: Marsh, Capen & Lyon, 1837), p. 202.

ing schedules and deadlines, requiring a manager who can motivate a team of craftsmen and company men to move at a faster pace.

These factors also describe modern political teams, which increasingly are also led by gamesmen.

Although most gamesmen have elements of the craftsman, the jungle fighter, and the company man, none of the others shares their unique qualities. Whereas gamesmen increasingly set the organizational style of flexibility, individuality, and risk-taking, other types imitate them but do not share their zest for this kind of life.

The modern gamesman is best defined as a person who loves change and wants to influence its course. He likes to take calculated risks and is fascinated by technique and new methods. He sees a developing project, human relations, and his own career in terms of options and possibilities, as if they were a game. His character is a collection of near paradoxes understood in terms of its adaptation to the organization requirements. He is cooperative but competitive; detached and playful but compulsively driven to succeed; a team player but a would-be superstar; a team leader but often a rebel against bureaucratic hierarchy; fair and unprejudiced but contemptuous of weakness; tough and dominating but not destructive. Unlike other business types, he is energized to compete not because he wants to build an empire, not for riches, but rather for fame, glory, the exhilaration of running his team and of gaining victories. His main goal is to be known as a winner, and his deepest fear is to be labeled a loser.

The games of business are both sociologically and psychologically different from other forms of play. In early childhood, play has the function of both expressing exuberance and mastering reality in the realm of freedom. In *Beyond the Pleasure Principle,* Freud described an example of an infant making a toy appear and disappear in order to master the recurrent trauma of the mother leaving him.* By the age of six or seven, many children's games, like hide-and-seek, have a new psychological function. They symbolize the struggle with authority, represented by the "it," or central person, who tries to limit the child's freedom. Children must learn to band together to free themselves from the authority. At this time, as Jean Piaget has pointed out, rules of reciprocity develop as an integral part of the game. Fair play becomes a basis for democratic moral judgments.†

As the child grows older, play takes two distinct paths. One is the disciplined development of spontaneous creative activity, which leads to the theological ideal of activity for its own sake, done out of love of beauty and wisdom. Examples are dancing, skiing, sailing, woodworking, etc. The most creative person is the "grave-merry" individual, writes the Jesuit Hugo Rahner, who "kicks the world away from him with the airy grace of a dancer, and yet at the same time, presses it to his heart."‡ In this sense of creativity, the ideal of making work into play is a noble adolescent dream, and we admire the scientists, artists, and craftsmen who come close to making it a reality. Thus, a group of leading American scientists in the middle nineteenth century called themselves the "Lazzaroni," after a society of Italian workmen whose goal was to make work into play.

If in fact scientists or artists fall short of the mark and are sometimes moved by baser motives, at least one can conceive of their work as disciplined play, although often science is in fact a more competitive activity. In the business world, there is less playfulness of this sort; the businessman generally wins at another's expense. In American folklore, Tom Sawyer

---

*Sigmund Freud, *Beyond the Pleasure Principle* (London: Hogarth Press, 1922).

†See Jean Piaget, *The Moral Judgment of the Child* (London: Kegan Paul, Trench, Trubner & Co., 1932).

‡Hugo Rahner, *Man at Play* (New York: Herder & Herder, 1967), p. 9.

was a prototypic gamesman-manager who motivated others to do his work for him, manipulating them, but at the same time making the boring work seem enjoyable.

The other type of play is the competitive game, which ranges from friendly tests of skill to warlike extremes of combat, where total aggressiveness is limited only by rules and penalties and the boundaries of time and space. In these games, there are plays, but little creative play carried out in the spirit of freedom. Although big business resembles aggressive-competitive games in many ways, it cannot be classified as a game, since it is not limited in time and space, and fashions realities that determine our daily life.

Yet business increasingly takes the form of interrelated games—the money game, the marketing game, the R & D game—all requiring specialized players. "What's your game?" has become a substitute for "What do you do?" On the higher levels, the corporate manager must respond to constant challenges having to do with new products, financing, decisions about production, labor costs, etc. Many businessmen can make sense of this crisis-style world only in gamelike metaphors. They will speak of the "game plan," of making "the big play." They will say, "We're going to have to punt now" or "Let's try an end around and see if we can corner a few more yards of the market." They will test out a new man by "giving him the ball and letting him run with it." Indeed, this language is increasingly the vocabulary of corporate business.

In the most dynamic corporations, managerial meetings have a locker-room atmosphere, where discussion of game strategy is punctuated with detached, mildly sadistic humor, employed by the superior to keep the inferior in his place. These little put-downs, which may be deeply resented by craftsmen or dignified company men, can be called "homeopathic doses of humiliation" necessary to maintain a minimum of hierarchy, to show who is boss, without having to humiliate the subordinate definitively by, for example, having him eat in another dining room or calling his boss "Mister Jones" rather than "Jack." Women who have reached top corporate positions have said that getting used to such joking is one of the hardest hurdles. Learning to accept ego punctures without being permanently deflated may be something acquired in team sports, and those who respond best are those who have played team sports seriously and can adopt the gamelike attitude.

One female executive on the way up told us how she fought back. Kidded about her short skirts, she put a shapely leg up on the table and asked her challenger whether he saw anything wrong with it. Although such a comeback to a superior is unusual, her gamy spirit won her points from the other gamesmen.

The semiconductor components industry is an example of an industry run by cool and daring gamesmen. Here we find executives who are highly imaginative gamblers. Like the auto parts maker, they sell vast quantities of their product (one company president called them "jellybeans") to relatively few customers, mainly those making computers, TV's, and radios (200 customers account for 70 percent of the business, according to this president). This produces fierce competition and pressure to lower price. Unlike the auto parts industry, here innovative craftsmen are the key to success, since the semiconductor component can be improved through research and development, and the customers can easily test them to determine which is the best for the price. On the basis of the test, customers will buy vast batches or none at all. The top executive must constantly weigh two variables that determine success or disaster. One is the level of design sophistication and the other is the capacity to produce large numbers of components. The overly cautious company man might produce an inferior component too hurriedly in order to have a product to sell, while the more scientifically oriented craftsman, driven by the hope of creating the ultimate design, might hold off developing production facilities until too late.

A spirit of intense competition for high stakes pervades the whole industry and is experienced on all levels. I asked the president of one semiconductor company what kind of people succeeded at this work and he said, "The competition is fierce; it's unbelievable. It has attracted an enormous number of bright people, but it's like Truman's kitchen, there are many dropouts and crack-ups."

It is common knowledge in the electronics industry that the components people are a special breed of gamesman. As if they did not have enough excitement at work, they tend to enjoy playing poker or tennis, games in which they beat others by capitalizing on their weaknesses. And they discuss one another in "game" terms, measuring their opponents as John Kennedy probably did when he saw himself up against Khrushchev or Castro. They say, "He tends to bluff in this kind of situation" or "He's going to think he'll get a scientific advantage here and so he's not going to produce in time, and I'm going to cut in here and zap him."

This spirit exists only in part because the industry is a young one and most of the top people know one another; the small, mass-produced technology and the specialized competitive market intensify it. In computer companies, where product lead times are greater and the customers' decisions are not made solely on the basis of cost and technical performance —programming, servicing, etc., are also important— the nature of the competitive struggle is considerably more relaxed. In some giant companies, the internal competition between project groups may be even greater than that with other companies.

In all the companies we studied, the spirit of competition prevails, sparked by either real survival conditions or by the executives' view of the expanding world market in which the company must either continue to grow or lose its position and eventually its profits. The gamesman's character also feeds competition. Even to enter the world of advanced technology, it is necessary to be competitive. But we have seen that the competitive urge is very different for each of the four character types. The following table summarizes these differences and the meaning of competitive behavior. Each type is motivated or energized differently, the craftsman by interest and pleasure in building and bettering the standard; the jungle fighter by his drive for power over others to escape being crushed by them; the company man by fear of failure and wish for approval; and the gamesman by glory and the need to be in control.

The gamesman's emotional attitude has meshed perfectly with the corporation's need for managers who could be turned on by the new technical challenges of the post-sputnik era and who could also excite others. More than any other types, gamesmen told us that the ability to dramatize ideas and to stimulate or activate others were among the most important abilities for their work. Charles L. Hughes, former industrial relations manager of Texas Instruments, wrote a book in the mid-sixties called *Goal Setting*.* He pointed out that extensive research showed that the kind of people who were most successful in the high-technology corporation were those "compulsively and habitually seeking to win." Speaking to older-style bosses and organization men who might be put off by the gamesman, Hughes astutely observed an advantage to the corporation in that the compulsive winner's main goal was not to become rich, but to win. For the gamesman, a high salary is important mainly because this is the way the game is scored, and he doesn't want to fall behind the others. He sees his salary not in absolute terms of becoming rich, but

*Charles L. Hughes, *Goal Setting* (New York: American Management Assn., 1965).

Roots of Competition				
Character Type	*Craftsman*	*Jungle Fighter*	*Company Man*	*Gamesman*
Typical meanings of Competition	Drive to build the best Competition vs. self and the materials	Kill or be killed Dominate or be dominated	Climb or fall Competition as price for secure position	Win or lose Triumph or humiliation
Source of Psychic Energy for Competitive Drive	Interest in work, goal of perfection, pleasure in building something better	Lust for power and pleasure in crushing opponent, fear of annihilation Wish to be the only one at the top	Fear of failure, desire for approval by authority	The contest, new plays, new options, pleasure in controlling the play

in comparative terms of staying ahead of others in his peer group.

The gamesman is not easily evaluated by traditional moral categories. In contrast to the authoritarian boss of the past, he tends to be unbigoted, nonideological, and liberal. He believes that everybody who is good should be allowed to play, and that race, sex, religion, or anything else has no bearing besides contributing to the team. Nor is he hostile. ("Nastiness and vindictiveness mean that person has already shown himself a loser," one gamesman told us.) Unlike the jungle fighter, he takes no pleasure in another man's defeat. But this does not imply that he is sensitive to others' feelings or sympathetic about their special needs. He is not compassionate, but he is fair. He is open to new ideas, but he lacks convictions.

Since he is so concerned about winning, the gamesman tends to evaluate co-workers almost exclusively in terms of what they can do for the team. Unlike softer or more loyal company men, he is ready to replace a player as soon as he feels that person weakens the team. "The word 'loyalty' is too emotional," said one gamesman, "and empathy or generosity get in the way of work." Nor does he share the jungle fighter's need for accomplices.

Although he may try to spark the "deadwood," the gamesman believes he is being democratic by giving others a "fair" chance to play the game. If a person, due to his background or temperament, never has a fair chance to compete against those gamesmen who are quicker and more driven, that means he belongs to an inferior class. The gamesman tends to classify people as winners or losers.

Many gamesmen operate well while young managers, but fail to resolve middle-age and middle-management crises. The ones who do reach the top are those able to renounce adolescent rebelliousness and become at least to some extent believers in the organization.

The typical gamesman's mid-career crisis exposes the weaknesses in his character. His strengths are those of adolescence; he is playful, industrious, fair, enthusiastic, and open to new ideas. He has the adolescent's yearning for independence and ideals, but the problem of facing his limitations. More dependent on both others and the organization than he admits, the gamesman fears feeling trapped. He wants to maintain an illusion of limitless options, and that limits his capacity for personal intimacy and social commitment.

This is one reason why imaginative gamesmen tend to create a new reality, less limiting than normal, everyday reality. Like many adolescents, they seem to crave a more romantic, fast-paced, semifantasy life, and this need puts them in danger of losing touch with reality and of unconsciously lying. The most successful gamesmen keep this need under control and are able to distinguish between the game and reality, but even so, in boring meetings they sometimes imagine that they are really somewhere else— at a briefing for an air-bombing mission, or in a hideout where the detested manager who is speaking is really a Mafia chieftain whom the gamesman will someday rub out.

Even such a gifted gamesman as Henry Kissinger imagines himself in an unreal, romantic fantasy. Ignoring the fact that he never travels without an entourage of his aides and the press, he tells an interviewer that he is like "the cowboy entering a city or village alone on his horse. Without even a pistol, maybe, because he doesn't go in for shooting."*

At their worst moments gamesmen are unrealistic, manipulative, and compulsive workoholics. Their hyped-up activity hides doubt about who they are and where they are going. Their ability to escape allows them to avoid unpleasant realities. When they

---

*"Kissinger: Interview," ed. by O. Fallaci, *New Republic,* 167:17–22, December 16, 1972.

let down, they are faced with feelings that make them feel powerless. The most compulsive players must be "turned on," energized by competitive pressures. Deprived of challenge at work, they are bored and slightly depressed. Life is meaningless outside the game, and they tend to sit around watching TV or drinking too much. But once the game is on, once they feel they are in the Super Bowl or one-on-one against another star, they come to life, think hard, and are cool. While other character types found in the corporation, such as the craftsmen or the more security-seeking company men, find such high-pressure competition enervating and counterproductive, for the gamesmen it is the elixir of life.

The gamesmen's yearnings for autonomy and their fear of being controlled contribute to a common mid-career uneasiness. Even the most successful gamesmen feel a kind of self-contempt that they are giving in, that they are performing for others rather than developing their own goals. A number of gamesmen respond ingeniously. Impatient with red tape and unwilling to be boxed in, some try to skirt authority to create their own organizations within the larger company.

Fred Gordon is thirty-six years old and manages four thousand people in a division of a multinational corporation. His goal is to have power. "I experience power," he said, "as not being pushed around by the company; it's a kind of freedom. Also, I can tell others what to do and set the direction and the strategy and the tone." As a young marketing manager, Gordon figured out that the way to the top was to get a relationship with a powerful customer to use against the company. "You need a very big customer who is always in trouble and demands changes from the company," he said. "That way you automatically have power in the company, and with the customer too. I like to keep my options open."

Gamesmen like Gordon try to create their own anti-bureaucratic teams, but in gaining their "autonomy," they may threaten the whole organization. Another such gamesman succeeded in forming his own "semi-autonomous" team, but his superiors complained that he was trying to set up his own barony and was making it more difficult to develop a more rational company-wide policy.

One gamesman near the top of a huge corporation has a recurrent dream in which he is a fugitive being chased by a powerful organization like the FBI or the CIA. But, in the dream, he knows he is secretly working for the organization, although those hunting him do not know it. He is testing the organization, its capacity to catch even the most resourceful individualists. He told me that he would leave the company if he didn't feel he could leave it any time he wished and make a good living elsewhere.

Such gamesmen are unable to resolve the conflict between their wish for total independence and their ambition to run the organizational team, which means satisfying their superiors and developing the team. They may create a successful project and even energize a whole company for a while, but over the long pull, some lack the patience and commitment to people and principles necessary to maintain a dynamic organization.

Bedazzled by the perpetually adolescent charm of the gamesman and sympathetic to his struggle against less attractive bureaucrats, our society romanticizes him. One might say that although we have no heroes because we have lost faith in our leaders, the gamesman is our favorite anti-hero. In the most popular motion picture of 1974, *The Sting*, two playful gamesmen, Johnny Hooker and Henry Gondoroff (played by Robert Redford and Paul Newman), confuse and conquer Doyle Lonnegan, the hated boss of a large gangster organization, dazzling him with a fake reality created by the fast-moving teamwork of many specialists using technology and sleight of hand. Like a modern morality play, *The Sting* presents the gamesman versus the old-style jungle fighter who built the organization. In this modern morality play, boyish and unprejudiced (black and white work together), informal gamesmen have the audience's full support because they are fighting killers. One quickly forgets that they started the trouble by ripping off the organization. Even though the master gamesman, Newman, is shown as bored and hung over when there is no action, one also tends to forget that these "heroes" are amoral, manipulative confidence men, lonely hustlers who drift apart after the game is over.

The fatal danger for gamesmen is to be trapped in perpetual adolescence, never outgrowing the self-centered compulsion to score, never confronting their deep boredom with life when it is not a game, never developing a sense of meaning that requires more of them and allows others to trust them.

An old and tiring gamesman is a pathetic figure, especially after he has lost a few contests, and with them, his confidence. Once his youth, vigor, and even the thrill in winning are lost, he becomes depressed and goalless, questioning the purpose of his life. No longer energized by the team struggle and unable to dedicate himself to something he believes in beyond himself, which might be the corporation or alternatively the larger society, he finds himself starkly alone. His attitude has kept him from deep friendship and intimacy. Nor has he sufficiently developed abilities that would strengthen the self, so that he might gain satisfaction from understanding (science) or creating (invention, art). In contrast to such aging gamesmen, there are seventy-year-old craftsmen whose goal in life is not winning, but making something better, and who are still energetic and interested in new ideas, although retired from the corporation.

Lundberg is now forty-six. Seven years ago, he was on top, the manager of a project that gained great profits for his corporation. He was a winner. Tall and blond, with an air of command, he had come to the company from the air force, where he was a pilot. Speaking of the past, he said, "I never wanted security; I felt we were all good race horses and we'd be allowed to run. I wanted to be part of the winning team. The corporation had begun to take off. It was wide open." Now, he has failed twice, and has been given a staff position with vague responsibilities. His superiors worry about what to do with him. He has become an alcoholic. His conversation was depressed. "I don't fear death now," he said, "but I fear discomfort. Hard knocks grind your ego down. There is a lot of pain there too. We sure had an ego then, partly because we were young."

Mitchell is still at the top at age forty, but is starting to worry about the future. Despite his success, he feels a failure. "I am considering whether all this is worth it. I started thinking about this four or five years ago. Before, I never thought about it. I feel a lack of joy. I don't see where all this is leading to." I asked him whether he felt his life lacked meaning. "Yes, it is running full tilt without direction. I'd like to do something that would make me *happy*. But I'm too lazy to do anything about it. I'd like to go fishing, but I'd probably go crazy in retirement. This environment is continually in a crisis mode. It's all high-speed. You can't talk about trivia. It turns me off when my wife wants to chatter. It's stupid when you think about it; what else can you do but listen."

Those who avoid middle-aged disintegration are the ones who have committed themselves to something beyond just winning games.

At the age of fifty, John Price, a gamesman with a company man's quasi-religious identification with the organization, became chief executive of the corporation where Ron Goodwin had failed to reach the top. Goodwin, we saw, was too idealistic and mild to achieve his aims. Unlike Price, he did not understand the game, its rules and boundaries, strategy and tactics. In his relation to authority, Goodwin was a courtier, while Price was more like a knight who had joined the Round Table.

Price told me his strength was solving problems

with others: "I have the ability to participate in a group in a harmonious manner which does not completely sublimate the ego. This is one of the most helpful qualities for a complex business. No one ever knows everything. An executive needs to be able to assess people and to be able to listen to what they say and evaluate it."

In contrast to Goodwin's warmth, enthusiasm, and idealism, the key term to describe Price's personality might be *controlled sensitivity*. Price does not waste a word. He can turn himself off and on. Even when detached, his radarlike sensitivity scans the emotional horizon. Whereas Goodwin believed he could change the world by humanizing the company, Price was convinced that the company already represents the best there is. Although he was modest about his own role, he felt deeply about the company, and his eyes watered when he talked about it. "What is central here," he told me, "is the idea that what we are doing is not only technologically important but socially important. We have a belief that we are inherently the best. We have a belief in excellence to support that. We are all very committed here. We don't see the end of this. The good we produce will probably reach a plateau someday, but we have a commitment to *growth*."

I remarked that there seemed to be a kind of religious feeling among top management, and he said, "There *is* a religious fervor here. It is the belief in what we are doing. We are doing much more than selling soap. We are at the cutting edge of society."

John Price was not opposed to humanizing the corporation or the world, and he respected those who undertook that mission. But it was not his. He was sympathetic to greater employee participation in decision making. "But I've tried very hard to see if there is anything more than rhetoric in this, and I feel it is not very practical except at the very low levels where people should have more of a say in determining how they work."

I asked him what he thought about the other issues that were so important to Goodwin. "A lot of it is very theoretical," he said. "It doesn't recognize the practical problems. Perhaps these issues are really way ahead of their time in relation to our sociological progress. Maybe if we were more affluent, we could worry about the social costs of the products we are making. Today we live in a competitive world."

Yet Price was open to change and was excited by it. He was proud that his sons had opposed the war, that they had sought more exploratory, less routinized education at their Ivy League colleges, and that his wife, a high school teacher, supported women's liberation. He saw the company like himself, responsive to new and reasonable social needs, just as it responded so effectively to changes in consumer demands.

What motivates Price? Not one simple motive. Like other executives, he said he wants a high income and financial independence, but unlike jungle fighters, there are limits to his ambitions, which are republican rather than imperial. He is also motivated by the game itself. Unless there is a contest, he said he gets too relaxed. "Everything is competitive here," he went on, and his Rorschach responses indicated that he is sparked, energized by the competition. He played football in high school and intramural sports in college. He loves puzzles and problem-solving, and welcomes the variety of problems at work. He likes to be where the action is, at the center.

Price is also motivated by the fear of failure. "I have always felt I must either move up the ladder or quit," he said. Besides the need for constant success, here is another theme common to the gamesman. He wants to believe he could leave if he did not make the top, but he knows he must keep on being promoted to keep his place as a respected member of the company. Unlike the functionary, he is too proud to accept a secure but humble place. His pride is maintained both by the respect of peers and by a sense (or illusion) of independence which compensates for unconscious feelings of being like an insignificant insect or small animal scurrying for food (images expressed by Price on the Rorschach).

I asked another gamesman, a corporate vice-president, to describe himself and he said, "I have a strong need to succeed. And a very strong need to be accepted by people. I feel some insecurity and self-doubt about how competent I am. I want to play the game if I can win and gain respect. If not, you don't want to play that game at all. You'd rather play one you can win." I asked if there was anything more important than winning. "Winning is really not it—it's not the right thing to say. It's really the need for respect from my peers. I'd rather be a highly respected Number Two than a poorly respected Number One." (You gain respect because you execute the plays and you are concerned about the total organization.)

As a child, Price dreamt anxiously of falling off bridges and of being chased, dreams of failure and competition. More recently, he dreamt of a spinning top. He asked me what it might mean, and I suggested that he was like a top which had to stay in constant motion; if he let up and relaxed, he would fall over. He agreed, adding, "I can't even take a vacation."

The dream might symbolize both the gamesman's psychic need for action and the corporation's demand that he keep moving to stay "on top."

Gamesmen like Price, who have reached the very top, take pride in their problem-solving abilities and coolness under stress (control) rather than their power (*machismo*).* They do not try to be glamorous.

---

*Dr. Ignacio Millán reports a dream of a Mexican manager of a multinational company in which he attacks a tall, blond European or American chief of the company who is sleeping beside him. In the dream the Mexican takes up a huge hammer. He recalled: "I raise the hammer with both arms and I strike the head of the stranger with all my strength. Despite my tremendous effort, something unbelievable happens. When

(In contrast to younger gamesmen on their way up with young and glamorous secretaries, the executive type invariably picks a plain, no-nonsense type.) The more adolescent gamesman still fantasies power and glory, and does not have the company man's belief in the organization. Although his passion to win may be enough to motivate a project team by offering others the chance to be winners with him, it does not serve to direct a giant corporation, to inspire thousands of employees, or to inspire confidence in bankers and large stockholders.

Gamesmen like Price are more independent and aggressive than the company men. I have asked them what they mean when they describe a successful manager as "tough," because while they seem to me detached, they also appear sensitive about hurting anyone's feelings. They lack the jungle fighter's willingness to destroy competitors or even to fire incompetents. (The executives of elite corporations hardly ever fire someone, unless they believe he is harming the company.) The toughness seems to be within the rules of the game. One top executive told me, "A tough guy genuinely induces fear in others. He has an

---

the hammer reaches his head, it hardly touches him. It only wakes him up. I feel terribly afraid and anguished. The foreigner looks at me steadily and without words orders me to hold his penis. I do it . . . His penis is flaccid. I strike it and his testicles with my fists, again and again. I feel furious and I see they are disintegrating but that there is no blood, and the man keeps on staring at me without showing any pain or emotion."

Besides expressing the repressed fury and humiliation the Mexican feels toward his foreign masters, the dream also revealed his experience of a totally different character type. The Mexican found that the executive's power is in his head. The Mexican's primitive force could not damage this, but only aroused the executive and provoked his retaliation. Forced to submit and humiliate himself, the Mexican tried to fight on a genital, animal level. Maybe he could triumph as a *macho* "Latin lover." But he discovered that the executive did not even need his penis and testicles. The executive could not be hurt at that level, and with this realization the Mexican woke up terrified.

aura of power, of being right. It is a strength of character, a winning attitude. Most people are backed off by it. You experience his inner violence."

Being tough in this sense is necessary to become a winner. Perhaps another reason why executives become tough and even subtly sadistic is because they have to accept constant humiliations. Their toughness is self-protective and their controlled meanness is a form of compensation, to reassure themselves that they have not been totally emasculated by the corporation.

The Rorschach responses of executives suggested that one of their most repressed feelings is humiliation at having to perform for others—from parents and teachers in childhood to the admired superiors at work —to be vulnerable and judged by them no matter how much the corporate policy emphasizes "respect for the individual." For example, on Card II, a corporate vice-president first saw two performing elephants, symbolizing strong and proud animals that have been trained and humbled. His next response was running tears of blood, symbolizing sadness, impotence, powerlessness, followed by rocket exhaust and flames, symbolizing phallic resistance, anger, hardening. He agreed with me that this represented the experience of castration and that it had led to compensatory toughness. Unlike the farmer or craftsman, the manager always remains in some way the schoolboy who is being judged on his performance. In this regard, it is interesting that the executive almost invariably mentions one of his superiors among the people he most admires, even when he complains about this man's treatment of him ("but if he weren't tough, we would not be where we are"). Rather than submit abjectly, he identifies with the aggressor.

Of course, in another sense, so-called "toughness" may really mean the courage to act on one's knowledge, in contrast to the soft-hearted alternative, which merely avoids having to take a stand. For example, a company-man executive saw that one of his managers lacked the technical knowledge and capacity to handle his job. Instead of stepping in right away, putting it straight to the manager and together working out a solution, probably a different assignment, the "nice guy" executive ignored the problem, telling himself he was giving the manager another chance. When the latter inevitably failed, he ended up with a negative report and a painful experience that could have been avoided if the executive had been "tougher."

The gamesman saves himself from the company man's surrender by emphasizing toughness and placing his primary value on fine-tuned self-control. By controlling himself so successfully and maintaining control over the organization, he begins to enjoy control for its own sake. The brain becomes the overwhelmingly dominant organ of potency. Others are judged also on their powers of control. Can they laugh at the hierarchical put-down without taking it personally? Can they take defeat as well as victory without losing their cool? Can they play the game, take the pressure, even when the results are unclear for long periods? Can they sublimate themselves harmoniously when need be and take over to analyze the problem and motivate others when that is needed? Can they communicate clearly? If so, they have succeeded in making themselves valuable and fine-tuned instruments.

Aristotle defined self-control as moderation and balance for the sake of healthy enjoyment of life. "Consequently, the appetitive element of a self-controlled man must be in harmony with the guidance of reason. For the aim of both his appetite and his reason is to do what is noble. The appetite of a self-controlled man is directed at the right objects, in the right way, and at the right time; and this is what reason prescribes."*

Executive gamesmen would agree with Aristotle,

---

*Aristotle, *Nicomachean Ethics* (Indianapolis-New York: Bobbs-Merrill, 1962), Book 3:11, p. 81.

but in their case, control has become as much an end as a means. Their own testimony, confirmed by the Rorschach responses, shows that the cost is dampened passion, emotional castration, and depression. More dependent on the organization than they realize for their life's meaning, their efforts at self-development make them valuable tools for the company. Outside the company, they have little social function or individual purpose. More than anyone else, they have exploited themselves.

John Price is a typical example of the gamesmen we interviewed who are taking over large corporations. Like most of them, he is a first son and Protestant. He attended an elite Ivy League graduate school, although he received his B.A. at a large state university, and he served as an officer in the Navy.

His whole life is organized to further his career.

Like most who reach the top, his wife is, in his terms, "flexible and supportive." He went on to say, "It is very unusual for someone to get ahead in the corporate world if his wife does not support him. They seldom get to the very top. People at the very top generally have very attractive wives who are respected. They are the kind of people others want to emulate."

Usually, the wives of these top executives are as intelligent, as energetic, and as competent at any activity they take on as their husbands are. They also spend time sitting on committees and performing civic duties that enhance both their own image and the corporation's as socially responsible. The most successful marriages are based on mutual respect for accomplishment.

The executive wives we interviewed were also just as oriented to success as their husbands, although this was not always their view of themselves. In one case, a gamesman executive told me that while he was competitive and analytical, his wife was emotional, compassionate, and intuitive. Later, when he was telling me about their leisure activities, he mentioned tennis.

I asked if they played together. "No," he answered with some embarrassment. Remembering that he had been a college quarterback, I was not surprised; she probably was not good enough for him. "No," he corrected me. "She won't play with me. She was nationally ranked." On meeting his wife, I discovered she was every bit as intelligent, analytical, and competitive as her executive husband. Forced to take the time to raise very small children, she was looking forward to when she could develop her own career.

Another executive wife's earliest memory was "I was not allowed to be leader of the line in the first grade and I was totally furious." She, too, saw herself as more oriented to the emotional than her husband, but it was a matter of degree and complementarity. There was enough difference between his tougher, controlled sensitivity and her more spontaneous subjectivity to create an exciting polarity; they both respected each other and enjoyed mutual criticism. Both were leaders who moved inevitably to the top of the organizations they joined. Neither was very sociable; they had few friends and spent most of their time together and with their children (taking trips, playing sports and competitive games—cards, Monopoly).

The executive wives we interviewed are women who like men. Most of them enjoyed close relationships with fathers who also liked them. Although they support the women's movement for equal rights, they disapprove of the "extremists" who hate men or practice lesbianism. They feel at home in a world dominated by men, and they admire their husbands.

The implicit marital contract between these women and their husbands is to become successful corporate models and to live a gracious, comfortable (though not opulent) life, with opportunities for travel and stimulating contact in the larger world of the successful (scientists, artists, politicians).

In bringing up their children, they encourage those traits and talents that will best prepare them to be winners like their parents. A gamesman executive's wife stated that her "number-one goal is to have a happy home so my husband and children have a springboard for success." Her husband told me that he feels a responsibility to push his children to succeed and achieve. This worked well with an older son who took after his father and was successful in sports, sciences, and school politics, but not with a more receptive, affectionate, and artistic younger son. With him, the father felt powerless and the boy escaped into compulsive eating and TV watching (his father countered by bringing home a TV camera and suggesting his son become a director).

Because this executive could not understand that his son was not motivated by problem-solving and winning, he was ready to conclude that the boy had no motivation. "I worry about him and I fear failure as a father," he told me. "I worry what people will think and what he will think." His wife also worried, but she more wisely decided that the son would be happier in a less performance-oriented culture. She said, "Unfortunately, a family can't be the best environment for all types of children."

The gamesman's attitude and talents fit the needs of the modern corporations, where his character has been developed. The gamesman qualities help him respond to constant changes in markets, methods, and technology. Since he is stimulated by the give-and-take of argument and the challenge of competition, he is less likely than more authoritarian jungle fighters or insecure company men to surround himself with yes men. He enjoys the give-and-take, the cooperative-competitive problem-solving, the trial by combat to assess good ideas and select comers.

So long as the corporation's relative standing is not threatened, the gamesman chief executive will favor programs that make the corporation more attractive to the brightest young people, and that will likely provide more chance for initiative and individual challenge. But here as elsewhere he will wait to respond to pressures. (One progressive top executive said that he was disappointed that the young engineers and managers entering the corporation in the late sixties did not demand more internal democracy and corporate social responsibility. But since they did not, the pressure for change was minimal.)

The gamesman will not initiate social programs that leave his company in an unfavorable competitive position. Nor will he pass up a chance for a big win in the market. He will trade anywhere he can, whether or not he approves of the regimes. (While older-style ideological managers and labor leaders criticize the Government for détente with the Soviet Union and China that they believe strengthens them and weakens us, the new high-technology executives complain that empty ideology and bureaucratic confusion prevent increased trade, which they maintain will liberalize the Communists.)

The gamesman will pollute the environment, even when he privately supports environmentalists, unless the law is such that each corporation must clean up its mess and none is penalized for being cleaner than the others. He will produce and advertise anything he can sell unless food and drug laws or other legislation stops him.

Even when he believes that the Government spends too much on weapons, he will make them. Even though he values privacy and is outraged by illegal intrusion of the state in the individual's affairs, he will build the technology that makes this possible. (A gamesman told me that his corporation had tried to build a new automated retail store system without hidden TV cameras to check employees as well as customers. Despite his distaste, his corporation had to build in the spying technology to remain competitive.)

But the new type of executive is ready and willing to play by the rules. One told me, "I like the game to be defined. Our main ability is that we know how to win at this game of business. Society can make any

rules it wants, as long as they are clear-cut, the same
for everyone. We can win at any game society can
invent."*

Given our socioeconomic system, with its stimulation of greed, its orientation to control and predictability, its valuation of power and prestige above
justice and creative human development, these fair-
minded gamesmen may be as good as we can expect
from corporate leaders.

---

*Note the testimony of Dr. C. Lester Hogan, Vice-Chairman
of the Board of Fairchild Camera and Instrument Corporation,
before the Subcommittee on Multinational Corporations of the
Senate Foreign Relations Committee, July 22, 1974, p. 3.

But Fairchild has found it difficult to obtain a clear
understanding of the government's position on the transfer
of technology—particularly semiconductor technology—to
Eastern Europe. This absence of a clear definition of
policy has been especially disappointing to Fairchild in
light of its 15-month effort aimed at working with the
government on a particular export license application,
which was recently denied, involving a proposed transfer
of semiconductor technology to Poland for use in consumer
products.

In matters of East-West trade, Fairchild has been and
remains willing and eager to play by the "rules of the
game" as determined by this country's policymakers. But
it would certainly like to find out what those rules are.

CHAPTER 6

A Creative Gamesman

All men have the capacity of knowing themselves and acting with moderation.

—HERACLITUS*

JACK WAKEFIELD is a crucial case for us to study in depth. Much has been written about craftsmen, jungle fighters, and company men, but little about the emerging corporate leader, the gamesman. But it is his capacity for evolution which will determine the corporation of the future. Gifted gamesmen, like Wakefield, express a mixture of traits. It is this richness of possibilities that gives the gamesman such flexibility and adaptability in a rapidly changing environment. Which of these qualities develop will depend on both circumstances and the individual gamesman's understanding of himself.

Wakefield appeared as one of the most creative and life-loving of the successful young managers we interviewed. Top management of a major multinational corporation saw him, at the age of thirty-two, as one of the young managers with the highest potential, a comer. He brought energy, verve, and originality to his work. He was a person who could motivate others to go beyond themselves. Furthermore, he was one of the rare young managers who expressed real social concern, as well as interest in his own self-develop-

*Kathleen Freeman, *Ancilla to The Pre-Socratic Philosophers* (Oxford: Basil Blackwell, 1947), p. 32.

ment. He was one of the few managers who saw the threat of corporate life to his own human development and worried how he could maintain his integrity as a corporate winner. Jack Wakefield is an example of the most productive type of gamesman. By describing his work and character, we will better understand that the two fit together and how the organization molds the character of its best managers.

Although he thought his high ideals got in the way of work and he worried about maintaining his integrity, Wakefield was deeply drawn to his work. He was both excited by it and highly rewarded because he did it well. In the end, he defined himself in terms of work. Away from work, he had difficulty connecting, either with his wife or with others who shared his professed ideals. Inside the corporation, his character fit the needs of the system, and he moved almost effortlessly. We shall see that over a period of time his ideals became blurred as he adapted to his work. His goals became defined more and more by the corporation, which had first call on his energy and thought.

The questions we shall ask are: Who is he? What happened to him in the corporation over a period of five years? How does he fit into the corporate psychostructure? What can we expect of him?

Jack Wakefield looks like Tom Sawyer grown up. You would not be surprised to see him with Paul Newman and Robert Redford hatching a plot together. He is extremely likable and seems open, yet one always feels in danger of being tricked or slightly conned. He is very seductive. He seems gregarious, yet when one knows him better, he is introverted and a little lonely. Like the typical gamesman, he is a collection of seeming paradoxes. He is idealistic, yet shrewd and pragmatic; cooperative, yet highly competitive; enthusiastic, yet detached; earnest, yet evasive; graceful, yet restless; energetic, yet itchy. Serious on the one hand, he is also boyish and playful, with a twinkle in his eye.

I first met Jack Wakefield in 1969, a time of turmoil and protest, when young people were beginning to attack the dehumanizing aspects of technology and militarism. Jack supervised about twenty people at that time. He had already had experience working with the president of the company, and had been sent halfway around the world as part of his training for top management. At this time he was managing the development of some of the newest projects in the company. He said that he felt under tremendous pressure. "It's like trying to innovate myself out of existence. Sometimes I think there will be so much innovation that we will end up not doing anything at all." He pointed out how new automated equipment had already knocked out the jobs of some of the other managers, "obsoleting them." Jack and some of the other managers in the company at that time thought that in the future it would be a privilege to work, since machines would do most everything. Jack grasped the purpose of the study immediately in terms of both the effect of work on the managers' character and social concern.

He pointed out that up to about three years ago he had not looked very closely at himself, but on one of his trips outside the country, he began to wake up to both himself and the social problems around him. He was particularly concerned about pollution, and he said, "The trouble with the engineering profession is that you can remain unconscious about the effects of what you make." Wakefield also said he didn't feel that advanced-technology corporations made products "that are all that useful to mankind. Of course some are, such as radar for airports, but a large part of the work is for the Department of Defense. I don't like that work, and I can feel we could use these things differently."

Wakefield said he believed that all products one creates should be a contribution to society. He told me that he had recently invited the leaders of the local university SDS to lunch with his group of engineers. I asked what happened.

"Well," he said, "the guys felt they learned a lot. They felt there were a lot of grounds for agreement between them and these students. Both were worried about pollution, and both felt that individuals should be more involved in making social decisions. Overall, there was a feeling on both sides that there is possibility for good technical change."

Wakefield noted that some managers believe that anything that they can build and sell, anything that can be technically created, should be made. They give three kinds of arguments: (1) Science is pure and based on rational circumstances. If you do it right, you get the right conclusions. If you can make something better, you should do it and it will benefit people. (2) This is a purely technical decision, and those who don't understand shouldn't be allowed to make decisions. (3) They argue that unless they keep making new things and what is technically possible, they will lose their jobs and they will have nothing left. This group is frightened by the idea of students dictating what they will do.

In contrast, Wakefield said that these are all social and political questions, which should be decided publicly. Sometimes he thought about going into politics in the future, but he decided he needed to make some money first.

I asked him how his work was evaluated, what he had to do to get promoted. He said he thought the promotion system was fair. It was based on the contributions one made to the success of the company. "Basically, we are evaluated in terms of the excitement we create in the company." Later, when Wakefield was helping me to design the first version of the interview questionnaire, he had much more to say about how his work was evaluated. I asked him to describe the criteria of success again, to think over how the work he did was evaluated for purposes

of promotion. He wrote down the following three
criteria:

(1) Success (i.e., sales) of the product line which
my group designs and develops.

(2) The technical contributions of these products
which excite top management and cannot always be
measured in sales. It is a new and exciting product
line and the sales are increasing rapidly—so promotion has been rapid.

(3) "Growth" of the people working for me.

Which of these criteria was the most meaningful to
Wakefield? His answer was "The growth of the people working for me and providing the right environment for them to enjoy their work."

After going over the first draft of my questionnaire, I asked him whether any aspects of his work
had not been covered. He said the questionnaire was
fairly good but there were two areas that should be
included:

(1) Do you have control over the way your job
and its evaluation is done within certain boundaries?

(2) Do you shape the characteristics of the product
you are working on in a relevant manner?

For Wakefield, at this time, one of the most important questions about work was whether the worker—
at least the engineer or engineering manager—had
some say in determining the form and content of his
work.

WAKEFIELD'S CAREER

Wakefield had been working for the company since
he left graduate school. He had studied physics first,
then electrical engineering and business administration. He got his first boost when he developed a new
product. Then he got into operations research where
he found ways of using the computer for business
prediction, and quickly saw the weakness of overcen-
tralized computer methods. Early on, he envisaged
the possibilities of decentralizing computer use, with

ideas that did not bear fruit until years later when new technology allowed them to become workable. In fact, at our first meeting, he told me a dream he had had of a solution to a problem using a decentralized computer system. His innovative work and the excitement he generated brought him to the notice of the president of the company and for a brief time he worked on his staff.

Before going more deeply into Wakefield's values, attitudes, and behavior, we might describe how he sees himself and how others who work with him see him. Two years after the first interview, he continued to be promoted rapidly, and was then in a new division where he was managing more than one hundred people. How would he describe himself?

"I'm a fairly open person, tending toward the serious side. I think a lot. I feel I say what I must say. I guess I'd say, well . . . some of my attitudes are shifting. Here you need to think your purpose is to generate the momentum toward goals the marketplace tells you to seek. I stepped into two jobs where the people before me had no interest in people, no concern about where they were headed. I experienced enjoyment in the people as well as in getting things done. But I look forward in the future, maybe in a year or so, to participating in some kind of program, where I can take some time off from the company and work for social goals."

A year later, Wakefield had been again promoted to a larger job, one that involved reorganizing a department that had a great deal of trouble producing the right product. He had moved from developing small instruments to his first love, computers. He described himself as follows:

"Working in a small-instrument lab, I was a perfectionist. Here in the computer industry I'm a freewheeling game player. I like to fire people up, give them reasons to extend themselves. I like to spend time with people, but it's hard on my life at home, you burn yourself out. That's why I read at home. I retreat into myself. Also, I'm a person who tends to get involved with sophisticated things, with a technical flair. I couldn't work in a shoe store. I like the technical stuff. It's the frosting on the cake that completes the whole story."

Wakefield had become totally wrapped up in the problem of his new job and the need to create a new product that would succeed in the marketplace.

What position would he like to reach eventually in the company?

"I didn't ask for this job." (Note: A theme in Wakefield's conversation was that he's not ambitious. He likes to get things done, and when he succeeds, they just put him in higher and more responsible jobs.) "I got my motivation up and got a real swinging group going. I'd like to see it succeed. Then I'd like a sabbatical of one or one and a half years. Maybe I'd become a dentist in a town of about a hundred thousand or so. I've been around a lot. Maybe I'd go into law. Being a vice-president doesn't do it for me. I want to *dramatically* change careers at least once. I don't see anything to make me stay here forever. I left pre-med because it wasn't creative and I went into physics because it was more interesting. Now I've been creative in the organizational sense, the people sense, the new-product sense. Now I want to get entirely into the people kind of thing."

A year later, Wakefield felt he had almost decided to go to law school. He took the law aptitude test and applied to graduate schools, and could have gone. At that time, the main reason to go to law school was the ultimate goal of doing something for the environment, of using his combination of technical and newly gained legal abilities to help develop laws to protect the environment. Eventually, he decided against going to law school, and we will discuss the reasons later.

How did those who work with, for, and on levels above Wakefield see him? Essentially, he was appreciated and admired by many, although there were some criticisms. Let us start with those on levels above him. The president of the division said, "He is bright, dedicated, and loyal. He is smart, a real spark plug. He is hardworking to a fault. I worry about him. He spends his weekends on the company work." However, another top executive, who had been his manager in the past, said, "He is very complicated and more self-centered than others on his level. It bothers me that he says one thing to me and another to someone else." This man responded to the quality in Wakefield of giving people what they want, of selling himself in such a way that one does not quite trust him.

The people on his own level were generally favorable. A manager from another division who knew him said, "He is one of the people I most admire because of his ability to get other people motivated. Right or wrong, he can manage to get almost anyone excited about things. He's a good guy. I like him personally. He's also very adaptable. He moves from one technical area to another without any problem. He reaches sound conclusions when he gets to them. He looks like he knows what's going on. People have faith in his data base. His perceptions are very good when I calibrate them. I try to do that myself. When there's a conflict, he talks about it. Jack is very open about those things. He is very bright. His overall plans are always well thought out, and he is sensitive to people."

Another manager on a parallel level said, "Wakefield is extremely adept as a technical, managerial individual. He is very aggressive. Yet there's not a trace of jungle fighter in him. He's active, extremely active. In a word, he is a winner in the American sense of the word. Well rounded, very complete as a manager."

Those who work under him were generally favorable, although there was some criticism from the traditional craftsmen. We'll start with the critical comments. One craftsman said, "We get along fine. He might tend to make decisions a little more hastily than I would, but that's his job. He's a considerable improvement over the last manager we had here. He takes the broad view. I've seen him make decisions on the short range, and compared to what we've had in the past, he's OK. He's sometimes somewhat abrupt, but that's in keeping with managers in general." In a similar vein, another craftsman: "He's more capable than the one before. The only thing I find a bit difficult is to get him to stop talking about his grandiose plans and get him to worry about the little day-to-day plans. I had a personal interview with him recently, and I didn't have as much time to talk about what was bothering me as he took to tell me what's in the works for the future."

Another somewhat critical craftsman on the lower level on the theme of lack of contact: "Wakefield's a very bright and self-assured guy. He obviously has a big job taking over this division since it has grown so rapidly. Probably he has been more severe than he would have been if he had been able to control the changes more. He is a very good, politically oriented guy, who gets along quite well with top management. He probably works better with them than with the people under him. I guess we don't see much of him on this level, so in terms of personality, I can't really comment too much. He seems a very fair guy. He's certainly open-minded and willing to listen to different viewpoints."

Those were craftsmen-engineers on the bottom of the technostructure. The lower-level managers under Wakefield were much more positive. A company man stated: "He is a very reasonable manager who's been around a while. He's extremely outgoing, very dynamic in the way he manages. He has a lot of good ideas; he's a believer in people, interested in people. To wit, his periodic interviews with those working under him. He helps our approach with the outside world. He is not politically always in the middle of the road; he takes stands; he has tremendous respect for the engineers' rights. He's well respected in the company and has tremendous ability to express himself. He can look at a person in the organization and get to the meat of the matter, where improvement is needed. He has a tremendous sense of fairness; he doesn't like to see things too lopsided."

Another manager: "He has good organizing ability. He's very smooth in personal relationships. He's aggressive; he has creative ideas. He understands well what you have to know to be a good manager, and he supports the people who work for him."

Thus, the general view is of an aggressive, articulate, highly intelligent, and competent manager. The heaviest critique of the craftsmen is the general critique they have of gamesman managers, that they are being pushed around and manipulated. But even those who are most critical about Wakefield generally recognize his talents. And generally they like him. For example, one of the most discontented young managers stated, "Wakefield is somewhat of an opportunist, somewhat of a politician. He should be more involved in actual things. His philosophy of management is to get the best people around him and let them do the managing. [Wakefield would agree that this is his philosophy and he would defend it.] He is very invigorating, very interested in people's work. I don't know whether he believes it, or whether he's just enthusiastic in order to stimulate people. Whatever the reason, he is very enthusiastic, and he is likable."

If some of his subordinates viewed him with mixed emotions, the very attractive young secretaries who have worked for him had no doubts. With them, he was a hero. What do you think of Wakefield? One secretary, herself a hip gameswoman, said, "Oh, boy. He is very deserving of respect. Like I don't hesitate in believing anything he says. Like a Hercules-type image. He just seems to be right on. He's sensitive. If Jack says something, it's accepted as far as I'm concerned. Maybe I don't feel that way, the way he says.

Well then, I'd question my own feelings, because when he really thinks, he's very sharp. He says witty things right off the top of his head. I find them very real, very upfront. One of the few people I know who doesn't seem to be playing political games. When I worked for him, he wasn't like a boss. It's hard for me to see him as the head of a division now. He's too real for that job."

Another secretary said she will continue to work in the company only so long as she can work for Jack. She described him as "Friendly, witty. I admire him because I think he's superintelligent. It's funny to watch him write something down on a piece of paper; it just snowballs. He's an excellent leader. He takes an interest in the people who work for him. He surrounds himself with good, strong people, as opposed to the kind of guy who surrounds himself with yes men. I admire his loyalty to the company. He's just a really good guy. I could go on. Human. I like that one, yes, he's very human."

On the other hand, his wife's description of him suggested that he does not shine so much in a day-to-day intimate relationship as he does being the boss in the office.* His wife, Jane, said, "He's very serious-minded. He's very mechanically oriented, and intellectual too. He's a very versatile person as far as I can see. But as far as I'm concerned, he is extremely inconsistent. Not in business, but as . . . He's an extrovert at work, but an introvert at home. I hear the guys at work talking about what they do at work, and it just doesn't jell with what I see here at home. I'd say he's a good family man. He's a very project-oriented person. He's not a demonstrative person as far as . . . neither one of us are. He's more demonstrative with the children. I think he's pretty much a person unto himself."

At work, everyone agreed that Wakefield was exciting, energetic, brilliant, and these qualities were

---

*Jane Wakefield was interviewed by Cindy Elliott.

particularly appreciated by the executives and his peers. Craftsmen lower down in the organization questioned whether they were not being hustled. At work, he seemed like a person who is really open and interested in others, but at home he seemed to avoid intimacy.

From the start, Wakefield presented himself as a man of ideals. He told us that he is not working just for the profit of the company, but that he wanted to make a social contribution. This was one of the aspects of his character that made him so attractive. Let us examine these ideals and then compare them with his behavior, both at work and outside work.

Wakefield's ideals and values can be organized in terms of four main themes: the individual, leadership, social responsibility, and concern for people.

The type of society Wakefield considered ideal would be "a society that places recognition and emphasis on the individual. I know that society requires institutions and institutionalization. But I believe these institutions must constantly be tested in terms of their viability for the individual." However, his concept of the "individual" sometimes seemed so vague as to be almost meaningless. Like many corporate managers, particularly the gamesmen, Wakefield thought of individuality in terms of having freedom to do his own thing within the large corporate structure. His fear was that he was going to become a part of the machine, an organization man. We recall that in responding to the first questionnaire, Wakefield emphasized the importance of having a say over the form and content of the work. Individualism also means not getting submerged in the corporate group, but being recognized for one's abilities and suitably rewarded.

Wakefield described his basic philosophy of individualism as follows: "I have an optimistic human attitude. There are a lot of things the individual can do, and there are some things only the group can do. I have a human-oriented philosophy with a lot of optimism mixed in. *The Plague*, by Camus, represents my view. A lot of things come up against you, and you just have to keep trying."

In my first interview with Wakefield, he stressed his belief in a system where all citizens had a chance to make decisions about questions that affected them. Part of his individualism was expressed in a kind of libertarianism, a rejection of laws and regulations that make people conform to institutional demands. He criticized school systems based on rigid discipline, in contrast to those that would allow students and teachers full freedom to develop their own interests. He was sympathetic to the rebellious ideas and actions of the young and considered that sometimes disobedience to the Government is justified. In his later interviews, there was much less talk about democracy and more emphasis on the importance of good leadership if a society is to progress.

Wakefield, like other gamesmen, wants to be the boss. However, all the gamesmen insist that they do not want to have power over other people. Their reason for being the boss is either the negative one of not wanting to be pushed around by other people, running one's own shop, or the more positive one of believing that they are better suited than most people to exercise leadership for the benefit of others, such as the craftsmen, who lack both vision and motivation to conceive of projects and to work for common goals. The people whom Wakefield most admired were all leaders. "I admire JFK, first of all, for a lot more than making policy and the right decisions. He knew something about the art of leadership; he knew how to motivate people. He was also very well read as a President, very thoughtful guy. He built a good staff, he had ideas, he was a philosopher. I'm always more receptive to guys who are thoughtful. He also had a majestic air, definitely. Bobby was a deep thinker, but he was not in the same league as JFK. I once met him on a plane, but he did not have that leadership magic."

The second person whom Wakefield admired was

the president of the company. "He's an entirely different kind of personality from Kennedy. He's a much colder kind of person, but you knew exactly where you stood. He's able to say what you can't quite grasp yourself. He digs to the heart, and clarifies. But in the final analysis, he lets you make the decision." Two years later, when Wakefield was getting closer to the top, he became more critical of the president. Seen close at hand, the president was keeping him and the other younger managers from exercising any real power at the top. At that time, they wanted more say over how large sums of capital were going to be spent, and who would get the stock options.

Still, he felt that the president was a "true individualist, a person who had ideas which were solid, not a lot of bullshit or fast dealing." Even if he didn't *like* the president so much, once he got into top management, he still *admired* him.

Wakefield defined his own philosophy of leadership in terms of how well the leader develops his followers to become leaders themselves. "I take a look at people. Are they building a purpose? Do they have a philosophy? Do they try and take a complex thing like Here's the world and here's what I can do? Do they try to figure out What am I doing for that world? Do they put the meat on the bones? Some people can do it and some people can't. That's one way of judging potential. Anyone with absolute power can rule for a while, but his good friends will leave him if he can't develop them. In my work I have to communicate with a lot of people. I have to understand and accept the ideas of others. I must spread credit. I need to stay out of the picture and give everyone credit. Most important, they must be able to maintain their own enthusiasm. I can't stand a guy who lays down. That's when I become cordial to treason. If some manager takes power and then he lays down on the job, others should take the power away from him. Some highly creative guys have their ups and downs. But the higher you go, the longer the efforts must last. That's why I admire JFK. He hung in there. The downers are where I have to take steps."

Wakefield also said that one of the jobs of a leader is to separate a rotten apple before he contaminates everyone else. Wakefield had come to admire Eric Hoffer, the author who also has little patience with weak people. "The more I study him, the more I admire him. He's really ahead of his time. The masses want freedom from freedom. People go under a dictator because they're looking for comfort. People aren't strong enough to exist in chaos. It makes me think that a socialist dictatorship might just work."

For Wakefield, leadership requires being aware of the forces influencing social change (currents) and having some power to affect change. "The U.S. was on top before because it was riding the currents of history. Now we are not so much. We're not so free to do anything we want. The United States has been trying to buck the events of history instead of going with them. We should ride the currents and shape them." Wakefield went on: "Power is an essential fact of life. You can't do anything in a staff position in life. You have to have power. But getting power assumes you have a responsibility for what you do with it. You have to have philosophical goals. Power has to nestle somewhere, and I'd like to see it nestle with honest, sincere people who have a philosophy I understand. I could go on for a long time about power because I've thought a lot about it. I don't like Nixon because he doesn't have a basic philosophy. I really try to communicate that here, that you have to have one."

Thus it would appear that Wakefield believed that a humanistic and optimistic philosophy which stresses individualism is basic to legitimizing his power over others. Furthermore, he was concerned with using power for social betterment. But what did he want to do for society?

He had already spoken about the importance of

cleaning up the environment and of measuring social institutions in terms of their effect on the individual. He went on. "The United States would be nice if we could lay claim to three things. One, the people should govern themselves. Two, we should apply technology to increasing the joy of living. We have a national culture and society such that we could have an Athenian-group type of life if we wanted it. Three, we have a powerful company—I mean country, which can help other companies—that is, countries, advance their civilization. I don't know what this hangup on company means . . . We can apply a philosophy of individualism to our country, using new technology. For example, we might be able to have people live in one place and have access to all of civilization. We could move the information instead of the people. Electronics would move the information. People would not have to live in the city. Or I think, for example, that this company should move its plants out into rural areas instead of near cities. We could use the company resources to make it happen. Why, we might even have a situation where everyone could work at home using the new technology."

This last idea seems an almost bizarre carrying of individualism to the extreme, or rather an interpretation of individualism as isolated work remaining under company control. Who would want to stay at home all day doing his work, when in fact one of the most enjoyable aspects of work for many people is the chance to meet people and socialize? Although this form of individualism has the advantage of freeing a person from policemanlike supervision, it would end up strengthening centralized corporate power. Workers would find it much harder to join together if they had complaints against management.

In terms of real activity, Wakefield had done little to actualize his social concern. He had been involved in ecology groups and had participated in lobbying. He had seriously considered developing a whole new career centered in public service with the goal of helping to develop his social values. But so far he had not done so.

Unlike most gamesmen, Wakefield's values included concern for people. For him, consideration of others and love were among the most important virtues, and betrayal of a friend was one of the worst evils, even worse than murder. What was his definition of a good friend?

"There's a difference between good friends on the East Coast and good friends on the West Coast. Here in the East, you have a few good friends for life. In the West, there is damn little that is close. People really move around. A close friend is one who is honest with you. There is no falseness nor flattery. You have to have something in common—like the ecology movement—something you believe in. Some of our friends are working people from the company. There are skiing friends. They are honest . . . friends who share activities. Yet friendship is often transitory. A couple of dozen people are really close friends."

After starting out with a clear definition of friendship in relationship to honesty and shared interests (although he left out any affection or intimacy or even really caring what happens to the other person), Wakefield ended up rather vaguely, implying that while he and his wife had many friends, they come and go.

Wakefield in his managerial philosophy expressed concern about people. "My managerial philosophy is based on a sincere interest in people. You can underline sincere. You have to enjoy people, enjoy them as much as they do themselves. Given this, you must also do everything possible to help them get ahead. You must get ahead of them and eliminate the roadblocks for them. I always step back and say, 'What are we doing to develop our people?' You need to be pretty organized yourself. You need to communicate your plan in a motivational way that gets people moving. People are afraid of freedom, and it's damn hard to innovate in a blue-sky environment. I'm most distressed when I don't understand the corporate strategy. Everyone is uneasy and needs to know where things are going."

A number of points or comments need to be made about this statement. One, he talked about sincere interest in people in terms of enjoying people and helping them get ahead. This assumes that getting ahead is the most important goal for everyone. It may be the most important goal for the company to make sure that people move ahead and want to move ahead, but is it important for the craftsmen? Our findings show that for many craftsmen, having a chance to do their own thing is more important than promotions.

Second, Wakefield believes that people are afraid of freedom and can't innovate unless they're motivated to do so in terms of the corporate goals. But when do they ever have freedom to decide themselves what they want to make? What if the things they want to innovate and create are not things that will gain a big profit for the company? It is not that people cannot innovate in a blue-sky atmosphere, or that they are afraid of freedom, rather it is that if you want to be sure that they do what the company needs, you can't let them go off by themselves and decide themselves what they're going to do. You have to get them to want to get ahead, to want to be promoted, and to be motivated to do things for the good of the company. Their goals must fit the corporate strategy because they're persuaded that it is in their best interest, whether or not it is.

The point here is that Wakefield never questioned the basic system. He saw people as weak only because they did not understand the corporate strategy and did not adapt themselves to it. Thus, they needed to be pushed, juiced up, and "helped."

Wakefield and many other managers, particularly the gamesmen, talk about the loss of individualism and the importance of being an individual, but they go around trying to organize everyone so that nobody else can be an individual. What they want is autonomy for themselves. This means having their own shop within the organization, and being free of bureaucratic pressures, of being pushed around by those higher up in the system. They rationalize their ambitions and character needs by seeing other people as weak and in need of direction and leadership.

In fact, would there be any motivational problem in the organization if the craftsmen could choose their own projects and work together at their own pace? If they did not need to adapt themselves so that the corporation could grow so much and gain such a high profit, what would happen? Would we all be poorer for lack of innovative products? Or might the craftsmen be able to develop their own projects which might turn out to be more useful to the society as a whole? Alexander Graham Bell developed the telephone in part because he was interested in helping people with poor hearing.

In the present system, there is some support for Wakefield's patronizing view that craftsmen would not be able to carry out large-scale projects without being organized and motivated by the gamesmen. Although they are interested in their own thing, many are rather hoarding and uncommunicative and find it hard to work cooperatively. Although they are concerned about how things work, and about quality, many do not consider the product's usefulness to society. Little in their education has encouraged them to consider the social usefulness of what they make. Quite the contrary. They have been trained in schools and corporations insulated from life and from real social and human needs. Furthermore, unless they are pushed to make schedules, they work at their own pace, which is usually slower than the schedules require. But this is only a problem in terms of a large corporation where everything is being rationalized and evaluated in terms of maximal profit.

However, Wakefield ignores evidence that craftsmen can work together if they are all committed to a project. He conceives of most workers as gifted schoolchildren frightened of freedom and in need of direction. As long as he can believe this, his views seem reasonable. If he respected the craftsmen's longing for autonomy, frustrated by the company system, then the contradictions within his own value system would become apparent. Like the other gamesmen who run modern corporations, Wakefield's ideology and character support hierarchy even though he is neither paternalistic nor authoritarian. He does not ask for personal loyalty, just loyalty to the project, and he does not seek power over individual people. He is not sadistic. His goal is an exciting and smooth-running team. It does not bother him that people move in and out of his organization, just as it does not bother the football coach that a different group of players plays on his team, as long as he can get good ones to play for him. For Wakefield, like a football coach, developing people really means developing them for the team (and we shall see that one reason he believes that this is positive for others is that he believes it has worked for him). Wakefield told me that the problem today is to motivate highly educated workers who create new products and new knowledge, and he has read Peter Drucker closely on this point. He realized that the modern "knowledge worker" will not accept paternalistic control. The semifeudal loyalty of the past would no longer work. Wakefield's approach was different. His job was to get the craftsmen motivated to give more to the group. He felt that he needed to figure out ways to get people into the competition and to get them excited.

Let us move now from Wakefield's philosophy and ideals to how he actually works, the style and content. We'll start with his intellectual approach. Wakefield noted that the following were his strongest intellectual abilities: (1) his systems thinking, which includes the ability to see the whole and not merely the parts, and the ability to integrate many ideas into the overall plan; (2) the ability to create an environment where others work better; and (3) the ability to understand another person's weaknesses and strengths in terms of the job requirements of the group. He underlined this last point because he was aware that this was also an area where he was weakest: his awareness of others' feelings and his ability to listen carefully to others. That is to say his understanding of other people was mainly in terms of how they could be useful to the work, not in other terms, of their feelings or goals outside of the work.

Wakefield has a systems mind. This means that he always sees details in terms of an overall picture. We have observed that those managers or engineers who have the systems approach to corporate questions express the same style of thinking on the Rorschach test. That means that they are not satisfied to see one or another detail, and in general they do not pay attention to tiny details, but look for the overall picture that the ink blot might represent. There are quite a number of individuals in corporations who have this kind of overall systems approach when they are looking at cards with no color, meaning in Rorschach terminology that they can integrate ideas into an overall system so long as they're in a purely technical situation, where emotional considerations do not enter. In some of these cases, when the cards are colorful and emotional responses are evoked, the systems approach breaks down and these people are unable to integrate their ideas. This is not the case with Wakefield, who in an emotionally laden interpersonal situation becomes dazzling and is able to integrate everyone's thoughts into some overall strategy.

Wakefield gave us a copy of a report he wrote for his division which lays out a business strategy for the future and attempts to educate the managers under him as to the reasons why they must develop their work in a specific direction, one that Wakefield considered will fit the requirements of the future market and of developments in technology (riding the wave

of the future). He started out with a history of the
use of computers and described why attempts to develop in certain directions failed. He emphasized the
importance of keeping in mind the user of the computer, and then showed that new changes in technology and the cost of computing make possible totally new solutions for decentralizing computing
systems. From this general analysis, he moved to
concrete examples, showing, for example, how new
decentralized computing systems can aid in factory
automation or in hospitals, research laboratories, transportation and utilities control, etc. Thus he saw a
change in the computer field to the point that the
user's needs were determining the structure of computing systems rather than as in the past when the
users had to fit their needs into a general-purpose,
centralized monolithic computer. From this analysis
of the developing trends in the market of the future,
Wakefield then turned to the practical implications for
his own division.

When Wakefield started describing what the strategy and tactics of his division should be for the future,
his language became more vivid and insistent. He
showed a remarkable ability to combine command
with technical language all in a graceful style. An example of his language in giving a command: "Swing
the LSI CPU design team hard into the mode of determining the architecture necessary . . ." Another
example: "There will be a relentless push towards having a minimal starter system underlying capability
which consists of a CPU, peripheral and software
combination which can do useful *work* as a human
computing tool . . ." Spiced among the commands
were also affirmative statements, noting, for example,
that "what is needed in the X program is a continuing,
creative effort to effectively enhance the exceptionally well done job by Jones . . ."

This business strategy report was a brilliant job,
complete with bibliography (with his usual considerable use of Peter Drucker's analysis of the future

requirements of knowledge workers). It combined technical analysis, strategic thinking, the integrating of details into a system, and, as always, was concerned with motivating the craftsmen. What was lacking in this total analysis of the future was any concern for the social effects of computers. The point was how to maximize profit and growth, how to win. This, of course, is standard for all industrial corporate reports, and Wakefield was no different. In fact, he was probably more aware of social factors in developing his market strategy than are most corporate executives.

The second ability Wakefield noted as one of his strongest was his ability to create an environment where others work better. One of Wakefield's secretaries described how he helped to create this atmosphere. "A lot of people are attracted to him. When he came here, it was the first time I saw the guys unite in respect. When he became the head of the division, he set up half-hour appointments with everyone in the lab. He wanted to know each of their objectives. He asked them what they liked and what they didn't like. No manager had ever taken the time to do it. Second, since there have always been changes going on, constant reorganization, Wakefield got us all together as a group and told us *why* it was happening. For the first time, people gained confidence in themselves. Everybody got the respect they deserved. Furthermore, he can explain things down to the level where even the secretaries can understand."

She went on to point out that Wakefield worked together with the attractive secretaries to help create an exciting and open atmosphere which helped stimulate the craftsmen to come out of themselves. "Wakefield has me throw a beer bust every six weeks or so. He has us [the secretaries] roam through the crowd and make sure people don't discuss business." There was a gamy, sexy atmosphere in the office. The men were encouraged to trade spicy, sexy repartee with the girls, who played a function that sometimes seemed a

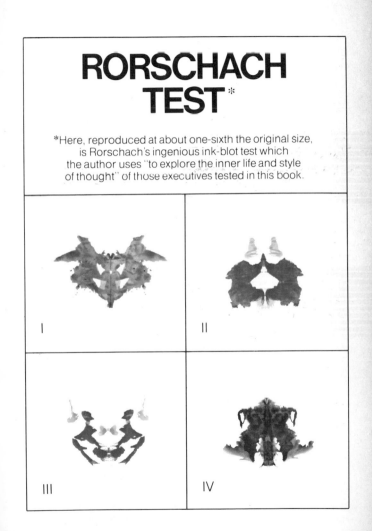

RORSCHACH
TEST *

*Here, reproduced at about one-sixth the original size,
is Rorschach's ingenious ink-blot test which
the author uses "to explore the inner life and style
of thought" of those executives tested in this book.

I

II

III

IV

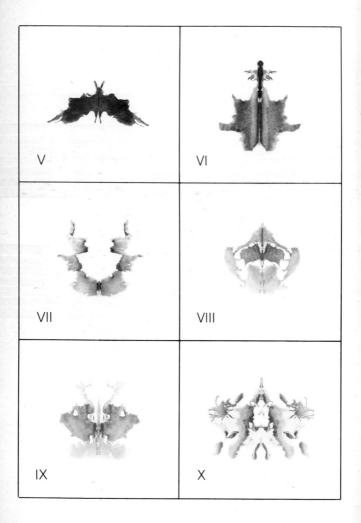

combination of Playboy bunny and housemother. The secretary went on: "When I first came here, I found that if I smiled freely, it would make the day for some of the guys. When I first started wearing hot pants to work, Wakefield kidded me about it. But then he would ask me to wear a certain outfit if he was going to have a bad day. I like being a girl here. I've never felt that being a girl has hurt me anywhere. They don't treat me as dumb or anything. They really appreciate it."

This secretary had discussed her function with Wakefield. She felt her main function was "to spoil them, to make life a little easier." She said, "If I come in here feeling bad, I can see the effect of it on everyone. When my engagement was broken, I took the day off because I didn't want to make a lot of people feel down just because I wasn't smiling. I feel I have a great emotional effect on the people here, because people are important to me. Wakefield has asked me whether I understand the power I have. He's told me that I can control whether they are up or down." (Note again Wakefield's flattery and exaggeration as a means of motivating the secretary.) She continued, "The managers have no time to be aware of the emotional things going on. To sum it up, I'm a sounding block. Even with people you don't know that well, it's not so much that you understand, but you're just there. They start talking about something, and then they get into what's really bothering them. Maybe that's what I do more than anything is just listen. Just listening does a great deal."

Wakefield has worked to create an environment where people work better, both by paying attention to everyone and clarifying their function, their contribution, and also by creating a seductive emotional atmosphere, using secretaries who worship him.

It was instructive to follow Wakefield as he interacted with his subordinates at a monthly strategy meeting. The purposes of the meeting were "planning and communications." He was using these meetings to develop a more open and friendly environment, where people could know and trust one another, and talk more openly about their mutual areas of interest. His innovation in this meeting had been to emphasize cooperative division-wide planning and to have every person there, especially those on the lower levels who might be involved in the area under discussion. Wakefield wanted everyone to feel a part of the project and to take more responsibility for its success.

This meeting lasted from 8:15 to noon. It started out with talk about a new product being developed, and it ended up with Wakefield spending forty-five minutes describing strategy for the division in the next few months. We will see the kind of atmosphere Wakefield creates in order to open up the craftsmen.*

Everyone arrived on time. Wakefield came in and sat in the row next to the back of the room by the wall. From there he could see everyone in the room, hear everyone without turning around, but he was kind of invisible to the others. He had purposely chosen one of his subordinates to be the nominal chairman of the meeting, while he was taking a role of being just like everyone else.

When Wakefield sat down, people became impatient, squirming around, looking at their watches, and looking significantly at him. Wakefield, however, was not apparently paying attention to anything. Finally, he said in a whisper to the person next to him, "Someone should tell George to get things started." People started looking at George. Then Wakefield said aloud, "Well, say George, why don't we quit wasting time and get started with this thing?" This forced George, the nominal chairman, to take a publicly active role, but all the emotional influence as the initiator and

---

*The description of the meeting is from notes taken by Mac Greene.

controller of the meeting belonged to Wakefield, sitting in the back of the room.

The chairman was a rather tight, tough character. He began with a spiel about how he wanted to encourage open, frank discussion. Everyone should freely contribute. Everyone should speak up about his ideas. He didn't seem to mean a word of it. The meeting started like a lead balloon. Wakefield was obviously dissatisfied, and he clearly could have done it much better if he hadn't resolved to keep a low profile. Although every word that the chair said was precisely what he wanted, the phrases were lifeless. The meeting proceeded until the coffee break at 9:15 with the group leader for the new product presenting detailed technical analyses and market forecasts. The purpose was for all the related project managers to see how this new product affected them, and to offer their observations, criticisms, and advice. But the people seemed restless and bored. Even Wakefield started to read reports about the project under discussion rather than listening to the speaker.

At the coffee break, everyone sprang out of their chairs. People were complaining about the meeting. There seemed to be a resistance to the whole purpose of the meeting. They were being forced to cooperate and they did not know how to do it. People were shy about giving their comments publicly. They preferred talking to one another privately.

One of Wakefield's chief assistants is Ray Schultz, the type of gamesman who is tougher, pushier, less seductive and supportive than Wakefield. He is playful, often a joker, but also like a fanatical football coach who has to win. Even more than Wakefield, Schultz cannot stand a situation that is static, where there is no action. He is the one who told us with a straight face that the three people he most admired historically were Vince Lombardi, Jesus Christ, and Harry Truman. He liked Lombardi because of his high ideals, Jesus Christ because of his incredible ability to motivate people, and Harry Truman was an ordinary man with whom Schultz could identify because he had guts and was a winner. Schultz is the kind of person who says he likes to put effort into things only if he's going to win. He doesn't like people who whine and he doesn't want to baby them. He told us he saw himself as a gamesman with a strong streak of jungle fighter in him. As we shall see, Wakefield used Schultz to perform functions that he himself could not do.

At the coffee break, Schultz promised to open up this meeting by shaking people up. He said what was needed was some tough action.

It may have been this threat by Schultz that helped to make the meeting after the coffee break more active so that some people started to speak more freely about their strategies and goals and to compare their products with those of competitors.

In the transitional point in the discussion, when the conversation lagged for just a minute, Wakefield made a strong contribution. He summarized the discussion up to then, describing the key points that had been made and fitting what had been said into the general strategy, emphasizing what was most important for the future. This contribution was in fact a decision to make compromises and trade-offs to settle conflicts about functions and schedules so that the project could move toward a final development of the product, but it was disguised as a summary and a clarification. From that point on, Wakefield's clarification became the ground of further discussion, but all the focus was on what Wakefield had said and not on Wakefield personally. After this clarification, others joined in and there was a great deal of joking. Someone mentioned that someone else was getting a lot of good feedback. Wakefield leaned over to him and whispered gruffly, "I'll say," giving the impression that he was privy to some secret. Everyone laughed.

As people began to open up, they began to make optimistic estimates of the future. Another manager, authoritarian and controlling, served a function in the meeting of always throwing cold water when spirits rose too high. The group was starting to get very enthusiastic. They were seeing their product as a real innovation, very useful, technically excellent, with elegant design, reliable operation. Furthermore, it would beat out IBM and other companies that were working along the same line. But this man broke in, saying, "I don't see how you're going to approach estimates like that. Aren't you deceiving people with figures like that? That's approaching the reliability of the dead." Of course, people jumped in to defend their estimates, but the effect of this kind of put-down was very useful. It forced everyone to be very careful and to stay close to the facts. It was a way of controlling a tendency to "specmanship," competing by promising unrealistic performance specifications. Lest this be too much of a downer, both Wakefield and Schultz came in with playful encouragement about how the new product would upset things within the corporation and make everyone reorient his thinking, since it would replace products already being used generally.

Wakefield began to flower out of his invisibility from the back of the room. He started making asides to various people, drawing them into the discussion, and maintaining a lively, low-key interchange with the public presentation at the front of the room. He particularly paid attention to the guys who were the most shy and uptight. By sitting at the back of the room, he was close to those people who normally sat at the back of the room so they would not be seen and so they could get out quickly. It was to many of these people that he directed some of his whispered asides and encouragements. In this way, he would succeed in getting some of these backbenchers into the discussion, referring to something they had once said to him or done that was relevant to the discussion at hand, and encouraging them to speak up.

Suddenly Schultz, who had been joking around, became a no-nonsense, hard-line businessman. This sudden transformation seemed to scare most people. "This schedule is too tight," he said. "There's not enough money to meet this schedule. Who made up this schedule? Who thinks we can make dates like that? The pipeline is clogged and you know that. [He was jabbing with his finger.] We're overcommitted now, and we don't know what the orders will be. It's impossible to schedule this. We can't tie ourselves to this schedule. It's not funded for this fiscal half. Who are we trying to fool with a schedule like that?"

Schultz sat back, his eyes flashing with a smug look that asked, What will you do about it now? Everyone seemed upset, as though their illusion had been shattered. But they pulled themselves together and agreed that they had to admit more flexibility into the schedule. Although Schultz pressed them to agree that their schedule was a complete fraud, they would not go that far. The project leader, who had started the meeting, repeated several times with a dazed look on his face, "Remember, we are serious about the project. Our assumptions could be vastly wrong, but we have to start somewhere. We are absolutely serious about this product."

The effect of this intervention, however, was to bring people down to earth. Like the earlier intervention, which had questioned reliability, this one questioned the whole idea that the product could be developed on an easy schedule, without pushing people to the utmost. The craftsmen had been brought out of their shells and now they were going to be challenged and motivated to step up the pace. Schultz pointed out to another manager, "You have on that chart that this other product is due in 1974. I want to change that to 1973. I don't want that kind of pressure removed from that project." Schultz kept on. He was warming up the meeting, keeping everyone off balance and under pressure. The craftsmen never opened their mouths again in the meeting. How did

Wakefield respond? Before, he had been acting as a kind of gentle stimulator, but as Schultz took off, he became harder and fitted himself into Schultz's tempo. The tone of the meeting became cooler and more efficient. Wakefield joined Schultz in challenging all kinds of assumptions.

The project leader tried to reassert his original estimate. But the challenge was making him give way on certain points, and he and his subordinates had to promise to commit themselves to work even harder. If they failed to meet the new schedule now, it would be their fault. They would be responsible. They had been warned. Wakefield also came in to point out to the project leader that the production department had to depend on the estimates of completion and sales. If things were going to be as good as he was predicting, then they would have to commit production in the future. Was he willing to take responsibility for this too?

The result was a reaffirmation of the product's value, but everyone had been scared so completely that they were easier to push into line in terms of the overall divisional requirements for timing and production capacity. After Schultz had led the browbeating, Wakefield stepped in and offered solutions which at that point everyone would have to accept gratefully.

The group's spirits rose again. They felt they had a winner. Wakefield pointed out how they had solved a problem that their competitor had failed at. He turned to the project leader directly and said, "It's a good system and it's gonna go. It's a winner." Somebody near Wakefield raised a question and he slipped directly into a tête-à-tête.

The mood was becoming more playful. Schultz's next challenge was not so scary. He said, "The numbers are still too low."

"Come on, Ray," said one of the project group, "it's only another fifty K."

Schultz laughed. "Fifty K here, fifty K there. *All right! When you're hot, you're hot!*" Everyone laughed and felt flattered.

Wakefield, speaking almost to himself, mumbled, "Even if it triples to a hundred and fifty K, the return will be incredible."

People then began to joke about all the new applications the product might create. Someone raised the possibility of environmental problems. What would be the tolerances for heat, humidity, dust, etc.? But the response was mainly boyish. At this point, no one was going to take this kind of problem seriously in comparison to the problems of scheduling and money. Schultz asked, "Do you mean will it run in the furnace or out?" Another man asked, "Can you run it under water?" But it was the end of the meeting. Wakefield came up to the front of the room. He congratulated everyone. "This is going to continually turn on the customers. It's an excellent program. It's the most exciting project I've seen at this company for years. We're in motion."

An aside from one of the younger managers: "Talk about local motion, you guys should come over and see Bob Burman's new secretary." Laughter.

Then Wakefield got serious. It was necessary to come up with a three-year plan. They would have to soon present the progress report to the president of the company. Wakefield stated that in this presentation he wanted the young guys out in front doing the presentation. He said, "I will introduce the guys and talk about their potential and growth and so forth." In this way, one might say that Wakefield would be showing the president of the company not only his success with products, but also his success in bringing along and developing new people. He then went on to give a strategy of how to present new material to the president of the company so that he would become most excited. "We give him the hard stuff in the morning and the exciting stuff in the afternoon. I've seen him go to sleep in these meetings. They don't do it right. It really turns the guys off and it's a big down."

At the very end of the meeting Wakefield discussed his plans for continual meetings that would allow people in different projects to meet those in other projects, to have some cross-fertilization and exchange of information. They needed also to have more interrelationship between development, marketing, and production.

After the meeting, Wakefield and Schultz discussed how it had gone. They felt the meeting had been only a partial success. The discussion of the new product was not the main point. The real goal of the meeting had been to get the shy and uptight craftsmen to work better together. Only that way could schedules be met and morale be raised. They felt that the meeting was only partially successful in terms of this criterion, since most people had not opened up. The pace of the meeting had been slow and without real enthusiasm. Schultz's pushing got some people responding in terms of having to defend themselves and commit themselves to a tight schedule. But it would have been better if they had not needed this kind of heavy-handed approach. Both Wakefield and Schultz believed it would take another year to open up the people satisfactorily. This meeting only reinforced Wakefield's view that the people needed strong leadership in order to become more cooperative.

Later in the day Wakefield presided over a meeting of his three top managers, including Schultz, in which they were going to assign people to teams to learn from one another and interact more. They all enjoyed this assignment, wanting to create exciting combinations of people who needed to know one another better and to keep apart those who might cause too much conflict. At this meeting, the managers showed their knowledge of the different people under them in terms of their strengths and weaknesses. They referred to the process of team-making as "packing in the brains."

In watching Wakefield at work, one was struck by how he responded to the different needs of different people. If he was talking about a problem with an uptight and controlling person, he played to the man's style, letting him think that he completely controlled the situation, encouraging him to take control. If he was talking with another gamesman, the conversation was hip and playful, totally different. In each case, Wakefield did not tell anyone what to do, but tried to state the situation in such a way that the other would see the answer and consider it his own solution.

For example, a manager came to see Wakefield with a problem. The manager, George Smith, just out of business school, was tense. He looked rather like a lieutenant fresh out of West Point trying to prove himself and keep everything under control. He had a customer problem. The customer had just installed a computer system, something wasn't working just right, and he wanted the company to come and fix it. Wakefield asked about the specific details concerning the service difficulties. He then asked whether these difficulties were specifically stated in the contract as the responsibility of the company. Smith, following Wakefield's train of thought, then suggested that maybe the customer was trying to beat the company out of some free service. Wakefield emphatically agreed, since that was the point he was trying to make without saying it. He then told a story about how one of their key technical managers had ended up spending a great deal of time helping another customer solve all sorts of applications problems that the customer maintained came from some initial faulty design. But the other company used this information to develop its own products. Wakefield eventually had kicked these people out, and he was now in the process of establishing a policy that key design people could not work with customers, who were often competitors. He intimated to Smith that brilliant designers were perhaps a little too naïve and nice to know when they were being exploited. Smith responded immediately to this idea, which fit his own prejudices. He agreed with Wakefield that these key design people had to be protected from aggressive customers, and people like himself needed to do the protecting. By this time, Smith was thinking that he had all along been intending to take a strong stand controlling the designer-customer interface. In this way, by understanding Smith's strengths and weaknesses, Wakefield had brilliantly solved a problem and made a new loyal ally.

We remarked to Wakefield that in contrast to his stated value that people should make decisions by themselves, he seemed to be very directive and manipulative. Wakefield responded, "I have to do that. It's not the way I'd like to do it, but this place was in chaos two years ago, and it takes a lot of work developing a good organization. People can't stand not knowing anything about what they're supposed to be doing. People are a lot happier being told what to do."

We can see that Wakefield's character, his game orientation, his joy of life, enthusiasm, and dazzling brilliance all served to make him effective as a top-level manager motivating a group of sensitive, rather closed but competent craftsmen. But just as he used himself as a key tool in his work, so his character was being molded in the workplace. Those traits and abilities that served the work were being exercised and reinforced constantly. The questions we will consider now are: What has been the human cost of his work to Wakefield? What has been the result to his own well-being of the character-development process going on in him? And which are the traits and capacities that have been left underdeveloped?

For a man such as Wakefield, with capacities and goals for understanding others, for love, intimacy, bettering the world, and helping other people, these are particularly important questions. In the best of circumstances, Wakefield, like the rest of us, would have to struggle to achieve these goals, to become the kind of person that he would ideally like to be.

It does not seem that either his background or work has oriented him in a particularly idealistic direction. Wakefield's background has elements in common with many corporate managers. He was the eldest in his family, brought up in one of the larger cities of the Midwest. With no more than a high-school education, his father, the son of a production engineer with only a grade-school education, became a success in the corporate world, moving from company to company until he became the vice-president of a small corporation. He was conscientious and conservative. "Even in his late fifties," Wakefield said, "he works harder than I do, easily seventy hours a week. For him, work is definitely a religion." Like many corporate managers, Wakefield never felt really close to his father, but he admired and respected him. His father traveled a great deal in his work and sometimes would be away from home for weeks at a time. Yet Wakefield enjoyed their time together, especially when they played ball or went sailing.

Wakefield's mother ran the household. "She was a fireball, full of energy and also full of prejudices, but she was like Archie Bunker in that she was also humorous. She reads a great deal, and she's a very neat and ordered person." Wakefield felt that both sides, the mother and the father, are in him. There are the ambition to succeed, the energy, restlessness, humor, desire to learn. On the other hand, receptive to changes in America and his corporate experience, Wakefield's own values have become more liberal, and he has become worried about questions that did not concern his parents, who took for granted the benefits of hard work and the success ethic. Although he was somewhat defensive when he talked about them, Wakefield did not criticize his parents. "All I can say is that those kind of people accomplished a lot of things." Wakefield knows that his parents grew up in a different time. He respected his father for becoming a success without a college education in the midst of the Depression, a man satisfied with living, who enjoyed his family, even though he had to sacrifice a great deal of family life to become a success.

Growing up, Wakefield was closer to his mother, mainly because his father was away so often. Even now, when asked about childhood, his answer carried a wistful echo of longing to be closer to his father when he said, "I just *never* saw him." His memories of his early childhood were vague. He felt that it was a happy time, mainly because his father was home more in those days, but he did not remember much. Few of the corporate managers we interviewed dwelt on their childhood or remembered it clearly. This may be because they live in the present and the future rather than the past. But another interpretation would be that they don't like to think of childhood because it was a time in which they were helpless, powerless. Perhaps their lack of freedom and self-determination now keeps them from remembering and experiencing feelings of childhood because they are too painful and too similar to work-related feelings of powerlessness that are constantly being repressed in the present.

Wakefield's earliest memory was of the first grade, when he was six. He remembered getting up early in the morning, when it was dark outside. "Mom cooks the breakfast and then Dad takes me to school. I first went to school at the age of five. I don't remember these things really. Dad had moving pictures of these events and I've seen them many times. I don't remember them personally." This earliest memory included some major themes in Wakefield's life. First is the importance of school and career. Second is the concern of loving parents, the theme of responsibility and love. Even though the father spent so much time away, it was a close and caring family. He remembered his relationship with his mother as "warm and harmonious," although not particularly intimate. She let him be by himself, roam around, but she was there when he needed her. When his father was at home, he was a teacher and a friend. Wakefield felt no resentment about his parents; they did their best. Nor did he particularly idealize them.

Finally, there was the theme of technology. He didn't remember living the childhood experience, but he did remember seeing the movies about it. His father was technically oriented and took movies of his family. And there is a sense here that Jack is the main actor, but in a kind of secondary reality of performance, which is the gamesman's primary world.

But Wakefield was also a rebel. In the first grade he was kicked out of public school as a hell-raiser. He was told that he got into a lot of fights. He was disruptive. He could not concentrate and was not able to learn. Then they sent him to military school, where he settled down. The conventional psychoanalytic interpretation for this would probably be to look for some difficulty in Wakefield's relationship to his father. Because Wakefield was close to his mother and his father was absent a lot of the time, psychoanalysts would inevitably talk about a failure of identification. But this explanation does not convince me. Wakefield never rejected his father, and despite the fact that the father was away so much, the mother always supported paternal authority. Wakefield cannot remember even one time when the mother put the father down or tried to usurp his place at the head of the family. Both she and his father were disappointed that he goofed off in school and was not concerned enough with getting ahead. It is notable too that his sister was never a rebel. "She was straight down the middle."

Wakefield is a person of exceptional gifts. He is brilliant, intuitive, and, above all, extremely energetic. The fact that most children adapt themselves so easily to the first grade and are able to sit in their seats without rebelling against their loss of freedom may speak as much of their fear, weakness, and adaptability as of their strengths. The early theme in Wakefield's life was not to give in to authority and to the institutional system. The theme becomes one of rebellion as a hell-raiser and then later, as we shall see, return (reconciliation) as a brilliant performer. Grown up, Wakefield was still struggling with this battle of childhood and adolescence. He still resented being corralled and organized by the system, yet its rewards and excitement always seduced him back into it.

Perhaps in another era more favorable to an independent career, he might have become an explorer. Even today, he said he is happiest walking by himself in the mountains. One might say that Wakefield's problem is not that he failed to identify with his successful corporate vice-president father, but to the contrary, that his failure is exactly that he finds no alternative to identification with his father, no way to find his own identity in some more personal and creative way. (Of course, we don't know whether Wakefield also sensed in his father a repressed rebelliousness and desire for freedom, but if this was so, it was completely unconscious, since his parents were outwardly shocked at his hell-raising and immediately sent him to military school.)

Wakefield's theme is one of both rebellion and overachievement. In military school, he was a model student. He had no trouble. He remembered particularly that he loved horseback riding because it absorbed his energy. Perhaps his overriding memory of his childhood was the experience of unbridled energy, the need to express it, and the extreme frustration of having to conform to others who operated at a much lower energy level.

He was sent back to public school in the seventh grade, and remembered coasting to the eighth grade. The rebellious drive popped up again in high school. Wakefield did not think that it had anything to do with a wish to provoke his teachers. He just wanted to be left alone and not be organized by the authorities, again the same theme but developed into a value of autonomy. "I liked to keep things at a challenging level," he said. Sometimes he would see it in terms of "just getting full of hell," which was the way his religious mother saw the problem.

In the tenth grade, Wakefield started drinking and smoking, and zoomed around the city in his hot rod, collecting traffic tickets. His grades were mediocre. When he was in the eleventh grade, the hockey coach and the football coach got together, saw this big, strong boy going nowhere, and challenged him to put his energy into sports. They told him they *bet* he didn't have the guts to play with the best, and Wakefield responded to the challenge. He became the offensive right end on the varsity, moving from the fifth string to the first string in one season. He made a hockey team that became state champions. This experience left a deep impression. Here were coaches concerned about him and, by their challenge and stimulation and teaching, motivating him to give up an empty, self-destructive, and rebellious existence, to develop himself and become a winner.

This is a typical American theme. Everyone acts out of self-interest and ends up happy. The coaches needed good talent and they saw this gifted, strong, and superenergetic boy who was just raising hell while he could be helping the team. The boy saw a chance to compete and gain glory and the esteem of parents, teachers, and peers. Everyone wins. Is this Wakefield's model for the development of the people under him?

That is hard to answer without knowing more. We don't know whether the coaches cared more about the development of the boy than they did about their winning teams. How important was winning to them? We once asked Wakefield about the extent to which managers like himself really affirmed and developed their subordinates as opposed to the extent to which they are just hustling and manipulating their people so that they would produce more.

Wakefield answered almost in a whisper, as though he didn't want anyone in the office to hear. He said he had thought a lot about this subject, and he felt that it was important for him to develop his people in a way that was broader than what was required by the business. He had sought help from outside and had planned a series of seminars and a retreat for some of his managers as an experiment. The purpose of this retreat would be the emotional awakening of middle management. In the series of seminars, they would explore their feelings, their perceptions of one another, and their unconscious values. He decided right then and there that he would put the plan into effect within a year. But a year later he said that his boss had vetoed the plan, and the reason seems clear. It is one thing to examine feelings, perceptions, and values of people who share the same basic goals. So long as people are committed to the team and to its goals, they can smooth out difficulties, especially the lack of communication that keeps them from performing their tasks better. But if you are willing to explore unconscious feelings and values that may be more critical of the organization than anyone is aware, you have entered into a dangerous exercise. You have to be willing to accept the possibility that some people will decide that they don't really want to play the game at all. Wakefield's view was still based on his high-school experience, that by playing more fully, one develops oneself and finds oneself. But this is not for everyone, and for anyone it has limits.

That summer after becoming a varsity athelete, Wakefield worked in a factory. He enjoyed communicating with the workers and the experience of being able to do hard man's work. Back at school his senior year, he got the top grades in his class. No one could believe it. From then on his helter-skelter, undisciplined attitude never re-emerged. Despite his poor grades in the first part of high school, the principal wrote a special recommendation guaranteeing that Wakefield would be able to do the work at college, where his grades were in fact all A's and B's. Before that no one had ever thought he would make college.

Wakefield is more ambivalent than most gamesmen about winning as a goal in life. As a child, he enjoyed sports such as sailing, swimming, and diving, which did not require competition to be satisfying. Even grown up, the outdoor activity he most liked was mountain climbing. The strong desire to win emerged in high school only when he was challenged by the coaches and joined the teams. Unlike the jungle fighter, he gets no pleasure in defeating another person. He doesn't like playing cards, and he doesn't like chess. In a way, his work has become the natural extension of team sports. Work is the game. Outside of work, he loves skiing and mountain climbing, individually oriented activities where he can be alone and compete against the elements but escape from the pressure of competing against people.

For Wakefield another life theme was that of being with people in the game versus the need to be by himself, alone. The mode of relatedness with teammates in the game is cooperative and interdependent, but not intimate. You have to be fair, but not close personally. "I was always considered a good sport and a good team player," he said. "I always took the dirty blocking assignments, but never bitched. And now I always like the guys working for me. I'd be perfectly willing to work for them, if it should be practical." Here Wakefield spontaneously associated his job and his willingness to share the dirty work to football and his willingness to take the dirty blocking assignments. The value of the game has been to develop reciprocity rather than to try to lord it over anyone else. If you dish it out, you have to be willing to take it. Gamesmen like Wakefield have the values of healthy twelve-year-olds—fairness and independence from authority are central. They despise the kids with special privileges, those who sidle up too close to authority, the teacher's pets. Although he wants to be a leader, Wakefield remained ambivalent about authority. He said he does not have a power drive, that he has never sought promotion, and he doesn't think about moving up the ladder.

Wakefield's responses to Rorschach tests given in 1969 and 1972 expressed these main themes of independence versus cooperation at work, aloneness versus relatedness.

In the first Rorschach, taken when Wakefield was thirty-two, the main themes involved trying to integrate the desire for freedom and self-expression with the need for relatedness. The responses were of a person who, unable to be deeply intimate, was running away, detaching himself from really close contact with another person. There was a suggestion that he saw intimacy in terms of being hunted and trapped. On Card V, Wakefield saw a bunny and a deer running away. The animals on Card VIII were small, either moles, beavers, or raccoons.

A second theme was cooperation, people working together. Here there was no conflict; Wakefield could express himself unambivalently. The figures on Card III were carrying a basket together.

A third theme was excitement and competition. On Card II, Wakefield saw two Samurai warriors hunched over in combat, a striking symbol of the corporate game. Many corporate managers see the Japanese semifeudal corporate model as the essence of the corporate spirit. Here is the Samurai, an individualist, technically proficient, a hired warrior, aggressive but not destructive, yet hunched over and submissive, not fighting his own battles but rather those of his lord. This symbol also expresses respect for technical expertise in a world of male competence in which people in close quarters remain distant from one another. On this same Rorschach card, some executives see trained bears or elephants, symbolizing that their passions and instincts have been tamed and socialized so that they perform for the company. That image is disturbing, consciously or unconsciously, for the company man who feels in this way castrated and humiliated. But the Samurai, while submissive, is still more spirited, more independent and zestful within the system.

There were other themes that also showed attitudes and possibilities which Wakefield might or might not develop in the future. The theme of potency in terms of engineering knowledge was expressed on Card VI, where Wakefield saw a turbine of a jet engine, and on Card VIII, where the top detail "could be a rough image of the new superengine transport delta wing."

His percepts also expressed beauty, delicacy, and love of nature. Yet it was nature at a distance or combined with technology. On Card II, a snow-capped mountain was seen from an airplane. On Card X, microorganisms were observed through a microscope. One of the most creative perceptions was on Card IX, where Wakefield saw a fountain with three different jets. The water was spraying at the top, tumbling at the side, and coming out at the bottom, colored by different lights. On the top was foam. Here is an expression of disciplined energy, beauty, exuberance, and technology, a symbol of emotional release, love of life, and technological innocence. Another theme was, like that of Steward, the craftsman, authority as protective. On Card IV, Wakefield saw a shade tree, like an elm or an ash. This is a card in which power-hungry jungle fighters like Phil Bass saw crowns, castles, stone idols, or powerful animals. The Rorschach responses in 1969 supported Wakefield's contention that he did not seek power as status or control over others, but that he did have a vision of leadership in terms of responsibility, protection, and stimulation. The question was whether the corporation would allow him to develop these productive and positive strivings.

Three years later his Rorschach responses were

more troubled, less innocent, darker, and more ambiguous. Gone was the sparkling fountain. Instead, on Cards II, VII, and IX, there emerged the theme of animals being hunted, an image present in the first Rorschach but more dominant and pervasive in the second. One got the sense of someone who was fearful of being a victim, but who refused to become a hunter. On Card IX, he first saw a flower, then a large animal fleeing. "It is a buffalo or bull moose . . . I would not be a hunter."

Instead of the shade tree representing authority on Card IV, there was an image of a marshy scene by a lake with bushes and trees mirrored in the water. This is an image common to executives and it seems to express worried concern about authority relationships combined with self-preoccupation and turning inward, problems unresolved.

Later, Wakefield told me that during this period he felt he was beginning a crisis that he had still not resolved. It was during this period that he was questioning corporate life, wondering whether he could keep up the pace without burning out. No longer did he celebrate technology, and his pleasure in combativeness had faded away. The turbine and the Samurai were gone. Instead, he expressed a yearning to be alone with himself and in nature. Yet at the same time there was much less life and action in the second Rorschach than in the first. It was as though Wakefield was discovering that he could not develop more actively and fully in the directions suggested by the first Rorschach, but he had not yet found an alternate way to express himself. It was as though he was stopped in time and was looking into himself.

Wakefield was going through a period of loneliness.

About this time, he said that his idealism and sense of fairness seemed to be getting in the way of his work. He was also feeling the demand that faces all successful gamesmen—that he become more of a company man if he wants to move from middle to upper management. At this time he noted that he was suffering from a few problems common to gamesmen at this level. They reflected and expressed his depressive inward turning. He said he was often restless. He was overeating and becoming puffy-looking. He felt that he did not know what he wanted and that it was "too necessary to give in to circumstances." As a result of his conflicted feelings, he was becoming uptight, obsessively neat, and overly careful. (Like his mother. Was he mothering himself?) He could no longer trust his perceptions of what was important. Even the smallest details seemed overly significant. At the same time he found it more difficult to be by himself, and yet with others he was more closed and kept his feelings to himself.

Up to now we have not described Wakefield's relationship to his wife. This relationship highlighted aspects of his character and showed that the traits reinforced and developed at work made it more difficult to develop other traits and to achieve his goal of a loving relationship with his wife. This is less of a problem with craftsmen couples like the Stewards, who do not seek deep love and intimacy and are satisfied with respect, or other couples who are able to develop a stable and satisfactory relationship in which the wife is willing to take a mothering role. But neither cool companionship nor a mother-son relationship would have satisfied Wakefield. He sensed the possibility of a more intimate and profound relationship that would develop and grow and bring out creative aspects of himself and of his wife, Jane. Yet he had not succeeded. The polarity between them remained either adolescent sexual excitement or at times an unstable childlike dependency that Jane found unsatisfying, although she did not object to the idea of making the home a place where "the husband can come home and let down after work." But she was willing to do this only if she felt that Jack supported her independence and development, and was close.

Growing up, Wakefield did not have problems in going out with girls. But he did not have to work too hard to get along with them either. Handsome and dazzling, energetic yet sensitive and somewhat shy, the girls came after him. When he was fifteen years old, he was seduced by a girl who called him up and asked him for help with her homework. He dated a lot from the tenth grade on and had some steady girl friends. In college he slept with a few girls but it was all in the modern spirit of having experiences and fun together. The first few years he worked for the company he had many girl friends and then lived for a while with a stewardess. He worked hard at having fun. His friends would kid him and say that he'd better get married or else he was going to die of dissipation. But, in fact, his relations with women during that period, although exciting and enjoyable, did not demand a great deal of him.

Jane was the first deep love of his life and he experienced something totally new with her. But marriage has been difficult. In a way it has been frightening because it has demanded a different spirit; it has not fit into the context of a game.

Wakefield described love as having some of the elements of a close friendship but "more intense on every front. You become so identified with that person that part of you doesn't exist without that person." For someone who has always evaded intimacy and fears being trapped, such a feeling is frightening. Unless the marriage relationship leads to the development of new activities, learning together, sharing intimate perceptions, experience and knowledge that can be shared with no one else, then feelings of love and deep need might become enslaving.

Furthermore, the development of an intimate relationship would be much different from that exciting, sexy atmosphere of courtship, which in a way still exists for Wakefield at work, where adoring, mini-skirted secretaries constantly flirt with him.

How could Jane, having to keep up the house and care for the children, compete with all that? As long as Wakefield burned himself out at work, how could he find the energy and interest needed for the marriage? Instead, he would come home just wanting to get away from things. He said, "When I get home I retreat to myself. I go into a room and read." Jane said he was "extremely inconsistent . . . an extrovert at work, but an introvert at home." But he was bored at home partly because he was evading real intimacy, still depending on work for excitement.

In seeing Wakefield over a period of seven years, one noticed that the spontaneous, youthful drive and energy no longer existed in the old, limitless supply. For most people in their late thirties, energy is generated by the quality of one's relatedness to the world rather than as in the teens and twenties, when it is tapped from wells of natural exuberance. While the older craftsman gains his energy from his interest in what he creates, the older gamesman comes to depend more and more on the excitement of work, on being juiced up by the contest. But this very dependency also begins to burn him out, use him up, and leave him increasingly depressed. As long as Wakefield depended on the work game to energize him, Jane in a way would make it harder for him because she would resent his emotional absence; she would want a more stimulating relationship. She said, "Always as far as our marriage is concerned he says it's 'as soon as I get everything straightened out, then I'll have more time.'" She feared he was going to give more of himself to his work as he moved up higher in the corporation, and she said, "I don't care if he doesn't go any farther." Jane has become disappointed. She expected more. "Marriage was a big change. We didn't know each other very well. It makes it harder. People aren't exactly as you thought they were."

Jane is a lovely, receptive, and life-loving person who, like Wakefield, appeared to have a capacity for real love. Before her marriage she was a teacher who deeply enjoyed her work with young children. She is slower, less brilliant and mercurial than Wakefield. Now she was becoming disillusioned. A recent dream was of a peach tree full of peaches. "I woke up thinking the peaches were all gone," she said. The peaches are like childish hopes that life will be sweet and easy with Jack. In the best of circumstances a peach tree is a poor symbol for mature love, but at the time of the dream, nothing had taken the place of Jane's early receptive, immature hopes.

The main point was not that work drained Wakefield and didn't leave him enough energy for his wife, although this sometimes happened. Rather it was more that the work reinforced and supported an attitude that was largely in contradiction to what would have been needed to develop a more loving, intimate relationship with Jane. Work was exciting, intellectualized, and allowed him to remain detached. He was worshiped and admired by the secretaries, who demanded nothing from him except a few jokes and some flirtation and who followed his every order with gratitude for being allowed to serve him. His relationship with women at the office was not a relationship where intimacy would require equality and respect for differences, loving interest, and full commitment. That kind of relationship depends on developing attitudes that are not needed in the office, where Wakefield's secretary saw him as a "higher type of person" because of his education and intelligence. She and all the others who worked with him in the office reinforced his dedication to the work, and they all hoped that he would rise in the company.

Wakefield's work, like football and hockey in high school, developed positive character traits in him. He considered that his work had helped him to become more flexible, yet systematic and self-controlled. It had developed his ability to take the initiative and feel pride in a good performance. Through the work, he had experienced and exercised his potentials for creative thought and leadership. Marriage offered an opportunity for a totally different type of development, but if a person like Wakefield cannot respond to the new challenge, then marriage can soon become boring.

At age thirty-five, Wakefield defined a good marriage in terms of "a respectable sex life, active but not calisthenic exactly, but active. There are things you can do together that you can build a relationship on. The idea of having children eventually. That's very important. Having sons has added a new dimension to our marriage." What this description stated was that marriage was limited to a good sexual relationship and having children. And in fact Wakefield felt that his marriage improved considerably when his boys began to grow up. In our last conversation he remarked, "The key thing about marriage is not just love. The children add a whole new dimension. It's exciting now." He could play with the boys and horse around. At home he could become a father-coach.

Jane's definition of a happy marriage did not even include sex. She said, "When two people enjoy each other. Also children are important. I think mutual respect is involved. You know, if you love each other and enjoy being together and respect each other, you work out problems." One might ask here what it means to "enjoy being together." Is this a matter of vibrations or does it also include shared activities which are enjoyable? Furthermore, was Jane waiting too passively for Jack to put more into the marriage? Was she becoming boring because she no longer had a job and lacked activities that might make her more interested and interesting? For love to develop after the first romance, it may be necessary that both man and woman develop equally, so that they meet together as emotional and intellectual equals who respect each other. Jane, unlike Betty Steward, no longer worked at her job and has not found another way to develop herself. She is also a person who needs more stimulation and challenge. If she became boring to Jack, the relationship might become one of fondness, mutual responsibility and caring, but the implicit marriage contract would change. No longer would it be a contract based on equal love and mutual development with constant challenge and joy, but rather it would become a contract to keep a good home, bring up the children well, and support the husband's struggle for success, which would allow the family to have security and enjoy many good things.

Failing to develop a new type of relationship, the Wakefields are likely to settle into a pattern dictated by their childhood experiences and the unrelenting pressures of Jack's work. He will seek a refuge and mothering at home, where he will become a responsible father and provider. Jane will develop herself as a loving mother and homemaker. Reasonably satisfied, both will sometimes feel that compared to the promise, something has been lost.

A key social and emotional problem in America today, even with people as sensitive and with the capacity to love as great as the Wakefields', is how to develop a loving relationship between the sexes beyond the traditional roles.

At age thirty-six, Wakefield felt that he was in a critical period of decision. He was no longer a boy but not fully a man. He felt that he was losing himself in the organization and that his marriage was souring. One of his goals had always been to start a new career. Like many gamesmen, the idea of keeping his options open was very appealing. Now, he and Jane had gotten involved in the ecology movement. This involved attending meetings together and talking about them afterward, and it brought them closer. Wakefield felt that here was a chance to do something to realize his values and make a social as well as a professional contribution that would make him proud of himself. He had thought about it for a year and had talked with people whom he respected in the Government and in the ecology movement. They had told him there was a need for leadership by technical people in this movement, particularly someone with both a technical and a legal background to work for environmental protection. Wakefield had become more and more excited by the idea. He had decided to take the law school admittance test and go to law school with the eventual goal of joining a group specializing in consumer protection, with particular reference to questions of computers and privacy.

Wakefield considered that his thirteen years in the company was long enough. Furthermore, he felt that he had reached the level of middle management where he had the greatest freedom to run his own projects and his own show. If he went farther up, he would have to give up independence and become more integrated into the Round Table of top management. He told me that when he looked above him at the corporate vice-presidents, "I don't see any happy faces."

I asked Wakefield whether money wouldn't be a problem if he left the corporation and went to law school. He said no, he had enough money for the law-school years. If he cashed in his shares, his savings, and some severance pay, he could make it through law school. It is worth emphasizing that Wakefield is not greedy. Becoming rich has never been an important motive at any time in his life.

Success certainly means security, for him, and as with all gamesmen, pay is one of the rewards for winning, but his goal is not to be rich. Yet, in the end, the financial sacrifice and threat to security did play a role for Jane perhaps even more than for Jack.

There were those who always doubted that Wakefield would really leave. His secretary was one. She said, "Jack just finds it too exciting to leave." And, as he put off leaving, debating the pros and cons, he became even more successful at work. The problems that had plagued him the two years before began to disappear as the organization got into line and the products began to sell. He started to think that he was in fact the kind of person who could be successful in top management. After all, the computer business was a new kind of business that required a different kind of person, not the old-style company-man executive or the brilliant craftsman-entrepreneur, but his kind of future-minded, cooperative leader willing to take calculated risks. "After all, this is a risk-taking business," he said. "We bet the corporation on a new generation of computers every few years. To develop computers means one commits oneself to a constant planned revolution."

When Wakefield told me in 1973 that he had applied to law school, I too was doubtful that he would really leave the corporation. He seemed much more content than he had been a year or two before. He no longer worked so hard. He took weekends off. He felt the symptoms that had bothered him before were now gone. He was more relaxed, had opened up a great deal, and had come out of his depression. At work, his philosophy and leadership were determining the direction of the division. Somehow, the idea that he was going to leave and go to law school just didn't fit with his enthusiasm about his work and his future in the company.

I also doubted that he would leave to dedicate himself to a social cause, since nothing in his background or experience supported deep concern for the effects of the company's products on the world. He was relatively unaware of what went on outside of his own rather protected world. He was extremely self-centered, constantly worrying about his own career integrity, with very little concern for the poor or for people in the rest of the world. This self-centeredness, this self-protectiveness, acted to keep him from deep intimacy with others and from a deeper relatedness to the world. Although it is unlikely that he would try to change the world, I do believe that Wakefield would support a movement to humanize technology in the corporation, since he is not greedy for money or power, and he does believe that corporations must be regulated by society.

There was another sign of adaptation. Wakefield no longer had disturbing dreams. When I first met him, he used to have many traveling dreams, as well as dreams about problems at work, some of which he would resolve in his dreams. Later, in the midst of his crisis, he would dream he was visiting a strange, unearthly place, that he was not in a real world. This expressed the feeling that the corporation was an inhuman place where he did not belong. The earlier dreams of visiting many places and flying are common to gamesman managers who are always moving around, never in one place, always restless. But this time when I talked to him, he said he no longer dreamed. This too I had heard from other gamesmen who have adapted themselves and no longer want to think about a troublesome reality or deep experiences that would cause them to change their way of life. In another company, after interviewing one gamesman who complained about his lack of goals and his wish to do something different, I suggested that that night he might have a dream that would tell him what he really wanted to do. It often happens in psychoanalysis that one can suggest that a patient have a particular kind of dream, and if he concentrates before going to bed, he often will have a dream that symbolizes the question or conflict. In this case, the manager woke up a half an hour ahead of his usual time but remembered no dream. I suggested that he try again, and he woke up fully an hour before the time he usually would get up, but still with no dream. The third night the same thing happened, and he said to me, "Maybe I don't want to know what I really feel."

A year later, in the summer of 1974, five years after I'd first met Wakefield, I called him up and asked him what had happened about law school. He said that he'd gotten a very good score on the law aptitude test, in the 700's. "But law school does not seem so glamorous now as it did before. In the end I didn't even apply to law school. I'm now much prouder about what's going on here in the company. I don't know, maybe Watergate made the law not so attractive as it was before. Maybe I'd prefer to be in psychology. I'm still ready to make a change if it were the right one." But Wakefield went on to tell me that he was putting more of his energy into making the division a better place to work, to improving the quality of work for all the workers. He was trying to develop flexible working hours and sabbaticals for the managers. He had tried to gain a greater say on the part of the middle managers in regulating their own salaries and stock options, and to a certain extent he had succeeded.

But then he went on to say, "Doing my own thing, finding out what I want to do, that's still the main problem. I know I have to get out of this environment. It is a total environment that catches you up fully. A number of people here are taking sabbaticals. Maybe that's what I should do."

Unsentimentally viewing Wakefield's struggles to find his autonomy and individuality, we can say that it is exactly his concern with social issues that would make him more valuable on the top levels of the company management. Many gamesmen who are able to motivate craftsmen in project teams remain purely inside men, who can only function within the corporate game. It is a rare person who combines the talents and skills of Wakefield and also is responsive to social issues. This openness helps him to understand changes in the market, and equally important, it puts him in touch with the currents of the young, so that he is better able to attract and manage the most brilliant young college graduates. The learning that has gone on in his flirtation with change, in law and ecology and maybe, in the future, psychology, will serve him well in the top reaches of corporate management. The idea that he could leave and change careers was an illusion he shares with many top executives, who like to feel that they are still independent individuals, that they are not fully company men.

How did Jane feel about Jack's decision? Mostly she was relieved that their financial security would not be threatened. She pointed out that Jack had discovered that lawyers aren't in the best of favor these days. "Anyway, the market is glutted with lawyers, and maybe once he found out that he could do it, the attraction was less for him. He would have really liked the work, the courses and all, but he decided that there was not much future in it. I felt pretty relieved about his decision, because of the financial standpoint. For three years he wouldn't have worked and we would have had to finance law school and at the end of the time we wouldn't have had anything left. If it had meant that much to Jack, well then, OK. But I was relieved when he decided against it."

Were they still working together, studying questions of the environment, of ecology? "I still do a lot of reading," Jane said, "but I get discouraged because it seems that nobody really knows anything for sure in this field. I'm still interested in it. I read books on it, but I haven't kept up with it. The group I was in disbanded. But there's a group here of people who distribute food and are interested in healthy food. Anyway, I'm so busy with the children. They're really quite demanding at this age. But as far as having anything organized in ecology, I have no time or maybe I don't have the interest anymore. There's plenty to do with the kids."

What about Jack's relationship with his family? "It goes in spurts," Jane answered. "Last weekend he spent the whole time on company work, but this is true of most husbands. Every woman I know complains that her husband isn't home enough. It's a universal thing . . . sometimes I think it's getting to be too much, but basically I'm satisfied."

Did Jane think that Jack would ever really change careers? "He's thought about medicine, law, dentistry. But these things, they take so darn long. If he were a dentist, I know he'd go buggy, he would get so tired of the routine. He might go to another company in the same field, but the company he's in is a pretty good company. He wouldn't find any better. He's talked about starting a smaller company. That's risky, and it hasn't materialized yet. I don't really worry about it. As things stand, I'm happy. This situation is ideal for me. The kids, the house, the neighborhood, the school—all of it is ideal for me. I can't imagine a situation that's better. I'm home all day here with the kids."

Have things changed in the last two years? "No, things haven't changed really, except I'm so tired at the end of the day with the kids. Jack is pretty secure in his position. He can kind of make things go his way a little bit more. I'm not pushing for a change. I don't want any major changes. He's spending more time at home, and part of it is due to circumstances. Daddy does have to do his part; he's kind of forced into it because the kids demand that he be around and pay attention to them. He's home more, there's no doubt about it. And I'm happy. I'm not ambitious. I really do enjoy the children." And she sounded as if she really meant it.

In sum, Wakefield's character fit his work and equipped him to move even higher on the corporate ladder. The motivation for change was just enough to flirt with different possibilities and learn things that in fact would be helpful to his career. But the conflict was not great enough to cause any deep suffering, or to motivate him to dedicate himself to social betterment. Furthermore, he could rationalize that by staying put, he was helping to develop the people at work. This development would be similar to that in his own life which turned him from a rebel and hell-raiser into a productive and successful manager. If the company and the work had encouraged it, Wakefield could have developed his idealism and love of life in cooperative, socially progressive projects. But those were not the character traits required at the top.

At this point, I sent the chapter to Wakefield, asking him to let me know if he thought I should change anything or whether its publication might in any way hurt him. If so, it would not be printed. I nervously waited, but he did not reply for months, and with the publisher waiting for the manuscript, I sent a second letter. Shortly after, he called. He hadn't gotten around to reading it, but when he finally picked it up one night, he couldn't put it down. He started at nine and finished at one A.M. and Jane kept asking why he was laughing so. He said, "I never realized how those meetings must seem, and the sexy secretaries." Jane has now also read the chapter and both thought it helpful. "Few people," Wakefield said, "ever have such an opportunity, of someone analyzing their lives in a way that helps them see themselves so clearly."

Wakefield questioned one conclusion, that he would ever enter top management. "It's like a club," he said, "and maybe you can't enter if you are too concerned with humanization. I would like to feel it is true, but in fact those few managers who do push hard for more social concern and responsibility on the part of their companies are never quite fully trusted by their top-level managers even though they may be highly respected and liked in all other respects."

CHAPTER 7

The Head and the Heart

'Give thy servant, therefore, a heart with skill to listen, so that he may govern thy people justly and distinguish good from evil. For who is equal to the task of governing this great people of thine?' The Lord was well pleased that Solomon had asked for this, and he said to him, 'Because you have asked for this, and not for long life for yourself, or for wealth, or for the lives of your enemies, but have asked for discernment in administering justice, I grant your request; I give you a heart so wise and so understanding that there has been none like you before your time nor will be after you. I give you furthermore those things for which you did not ask, such wealth and honor as no king of your time can match. And if you conform to my ways and observe my ordinances and commandments, as your father David did, I will give you long life.' Then he awoke, and knew it was a dream.*

—I KINGS 3:9–15

God brought you forth from the wombs of your mothers. You did not then know anything. And He gave you hearing and vision and hearts . . . and you are little grateful.†

—IBN KHALDŪN

The men of old, wanting to clarify and diffuse throughout the empire that light which comes from looking straight into the heart and acting, first set up good government in their own states; wanting good government in their own states they first established order in their families; wanting order in their families they first disciplined themselves;

---

*The New English Bible (New York: Oxford University Press, Cambridge University Press, 1970), p. 377.

†Ibn Khaldūn, *The Muqaddimah*, Vol. II, abridged ed., trans. by Franz Rosenthal, Bollingen Series XLIII (Princeton: Princeton University Press, 1958), p. 407.

desiring discipline in themselves they first rectified their hearts.*

—MENCIUS (MENG-TSE)

WE HAVE SEEN that at the top levels of the corporation, individuals must be highly motivated to do what the organization requires of them, and that in the process of reaching the top, managerial character is refined.

Overall, there is a threefold process of social (in contrast to natural) selection that includes organizations, character types, and attitudes. One part of the process has to do with which organizations survive and prosper. Another part has to do with which character types are selected from the available population to man these organizations. (Over a period of time, the adaptive companies tend to be the ones with structures, cultures, and kinds of people that best fit the requirements of the market and technology, and that best succeed in creating an atmosphere that encourages productive work.) And the third part involves an internal selection process whereby those traits that are useful to the work are stimulated and reinforced while others that are unnecessary or that impede work are frustrated, suppressed, or unused and gradually weaken.

Any organization of work—industrial, service, blue or white collar—can be described as a *psychostructure* that selects and molds character. One difference between the psychostructure of the modern corporate technostructure and that of a factory is the fineness of fit between work and character demanded of corporate managers and engineers who do "brainwork," in contrast to factories, where only minimal compliance is required to perform the simplified, repetitive tasks.

---

*Quoted by Archibald MacLeish, "An Age of Adolescence," *Washington Post*, January 21, 1974.

The concept of a psychostructure which selects character types for different roles resolves an argument between the sociologically minded, who claim that the role determines behavior, and the psychologically minded, who claim that personality determines behavior.* Although there is leeway in any

---

*Examples of the sociologically minded are such astute observers of corporations as Paul Baran and Paul Sweezy, who in *Monopoly Capital* (New York: Monthly Review Press, 1966) contend that psychological motivations are unimportant because the large corporation is like a baseball team where each player's behavior is dictated by his role, the rules and events of the game, and not his individual motives. ("A professional baseball player makes his living by playing ball. He may detest the life and stay with it solely for the money. Or he may love the game and be quite willing to play for nothing if necessary. It makes no difference at all when he gets out on the playing field. There his objectives are no longer dictated by his personal feelings and preferences; they are laid down for him in the baseball rule book," p. 41.) What Baran and Sweezy leave out is that the process of selecting players for each position in the corporate game (which is closer to football than baseball) is based on personality as well as skill.

Dr. Arnold J. Mandell, chairman of the Department of Psychiatry at the University of California, San Diego, actually studied this process of social selection in a professional football team and reported his findings in "A Psychiatric Study of Professional Football," *Saturday Review/World*, September 5, 1974, p. 13.

I began to differentiate the personality profiles of these men independently of any prior knowledge about the specific requirements of their individual positions. Before long a personality classification in relation to position began to emerge. The consistency of the patterns seems explainable on the basis of the selection that occurs before any professional football player gains a regular starting position in the NFL [National Football League].

Every year several thousand college football players are eligible; not more than 600 are seriously considered, and of those, 50 to 100 make it to the NFL. The selection goes on year after year. A player maintains his position by winning individual battles week after week on the field, where his performance is witnessed, filmed, and "graded." The crop of players is weeded systematically. The athletic difference between those who remain and those who are dropped is amazingly small. When it comes to making it in the NFL, practically every owner or coach with whom I've talked says, reverently and resignedly, "The game is

role for some differences in style, intelligence, and character, as one moves up in a competitive and selective organization, these variations become less important. The higher you go in a large electronics company, the more likely you are to find the gamesman. At the top of the organization, you might conclude that the chief executive officer's behavior is determined "psychologically" by the way his personality responds to pressures, opportunities, etc., but that conclusion would leave out the fact that his personality has been selected exactly because it fits the requirements of the role. Inevitably, the chief executive of the modern corporation will be one who is responsive to the requirements of various corporate departments, a person who can be trusted to protect the company's growth and profit, who can inspire employees and stockholders with a sense of purpose, who takes calculated risks, who is controlled and can control gifted technical people without dampening their enthusiasm for innovation. However, the personalities of the executives molded in the course of their work also maintain or modify the organization.

We gave most of the 250 executives, managers, and engineers we interviewed a list of character traits and asked them to check both those "important for your work" and the ones that were "stimulated or reinforced by your work." Table 7A shows that in general the traits considered most useful for work were the ones most strengthened. Now, if we consider the traits marked by the largest number compared to those which few or none considered to be stimulated by work, the following pattern emerges. Corporate work in advanced technology stimulates and reinforces attitudes essential for intellectual innovation and teamwork, qualities of the head. And those are the traits required for work. In contrast, compassion, generosity, and idealism, qualities of the

---

in the mind." In addition to athletic ability, motivation, and commitment, the player needs a personality that meets the requirements of his position.

heart, remain unneeded and underdeveloped. (See below.)

A notable exception to this rule is that while honesty is considered important for the work by 72 percent, only 12 percent consider that corporate work develops honesty. This means that while honesty is essential to team building and planning, it does not always help in selling oneself and the product.

The most positive aspects of corporate character development can be defined in terms of competence, confidence, and openmindedness. Top corporate managers are cooperative and able to communicate well. Most enjoy their work. Some are brilliant and innovative, even dazzling in their ability to understand complex sociotechnical systems.

They are not overly destructive, overly dependent,

Table 7A • CHARACTER TRAITS VERY IMPORTANT TO WORK AND STIMULATED BY WORK

Qualities of the Head	Very Important for Work (Percent)	Stimulated by Work (Percent)
Ability to take the initiative	91	58
Satisfaction in creating something new	74	51
Self-confidence	86	50
Coolness under stress	71	40
Cooperativeness	74	37
Pleasure in learning something new	68	35
Pride in performance	88	35
Flexibility	76	33
Open-mindedness	81	30
Qualities of the Heart		
Independence	45	21
Loyalty to fellow workers	47	18
Critical attitude to authority	21	17
Friendliness	35	16
Sense of humor	53	14
Openness, spontaneity	46	14
Honesty	72	12
Compassion	18	4
Generosity	13	2
Idealism	9	1

or grandiose. Few are either exceptionally greedy or hungry for power. Yet they are not a particularly happy group. They lack passion and compassion. They are cool or lukewarm. Intellectually open and interested, they are emotionally cautious, protected against intense experience.

The corporation is of course not fully responsible for the character development of those who work there. Character is formed first in family and school, and the type of person who chooses to work in a corporation has some idea of what to expect. He or she enters with character traits common to young Americans who pass all the exams and get high grades at colleges and universities. The corporate individual must be competitive and highly intelligent in terms of intellectual problem-solving. But most young people are a mixture of still-malleable attitudes. Upon entering the corporation, they still have the chance to become more idealistic and just or they could become disillusioned and self-serving. The traits stimulated in the corporation will in many cases have a decisive effect on the kind of people they become, not only as managers, but as citizens, husbands, wives, fathers, and mothers.

On the basis of the total interview, we rated managers and engineers on the level of their productiveness in both work and love (*agape*). The results are shown in Table 7B. Practically none of the managers are to be found at the extreme of either scale. In terms of work, none expressed the deep interest of a scientist passionately searching for the truth, but none rejected work totally. In terms of love, none were deeply loving, expressing the kind of interest and creative support of another person that implies profound knowledge and care together with transcendence of egoistic concerns, but practically none were rejecting of life or misanthropic.

Significantly, the corporate group was more productive in terms of work than of love. As Table 7B reports, 80 percent expressed at least moderate in-

Table 7B • PRODUCTIVENESS IN LOVE AND WORK

Work Scale	Percent
Deep scientific interest in understanding, dynamic sense of the work, animated	0
Centered, enlivening, craftsmanlike, but lacks deeper scientific interest in the nature of things	22
The work itself stimulates interest, which is not self-sustained	58
Moderately productive, not centered; interest in work is essentially instrumental, to ensure security, income	18
Passive unproductive, diffused	2
Rejecting of work, rejects the real world	0
	100

Love Scale	
Loving, affirmative, creatively stimulating	0
Responsible, warm, affectionate but not deeply loving	5
Moderate interest in another person with more loving possibilities	40
Conventional concern, decent, role-oriented	41
Passive, unloving, uninterested	13
Rejecting of life, hardened heart	1
	100

terest in their work compared to 45 percent expressing moderate interest in another person. The same individual who spoke with imagination and animation about work was blank about love or defined it in dry and bureaucratic terms, for example, "Love is a mutual relationship involving two people most frequently of opposite sexes that involves sexual attraction, compatibility of personalities, common interests."

The most loving were not the ones who moved up the ladder rapidly. Corporate work stimulates and rewards qualities of the head and not of the heart. Those who were active and interested in the work moved ahead in the modern corporation, while those who were the most compassionate were more likely to suffer severe emotional conflicts.

When I reported these findings at a seminar of top managers at one company we studied, they were touched and worried. Many managers consider themselves religious people or humanists. The contradiction between the effects of corporate life and their religious values troubled them, and typically they looked for a managerial solution. How could they change their work or institute new programs to develop the heart? The question took me by surprise. I did not have an answer and had assumed that this was not possible in our system, but since then the question has made me think about what it means to develop the heart and why this is so difficult, almost impossible, within the corporate system.

People think of qualities of the heart as opposite to those of the head. They think heart means softness, feeling, and generosity, while head means toughminded, realistic thought. But this contrast is itself symptomatic of a schizoid culture, in which the head is detached from the rest of the body. In pre-Cartesian traditional thought, the heart was considered the true seat of intelligence and the brain the instrument of thinking. It is more precise to say that some kinds of knowledge require both the head and the heart. The head alone can decipher codes, solve technical problems, and keep accounts, but no amount of technical knowledge can resolve emotional doubt about what is true or what is beautiful. No amount of technique can produce courage. The head alone cannot give emotional and spiritual weight to knowledge in terms of its human values. The head can be smart but not wise.

The view that heart is opposed to head is also a symptom of the socioeconomic system. Getting ahead in school and organizations requires head but not heart, and it often happens that the people with the most concerned hearts are craftsmen-farmers or not careerists. It is not that they lack intellectual capacity, rather that society does not encourage them to think critically, to analyze and invent. They cannot move up the hierarchies of schools and corporations to gain access to technical, theoretical knowledge. And those few who do move up the hierarchies develop the head and not the heart.

Thus, it appears that we must choose between head and heart or at best find an unstable balance between them. Conventional wisdom states that the individual who remains in his head at school or work should act from the heart at home, as though it were possible to switch character like suits of clothing. But we would draw a different conclusion if work and education were organized to develop the individual's fullest creative and critical capacities. Although head and heart may never be integrated in the corporate system, there is no inherent contradiction between them, and as we shall see in Chapter 9, it is possible to experiment in reorganizing work toward this goal.

Considered as not separate from but integrated with the head (and the rest of the body), the development of the heart determines not only compassion and generosity, but also one's perception-*experience*, the quality of *knowledge*, capacity for *affirmation* (of truth or sham, beauty or ugliness), and the *will* to *action* (courage).

The quality of perception depends on our openness to experience. We can "see" that another person is sad or happy, but if our hearts are open to him, we also experience *with* him. Empathy and compassion, or experiencing together with another person, are activities of an open, listening heart.

Intellect alone organizes data from and about other human beings but it does not experience them. The knowledge available to the detached head is laundered of emotion. The head knows by inference, like a computer; sense data are filed into programmed categories. The intellect may examine human problems but they are abstracted, weightless. It must be emphasized, in a world where thought is detached from the heart, that affirmation is not just an emotional reaction, but an act of reason. The more we can experience reality, inner realities as well as the external one, the more information we have to understand the world, ourselves, others. We use our heads fully only if our hearts are strong. This is true about knowledge of the self as well as of the outer world, because with a detached heart we do not experience inner strivings directly, but can only deduce our motives.

Unlike the head, the heart is not neutral about knowledge. The heart wills and strives. Thus, the quality of the heart, its purity in Kierkegaard's sense, affects how and what we know.* If our hearts are full of childish strivings, our knowledge, especially about people, will be confused and distorted. If our hearts are weak and fearful, we will not want to know something that confronts us with our cowardice. If our hearts are envious, we will want to hide from the experience of "eating our hearts out." Thus, the heart is the seat of *consciousness*, in contrast to *conceptualization*, which is in the head. One reason why we detach head from heart is to avoid painful or confusing experiences of fear, greed, envy, anger, powerlessness, but we do so at the expense of remaining only half aware.

The detached head can neither affirm nor will. It thinks but it cannot act. Affirmation of convictions and rejection of evil must come from a strong and courageous heart, one that can experience the difference between truth and sham. But the will to destroy and to exploit others is also rooted in the heart, a hardened or anesthetized heart, which may be connected to a technique-oriented, option-seeking, neutral-knowledge head.

Affirmation is not a contradiction to a critical attitude. To the contrary, a critical attitude makes us either more sure of our affirmation or causes us to doubt it and to look for possible reasons why we have

---

*Sören Kierkegaard, *Purity of Heart Is to Will One Thing* (New York: Harper and Brothers, 1938).

been taken in. It is interesting that few managers report that a critical attitude has been stimulated by corporate work.

Neither openness to experience nor courage to act means that a stronghearted person is always right. The individual who can affirm life and truth may make mistakes. We may be fooled by illusions and wishful thinking, by a seductive, charming person, or by misleading events. The opposite of doubt is not certainty, but rather faith in our experience and the willingness to risk being wrong, and, worse, gullible. It is easier to take this risk if we know that with effort we can think/experience ourselves back to the truth. In contrast, certainty implies control and predictability. For both the detached intellectual and the hard-hearted fanatic, it is the facsimile of conviction. The fainthearted look for someone else who can affirm life for them as a substitute for their missing faith and capacity for critical reason. The fanatical embrace idolatrous causes.

To affirm an unconventional perception or feeling and to act courageously, independently, is based on the experience, the conviction, that it is life-enhancing, harmonious, and right. Note *Webster's New International Dictionary*'s first definition of courage, with its root in the Latin *cor* and French *coeur:* "The heart, as the seat of intelligence or of feeling . . ."

With a detached heart, an individual may be motivated by "guts," appetite, or fear. Although we sometimes use the term as a synonym for courage, guts seems to imply the capacity to risk oneself for a goal, whether or not it is good or just. In this sense, both courage and guts require bravery, but courage also implies more human qualities. Hardhearted fanatics or amoral secret agents might have guts. Unlike the root of courage, the concept of guts has a quality of adolescent toughness, like a strong stomach. In Spanish, the closest translation would be *muy macho*, or to have balls, for a man, and for a woman, *sin verguenza*, a person who cannot be shamed, who moves ahead to get what she wants no matter what anyone thinks. In these concepts, there is the implication of appetite, some form of greed, sexual or otherwise, combined with rebellious pride.

Guts may drive a young man to charge into the line in a football game or to dive from the high board. But if he risked his life for his friends, we would say he acted out of courage, even though it would be clear that such bravery required guts. Courage implies conviction. It may mean risking deep pain—contempt, rejection, loneliness—by expressing the truth to another person. It takes courage to oppose company policies that are harmful to employees or consumers or to leave work that is spiritually demoralizing. In contrast to guts, courage implies commitment to self (integrity) and to other people. In this sense, courage of the heart is related to both the intimate and the political, to both love and moral conviction.

Both literally and figuratively, the heart is a muscle. Without exercise, it tends to become weak. Overly protected, it becomes easily hurt. In common language, there is a term for a person with a weak heart, but a strong sense of guilt: a bleeding heart, typically a person with liberal beliefs who lacks the capacity to understand others and the courage to act according to his beliefs, so that he is easily manipulated by his guilt. The bleeding heart's guilt paralyzes his head, so that he often feels taken in when he has helped the underdog who is not grateful.

The exercise of the heart is that of experiencing, thinking critically, willing, and acting, so as to overcome egocentrism and to share passion with other people (justice-compassion) and respond to their need with the help one can give (benevolence-responsibility). It requires discipline, learning to concentrate, to think critically, and to communicate. The goal, a developed heart, implies integrity, a spiritual center, a sense of "I" not motivated by greed or fear, but by love of life, adventure, and fellow feeling. A strong heart is generally merry, with a sense of humor (another trait little stimulated in the corporation).

Why is it that the heart of the corporate individual remains underdeveloped? To try to answer that question, the findings of the study need to be integrated with what psychoanalytic experience teaches us about the heart. Psychoanalysis is a therapy of the heart. People who come for help suffer from passions or fears that conflict with the development of the heart. A psychoanalyst sees people who suffer from obsessive doubt, the inability to affirm and enjoy life. Others are people who live only in their heads and do not feel anything. Some have so hardened their hearts that they suffer chronic depression, at the extreme rooted in hatred of life.

There are three main reasons why the heart remains undeveloped. For some craftsmen and company men, the reason is dependency. For the jungle fighter, it is power-seeking. These are traditional causes for an undeveloped heart. The cause most applicable to the gamesman is careerism, the modern pathology of the heart.

DEPENDENCY

To exercise an independent heart, to experience our emotions and to understand others empathetically, we must be aware and independent enough to experience that person's emotional reality. Only then is it possible to respond helpfully. Erich Fromm has distinguished the humanistic conscience from the authoritarian conscience (or superego).* The authoritarian conscience is internalized fear of authority. The person does something because he has a bad conscience, meaning he is fearful that if he does not, father or mother will be angry and punish him. He

---

*Erich Fromm, *Man for Himself* (New York: Rinehart, 1947), pp. 145–162.

has the illusion that this is his own conscience speaking, but he is really talking to the internalized authorities, inside his head. A dependent, fearful person judges his acts in terms of authoritarian conscience, in terms of duties and oughts, rather than in terms of his own experience and judgment of what is right or wrong. Such a person is always listening for the authority either outside or inside his head, but he is not listening to his own heart. When such a person feels guilty, he never knows whether it is because he is not doing what the authority wants or he is not doing what his own heart tells him is right.

For the dependent person, the concept of responsibility means carrying out the demands of authorities. For the independent person, responsibility is the ability to respond to another's need, and conscience merges with consciousness rooted in reverence for life.

The development of the heart through overcoming fear and dependency is, usually, part of the normal process of growing up. This is particularly so if a person is not intellectualized and does not rationalize his fear in terms of making the authority into some kind of wonderful or godlike figure who merits total obedience. In cases where the authority is idealized and worshiped, it is of course much harder to overcome fear, especially so if the person feels so weak and worthless that he can do nothing by himself, like some of the company men who idealize and worship the organization.

Accounts of the corporation, like Alan Harrington's *Life in the Crystal Palace*, portray conditions that would favor passive-dependent corporate employees. While a few companies we visited have this hothouse, dreamy quality, most do not, and these conditions were probably more characteristic in the fifties, and then only in the richest companies. International competition and recession have combined to tighten up the corporation and to demand more from employees. Although extremely dependent individuals don't make trouble, they are liabilities when initiative and responsibility are needed.

Only a minority of those we interviewed (about 25 percent) appeared to be extremely dependent and childish. Most of them were company men or those craftsmen who were disappointed and grandiose, treating the corporation as a parent who would protect and reward them in return for obedient service. Often they were intensely fixated on their mothers and had transferred this dependency to the corporation. While the dependent company man idealizes the corporation as the mother, the grandiose person typically experiences more ambivalent feelings. Like a rejected child, he resents the corporation because he feels unloved, not admired enough. Uncooperative and overly egocentric, such dependent individuals do not rise very high in the corporate hierarchy; almost all of them are found on the lower levels.

Childish dependency and fear are not the main reasons why the corporate individual's heart remains underdeveloped. In fact, this problem is more prevalent in traditional village societies, particularly those with a history of colonization and forced dependency that has become institutionalized in the family, church, education, etc. The following story provides a contrast to corporate society and an illustration of how developing independence and critical thinking strengthens the heart.

Candido, a Mexican boy of sixteen, was a member of an experimental agricultural club that I worked with in the early sixties, together with volunteers from the American Friends Service Committee. He and the other boys, ages twelve to eighteen, were always fearful that they would not do the right thing and that their parents and other authorities would punish them. It is understandable that they felt that way, since in that village, which was once a hacienda (semifeudal plantation), authorities generally punished children whenever they disobeyed. Village parents did not try to help their children become independent of them. Rather they believed that children were likely to get themselves into trouble and do wrong unless they were fearful of being punished. Furthermore, independent thought and a critical view about authority were experienced as threats to the family and the community, likely to cause problems.

These fearful, "guilty" boys were unable to work cooperatively and to take responsibility for the agricultural project by themselves, when there were no authorities around to tell them what to do. Their attitude toward work was: obey the patron and avoid work when you can. As the project developed, they realized that their fear and rebelliousness crippled them from achieving their goals. In our weekly meetings, we discussed this attitude and how it was formed in their childhood and reinforced by cultural patterns. The boys began to talk together about their common condition, and as they became more conscious that they all shared fear of their parents, they felt less "guilty."

A key event in developing new consciousness was a meeting in which the boys' parents were asked to help with running the club so that we could leave. When the parents heard about the difficulties the boys had in cooperating and about losses of animals and crops due to negligence, they were all for giving up the club. They didn't want the responsibility and their immediate response was typical peasant self-deprecation and negativism.

"These boys are just egoistic and disobedient," one father said. "They cannot do it."

"Why do you waste your time?" asked another. "These boys are not worth it."

At the next club meeting, I asked the boys what they thought of their parents' response. One boy said the meeting was fine. He was immediately challenged by the others.

"What do you mean, fine?" one said. "They do not want to help us; they think we are no good."

Another said, "Already we know more about chickens than they do, and we have learned how to market the eggs. Why do we need their help? They would only order us around and take the profits."

At this moment, a new, independent attitude began to crystalize. The boys were not being rebellious or resentful of their parents. They were not blaming them for their own lack of development. Their criticism was realistic. They were seeing their parents as they were, and they saw, furthermore, that the authorities stifled their chances to grow. While before they could react only to commands, their new awareness produced a new kind of responsiveness.

One day shortly after the meeting, Candido came to see me and told me that for the first time he understood the difference between conscience as fear and conscience as an experience in the heart. He said that up to now he fed the family cow every day because he was afraid his mother would beat him if he did not. But he was beginning to experience his new knowledge, and he was losing his fear of his mother. Today, when he was thinking about the fact that he was no longer frightened by his mother, he looked into the eyes of the cow and for the first time he realized that the cow was alive and depended on him. In that moment, he knew that he would always feed the cow, not because anybody told him to, but because he would feel terrible if he didn't.*

It is normal that young children depend on and fear their parents and teachers. If there is any social support, the healthy person outgrows this by struggling to gain independence and to overcome fear. This support is lacking in a society based on au-

---

*For a fuller discussion of the boys' club project, see Erich Fromm and Michael Maccoby, *Social Character in a Mexican Village* (Englewood Cliffs, N.J.: Prentice-Hall, 1970), pp. 217–225.

thoritarian domination and colonization. In our
society, despite pressures to conform and media
manipulations of the mind, there is still support for
independent thought. Of course, no institution will
ever fully support independence. There will always
be some conflict between social pressures to conform
and the individual's strivings toward individuation.
Some patients in psychoanalysis typically blame their
parents and teachers for not making them more independent. But although authorities may be guilty of
terrifying a child and breaking his will, no one, not
even the most loving parent, can grant independence
to another person. We can try to create conditions
that do not oppress others or crush independence.
We may even encourage and support a child's attempts to individuate, but even in the best of cases,
we must all struggle for our independence, and in
the struggle develop courage.

Unlike the village boys, no one stimulates dependent corporate employees to organize projects in
which the members decide cooperatively on goal,
means, and meaning. Typically, no one in the company supports idealistic impulses to create a more
democratic workplace. Neither have corporate individuals at home, school, or work ever been encouraged to look critically at authority in terms of
whether or not it stifles their chances for fuller human development.

POWER-SEEKING

The most malignant reason why the heart does not
develop is because the individual hardens his heart
or, as in myths and dreams, replaces it with stone.
The heart becomes perverted as the will is directed
toward power. Perversions such as extreme sado-
masochism, cannibalism, and necrophilia describe
the human relationships of individuals whose hearts
are hard. Other people are used as objects or as
puppets. Even if they wanted to, hardhearted peo-

ple could not "listen" to the emotions of others because they would find it unbearable to experience the fear, envy, hatred, revenge they have provoked. They must surround themselves with admirers, and admiration becomes a drug for them to blunt the self-disgust they must repress.

For such people, repentance requires a total change of heart. They must change their minds, intentions, and actions. This requires the willingness to experience full self-disgust and turn to a new path.

How hardhearted are corporate managers? This is a complicated question. Many of the most hardhearted people in corporate roles are ambitious but neurotic failures, petty bureaucrats (hopeless company men) who have been so humiliated and discouraged by life and by their parents and bosses that they have chosen to use the little power they have to make others squirm. Only a very few of the individuals we interviewed expressed such destructive tendencies.

In contrast, some of the high-level power-seekers were more complex people, combining ruthlessness to outsiders with benevolent justice for their own people. Thus, the head of a major company, a lion-like jungle fighter, likened corporate growth to the conquest of Genghis Khan, and spoke coldly about the survival of the fittest, writing off the people of whole continents as "fauna" that no longer could compete with the new managerial breed for scarce resources. Yet the same man kept an open door at work so that any employee could seek "the king's justice," and he worried that his business-school-trained vice-president was unfeeling. In contrast to this industrial baron, the average gamesman would be both less imperial and less concerned about his employees.

While some corporate jungle fighters are exceptionally hardhearted and sadistic, on the whole, the modern corporate executive is much less so and is more concerned about being liked than the empire builder of the past. The modern corporation has been built in such a way as to minimize the need for people with a hardened heart. Still, the logic of corporations is to optimize profit and power, and the corporate managers must serve it. Most become comfortable servants of the company. Unlike the kings and conquerors of old or the modern robber barons, they do not boast of their glory or power. Many executives of elite corporations have never fired anyone, and if they are forced to, they feel terrible about it. Beneath the protective shell, they are rather softhearted.

Yet the managers admire and even idolize the powerful corporation and accept its goals as their own. For about half the people we interviewed, the corporation is the main object of devotion, and this orientation is more dominant in those at the top.

The process of bending one's will to corporate goals and moving up the hierarchy leads to meanness, emotional stinginess, but not full-blown sadism. Although more than a third of the managers expressed sadistic tendencies, they are controlled and channeled, employed within the game in the form of jokes and put-downs or in the service of the team against opponents. There is just enough fear and humiliation to keep the hierarchy glued together. If the corporation is destructive, it is because its products are harmful and its human effects damaging, not because those who conscientiously fill their roles and further their careers wish anyone ill.

CAREERISM

A corporate president remarked that if he thought of one word to describe his experience with managers over a period of thirty-five years, that word would be "fear." His thought fits our findings of the emotional problems most experienced by the managers and engineers. About half of those interviewed checked "anxiety" and "restlessness" as difficulties for them, and almost a third felt that "unwarranted fears" were a problem. (See Table 7C, p. 201).

Other symptoms shared by a significant percentage are also usually related to fear. These include overeating (32 percent), obsessive thoughts (19 percent), gastrointestinal symptoms (18 percent). And this includes only those who consider these problems to be a difficulty. Others experience fear but feel they have it under control.

Table 7C • DIFFICULTIES REPORTED BY CORPORATE MANAGERS

	Percent Checking Totals
Fear	
Often restless	58
Anxious	48
Have unwarranted fears	28
Detachment	
Keep your feelings to yourself	61
Difficulty saying what you mean	59
Avoid people	35
Lack of Self-determination	
Give in too easily to others	59
Don't know what you want	46
Other Related Symptoms	
Tend to blame yourself too much	50
Depression	44
Overeat	32
Lack sufficient energy to do what you want	36
Sleep badly	30
Obsessive thoughts	19
Gastrointestinal symptoms	18
Have thoughts of acting destructively	12
Sexual difficulties	12
Thoughts of suicide	5

Why are corporate managers fearful? Some are frightened that they will fail to perform well; they will lose a sale, miss a deadline, come up with the wrong answer. Someone above them will decide they don't measure up and "zap" them. (One manager said he felt as though he were continually walking down a dark alley, waiting for a bullet to come from somewhere.) Even if they are not afraid of being fired or sent to corporate Siberia, they worry that by not moving ahead, they will fall behind and be forgotten. The company will discover that they are not needed.

The sources of fear are three. One type includes fears that something concrete will happen or not happen—that the project will not succeed, that a sale will not be made, or that one will be found out in a half-truth or lie.

The second type is fear based on lack of knowledge. Many managers do not understand the business and their function in it. They do not know what generates income. They are afraid that they aren't really needed and that someone will discover it. The best way to overcome this fear is for managers and employees to learn together about the economics of the company and have the freedom to reorganize work so that everyone understands his function and has a chance to exercise it in the most satisfying and productive way possible. Instead, some managers mystify what they do, inflate their budgets, and build protected bureaucratic baronies. As a result, their fear increases and the company loses.

The third type of fear is more pervasive, a constant gnawing anxiety not usually tied to any particular event or knowledge, but to loss of control. It is anxiety about losing one's cool, clutching at a crucial moment, looking bad, saying the wrong thing (and in some cases revealing repressed envious, cannibalistic, hostile impulses). If the corporate individual could penetrate to the causes of this paralyzing fear and anxiety, he would find *careerism*. He is afraid that external events beyond his control or his inability to control himself will damage or destroy his career.

From the moment a person starts treating his life as a career, worry is his constant companion. Careerism can begin at age five, fifteen, or later. Why do children become careerists? Parents start the ball rolling by evaluating all their children's actions in terms of usefulness to career. Is he smart enough? Is her personality right? Can he sell himself? The parents, themselves careerists, threaten the child not with punishment, but with failure in the career market of school and workplace. In cases of extremely anxious careerist parents, children become so frightened they cannot learn in school.

In the early 1960's, CBS and the University of Michigan's Institute of Social Research presented a TV report called *Sixteen in Webster Groves.* The film makers chose one of the richest middle-class communities in America and interviewed the high-school students. They found the students obsessed with fears about not making good enough grades or getting high enough test scores to go on to elite colleges and eventually find jobs or husbands with jobs that paid well enough to allow them to live in towns like Webster Groves, Lake Forest, or Scarsdale. Only a few of the students were concerned with social issues— such as racism and poverty—and these were the outcasts from high-school society.

For a brief time, in the late sixties, the attitudes of students seemed to change radically because of a new spirit against racism and war. But even among the more socially involved in the middle class, the dominant orientation was careerist. In 1971, I spent the day with high-school students in another affluent suburb. Although these young people were more conscious of the larger world outside of themselves than the Webster Groves students had been, they too were anxious about their careers, fearful of letting down their parents and being labeled losers. Unlike the traditional academic program of Webster Groves, this high school encouraged independent study and apprenticeships in community and welfare programs in order to develop social responsibility. Yet many students doubted whether they really cared about their individual projects or community well-being. They questioned their motives: perhaps they were socially "concerned" only because they thought colleges would favor the involved student.

These students had become careerists, their life

decisions were determined not out of a sense of vocation, but in terms of career. As they progress through
college and workplace, the demands of career will
continue to take precedence; career will be the dominant value.

On the basis of national surveys, Daniel Yankelovich
and Ruth Clark reported that student interests were
changing rapidly at the end of 1974. They concluded
that student interest had shifted away from social
reform to focus on the self and its private vicissi-
tudes, that today's college youth have little emotional commitment to changing society and are, instead, preoccupied with their own career planning
and personal fulfillment. They write, "We see a growing majority of college-trained youth readying themselves for careers in the upper reaches of the social
order. The professional managerial and technical
categories are the fastest growing occupational
groupings in the country . . . increasing numbers of
young people are heading straight for these upper-
level niches, their eyes fixed on the goal marked
'successful career.'"* Careerism has emerged as the
dominant national orientation.

While in the past, careerism was a characteristical-
ly middle-class preoccupation, increasingly working-
class youth are also becoming careerists. They too fear
becoming losers, left behind in the dead-end jobs
that satisfy neither their needs for craftsmanship nor
their desire for respect. Schooling feeds the belief
that the rewards of successful performance on tests
should be career advancement, in contrast to the
goals of traditional craftsmen and farmers to perfect
their skill and knowledge and to build something
useful.

Careerism results not only in constant anxiety,
but also in an underdeveloped heart. Overly con-

---

*Daniel Yankelovich, *The New Morality: A Profile of Ameri-
can Youth in the Seventies* (New York: McGraw-Hill, 1974),
p. 22.

cerned with adapting himself to others, to marketing himself, the careerist constantly betrays himself, since he must ignore idealistic, compassionate, and courageous impulses that might jeopardize his career. As a result, he never develops an inner center, a strong, independent sense of self, and eventually he loses touch with his deepest strivings. Thus, 59 percent of those we interviewed checked as a difficulty that they "give in too easily to others," and almost half checked "don't know what you want." To stand up to others requires courage and to know what you want implies the sense of volition of a strong heart.

Erich Fromm has analyzed careerism in terms of the "Marketing orientation,"* pointing out that the individual's sense of identity, integrity, and self-determination is lost when he treats himself as an object whose worth is determined by its fluctuating market value. The marketing individual experiences or more likely represses a deep sense of shame, self-contempt, and guilt (self-hatred). The reason why 50 percent checked as a difficulty that they "tend to blame yourself too much" may reflect the authoritarian consciences of some, but more likely, many feel guilty because they have sacrificed self-respect. Their self-blame is not an irrational feeling, but a nagging sense of self-betrayal that they have chosen career over the higher needs of self, family, and society.

Careerism demands detachment. To succeed in school, the child begins to detach himself from crippling fear of failure. To sell himself, he detaches himself from feelings of shame and humiliation. To compete and win, he detaches himself from feelings of empathy and compassion. To devote himself to success at work, he detaches himself from family feelings. Ultimately, to gain his goals, he is detached from social responsiveness.

*Erich Fromm, *Man for Himself* (New York: Rinehart, 1947), pp. 75–89.

The psychological meanings of detachment require explanation. Detachment is sometimes a self-protective necessity. As David Schecter has pointed out,* the capacity for detachment allows a child to free himself from overattachment. Detachment also allows us to stand back from pain and humiliation and take stock of ourselves objectively. In this sense, detachment implies a temporary expedient; the individual is still capable of full experience and is not alienated from himself.

In one form of spiritual development written about by mystics, detachment has a totally different meaning; it implies not being attached to things and images, including self-images. In contrast to the careerist goals of the detached corporate manager, the spiritual aim is to overcome greed and fear and thus strengthen the heart. Free from possessive attachments, the mystic experiences self and others even more deeply; he is able to enjoy life more because he is not fearful of losing what he has.

The corporate manager is detached in order to succeed and to protect himself from uncomfortable feelings. Competition generates fear that must be neutralized if the corporate individual is to function. Other unpleasant feelings provoked by corporate life—humiliation, envy, hostility—must be kept under wraps.

Besides detaching himself from his own feelings, detachment protects the manager from being too involved with others' emotions. One manager was flabbergasted by the very idea of experiencing the feelings of his subordinates, of developing a heart that listens. "If I let myself feel their problems," he said, "I'd never get anything done. It would be impossible to deal with people." Other managers have thoughtfully considered the issue and told me that

---

*David Schecter, paper presented at the Vth International Forum of Psychoanalysis, Zurich, Switzerland, August, 1974. Prepublication.

unless one is detached, it is impossible to make decisions having to do with building new factories or changing technology in ways that will put many people out of work. In the long run, they claim, these decisions will be socially beneficial, but to carry them out, they cannot dwell on the suffering caused. But what if they did? Perhaps the corporate manager would have to experience something of the pain he causes. A strong heart does not imply that one shrinks from difficult decisions.

The process of detachment as it occurs in the corporate career builds a shell around the heart. Like the mythical King Midas, who turned his daughter into gold, the corporate manager can no longer choose when to be intimately related and when to be detached. A corporate president told me that despite his attempt to be a good father, his children resented him bitterly. "I don't blame them," he said. "Even though I appear frank and open, they know there is a shell around my heart, that they can't really touch me."

A majority of all those interviewed recognized difficulties that seem related to detachment. Sixty-one percent (especially craftsmen and gamesmen) checked as a difficulty "keep your feelings to yourself"; 59 percent (especially craftsmen) checked "difficulty saying what you mean"; and 35 percent (craftsmen and gamesmen) "avoid people."

The gamesman's detachment is different from the craftsman's self-protectedness. The gamesman becomes one with his role. Energized by the excitement and challenge of the corporate world and cut off from other emotional reality, his form of game detachment allows him to express enthusiasm within the game, to make quick decisions and to take risks. Detached from his anxiety, he feels free, unaware that his freedom is strictly proscribed by his game role, his alternate reality, and that he must cut himself off from ideas and impulses that might upset his fine-tuned equilibrium. Although they appear at first so open, almost all the gamesmen admitted that they have difficulty experiencing and communicating any feelings at all, so well have they detached themselves.

In contrast, craftsmen are more like traditional village people—farmers, fishermen, potters—who develop a protective wall around their emotions as an adaptation to an uncertain, dangerous world. The difference from the gamesman is that the more active and life-loving craftsmen value intimate relationships with those they trust, those they let inside the wall. In our interviews, we found craftsmen cool and distant until they felt one's interest as stimulating and not hostile or moralistic. Then they opened up. (The gamesman lives in an impermeable, transparent dome; the craftsman, behind a wall with a door.)

One of the first craftsmen I interviewed was closed and suspicious until he suddenly began to open up. His tone of voice changed. He became animated. When I asked what had happened, he first said "Nothing." When I persisted, saying I experienced him as having become much more open, he said he had been observing me and that I seemed to him a basically happy person with no ax to grind, so he had decided to open up. In contrast, gamesmen like Wakefield appear spontaneous, friendly, even intimate from the start, particularly if you are playful with them. But you seldom go deeper. When emotions are called for that he cannot measure out, the gamesman becomes evasive.

Within the corporation, the craftsman's emotional wall protects him from the gamesman's seductions and from being made anxious by his bosses. But such protection is costly. Within his psychological enclave, he remains vulnerable, suspicious, and emotionally childish. A self-protective attitude makes a person fearful. It is hard to be generous or idealistic behind a wall.

In some ways, careerists also wall themselves in. We asked managers to check the most important goals for them. Although the answers differed according to character type, some goals are shared by all types and some by none. The craftsmen want to see the concrete results of their work. The gamesmen want to be winners, to earn more money than the average, and to have an impact on the corporation. The company men want to be effective managers who develop people and gain the esteem of coworkers. The jungle fighters want power over others. The main goals stated by all corporate types are a *comfortable and protected family life, interesting work,* and *respect from superiors, co-workers, and subordinates* (which is a way of saying that they want to enoy life and look good). Their goal is essentially to have a protected but intellectually stimulating life. They are not very concerned with helping society. Only 7 percent considered it important to have work that is vital to human welfare. We asked if there was any project that an individual would not work on for moral reasons. Most could not think of one, or if they did, it was a project outside of their realm; an electronics manager rejected poison gas, and the manager of a chemical company said he wouldn't build an electric chair.*

The majority of managers in these high-technology companies believed that the U.S. overinvests in the military and they didn't like to think that what they were working on was for the military. They would much rather believe that what they were doing was bettering industrial productivity or medicine or improving communications in the world.

Typically, the managers underestimated the percentage of their sales to the military. In one company, we figured out that total world-wide military sales

---

*Since this was written, three General Electric managers, Gregory C. Minor, Richard B. Hubbard, and Dale G. Bridenbaugh, quit G.E. rather than continue to develop nuclear power plants. In his letter of resignation, Mr. Minor wrote, "My reason for leaving is a deep conviction that nuclear reactors and nuclear weapons now present a serious danger to the future of all life on this planet." *The New York Times,* February 3, 1976, p. 12.

were three times what an executive had told us. He accepted the calculations with sincere surprise.

Most important, the managers made no effort to learn the social/human effects of their actions in the United States and the rest of the world. So long as they remain unaware and unrelated, they avoid having to accept responsibility.

Nor were the corporate managers interested in scientific understanding. Although 32 percent considered it extremely important to explore and develop new ideas related to business, only 11 percent wanted to contribute to the advance of science, and hardly anybody wanted to be part of a scientific community. Science as the search for truth leads to questions of social ethics and ultimate purpose, questions that corporate managers and many scientists avoid. Although they admired men like Einstein and Bohr for their contributions to knowledge, hardly any shared the devotion of these scientists to the search and to the community of seekers.

In a fundamental sense, the goals of the careerists reflect their tendency to construct a protective enclave for their emotions, themselves, and their families. The corporate career becomes the means to avoid anguish and uncertainty. But the goals of intellectual stimulation and material comfort do not lead to development of the heart. They tend to make the person intellectually active but spiritually passive, emotionally stingy, and, at the core, flabby.*

The concept of friendship stated by most managers expressed goals of comfort and being supported by others rather than spiritual development; they wanted a friend whom they could depend on, who would always support them no matter what they did. Their definitions of a good friend were as follows: "Someone I can depend on when the going

---

*Crabs and lobsters are commonly seen on the Rorschach, representing greedy and hard-shelled animals that are soft inside.

gets rough." "I can confide in him. He will help me no matter what." "I could count on him for support." "You can rely on him."

Fewer than 10 percent spoke of a person who shared spiritual goals or, as Wakefield put it, someone who is honest with you, with no falseness or flattery. Another exceptional manager said, "A friend is a person who would be open enough to tell me what I need to do for growing and progressing in life. Not the kind of guy who doesn't care, not a neurotic relationship, where both like to go sailing or build model airplanes—and that's all that keeps them together. It has to go deeper than that." If you are concerned with developing your character, purifying your heart, you need a friend who both shares these goals and will be critical of you when you stray from the path. You need a friend whom you can trust not to support you always no matter what you do, but to tell you the truth and to be concerned about your soul. Otherwise, you are likely to find a "friend" who is so terrified of your disapproval or of losing the relationship that he will do anything to flatter you and consequently undermine your clarity and your ability to see yourself as you are. Such "friendships" reinforce the tendency to isolate yourself from the rest of the world, and support the illusions about yourself that rationalize spiritual stagnation.

It is not so easy to develop friendship. To be critical while not negative or unfriendly requires both concern and thought. It may take courage to tell the truth, just as it often requires courage to accept it. To accept criticism given in a friendly spirit, we must be willing to struggle with egocentric illusions about ourselves. Often, however, friends are uncritical because there is an implicit contract for mutual admiration or support against others, and to break the contract would dissolve the relationship. A hostile, unhappy jungle fighter once told me, "I have no friends, only accomplices."

Friendship based on shared goals of personal integrity and realism strengthens both individuals, just as a family whose main goal is the character development of each member, the development of both mind and heart, strengthens its members. in contrast to a family that has as its main goal becoming a shelter from the world, a winning team, or an entertainment center.

Although they wanted help from their friends, few of the managers we interviewed mentioned helping other people as a goal in their lives. This is in contrast to a study we did of workers in a Tennessee factory. While fewer than 10 percent of the managers mentioned helping others as a goal, more than half of the workers in the factory did.

I visited the factory once with a brilliant, highly successful manager, a man with a strong jungle fighter's streak that warred with his idealism. He was convinced that only after succeeding at one's career can a person develop greater concern for his fellow man. I argued that while this sometimes happens, more commonly, those who strive for success lose their concern for others. Among the working class, at least in rural areas, the bonds of brotherhood are more likely to be reinforced through union activity, church membership, a tradition among farmers of helping one another at harvest, barn building, etc. In the factory's community, people are esteemed more because of their concern for others than because of their success. During the visit, we attended a meeting of workers and managers, and afterward, on the spur of the moment, I asked a young black woman if she would tell me her goal in life. She answered: "Sure, I want a house and financial security, but I can't walk down the street with money in my pocket and not heed the cries of those who are in need. If I did that, I'd be nothing."

Corporate managers do not hear the cries because they have created protected enclaves where they can separate themselves. These enclaves, these isolated villages, grow up wherever there are large corporations. Indeed, corporations move out to the suburbs in order to build enclaves. Many companies that set up shop in other countries house their employees in enclaves where they are either totally isolated from the locals or live with native managers who are also protecting themselves from their poor compatriots. These little villages express spatially the psychic attitudes of the corporate managers who detach themselves from what goes on in the rest of the world.

After I spoke on this theme at the National Bureau of Standards, an engineer, John L. Berg, was moved to write an article for a local paper, offering the following definition of communities as contrasted to enclaves:

> I see communities as families reaching outward to neighbors or to satisfy mutual needs, neighborhoods reaching out to other neighborhoods to find solutions for everyone's problems.
>
> Enclaves, on the other hand, are neighborhoods that turn in on themselves. They set themselves apart from the surrounding communities and defend themselves against threats from those outside the enclave. Their attractive entry walls become symbolic bulwarks—sometimes accompanied by explicit no trespassing signs. To enclavists, property values become more important than human values.*

The enclave is more than the protected village or house in the country. It is a state of mind, the psy-

---

*John L. Berg, "Enclaves?", *Montgomery County Sentinel*, June 13, 1974, p. A-4. In *Sex and the Significant Americans* (New York: Pelican-Penguin Books, 1966), John Cuber and Peggy Harroff interviewed more than four hundred business, government, and other national leaders on marriage and family life. They wrote that "when some of these men talk about home and family they suggest an image of a feudal manor house; it is a place of protection, a base from which the expedition moves out and to which it returns for replenishment. If this seems vague and sentimental, it is because many of these men themselves are so. The only uneasiness they have about this way of life relates to concerns about how to strengthen, stabilize, protect, or adorn the manor," p. 117.

chic shell that isolates and protects the heart. Managers may believe that "home" is the opposite of "work," a place to relax and replenish themselves, but in a spiritual sense, their corporate offices, homes, and hotel rooms are all protected enclaves.

What happens to a person who spends too much time living in enclaves, hotels, jet planes, and corporate offices? When I get into this kind of life, I also escape into myself, away from the machinelike rhythms, antiseptic smells, Muzak, and tasteless rooms; it takes days to feel alive again, and for many executives, this atmosphere of the mechanical womb reinforces the detachment of their everyday lives.

The enclave protects a person from himself and the world. Many an American manager has moved from city to suburbs to leave the violence and decay, taking no responsibility for improving the city. Because he lives in an enclave, he continues fearful of those outside the walls who may be envious of him. Isolated from the poor, he lacks understanding (not to speak of compassion) about why they are poor and how the corporate system isolates them and insures their continued poverty.

Many corporate managers feel that since they made it through hard work, others should be able to do the same. Forty percent of those we interviewed believe "the fittest should survive"; they consider those who lack the attitudes and talents fitting them for a useful role at work to be inferior beings. This attitude was stated by a successful gamesman.

"Early in life one develops a competitive drive usually through athletics. People with this competitive drive have energy. We have speculated on why some people don't succeed here. They are usually foreign-born and blacks. First, they have a difficulty communicating. This is symptomatic of their lack of aggression and lack of a wish to learn. The second reason is fear and an inferiority complex. This is true of blacks and also of black Africans."

Even managers less harsh in their judgments expressed little or no responsibility to the poor. Nor had they thought a great deal about how to improve society to overcome injustices. However, a sizable number did support liberal national policies as the most practical and human solutions to national problems. Thus, they favored welfare, but combined with measures to limit future population. Thirty-five percent approved some form of guaranteed income where each person would receive the minimal necessities of life whether or not he worked. They seemed to envisage some kind of dual society, the winners and near-winners in their more or less secure enclaves and the loser-outcasts on the dole, entertained by the mass media—a modern version of bread and circuses.

But many managers—probably the majority—would be just as happy if all the unneeded people disappeared. The bluntest sound like the middle manager in charge of computer development who said, "We take enough Negroes into the company to keep them from burning down the cities, but we won't change our standard operating practices any more than we have to. I don't care about those guys. It'll be better in the long run. They'll be out of the world economy. It'll be better for us and for them— India, Asia, they'll be better off."

In no discussion with corporate managers have I found any serious consideration that the same factors favoring their success may make it harder for others outside the corporate system to live their lives. The disappearing farmer and craftsman, the small businessman who can no longer make a living in competition with giant companies, do not figure in the thoughts of corporate managers. Few worry that the new technology they create does away with jobs, many low-level jobs. They may boast that they are creating new and better jobs in communications and data processing without considering that the dis-

placed operators and counter checkers may lack the
education or aptitude for the new jobs. Instead, they
think about the needy in terms of freeloaders trying
to get something for nothing.

"It is a mistake for the Government to give money
to people who don't work," a top executive told me.
"Most people who get welfare could work."

I asked him, "What about old people, the handi-
capped, and mothers with dependent children?"

"This must be a small minority," he said.

I said that his view seemed a kind of social Darwinism which stated that those who cannot adapt to
the system should fall by the wayside and be sacrificed to progress.

"Yes," he said, "the system works that way."

I asked whether he did not feel any responsibility
to people who have been displaced by changes—the
craftsman, the farmer, or the businessman whose attitudes of independence, obstinacy, and frugality no
longer fit the available work roles. For example, the
shopkeeper wouldn't have the traits that would make
him a successful manager of a chain store where he
needed to operate in a network of industrial and
corporate relations. The argument interested him,
since his grandfather had lost his grocery store in competition with A&P, but he shook it off. "Those people
will survive somehow. It's the others who are the
problem. We have put a lot of effort here into training blacks for jobs, including technical jobs. But this
has been a very dubious success. The people do not
take to the jobs."

What was his view of his social responsibility?
"The only real priority is growth. Without growth
we cannot provide jobs or feed the poor. The main
purpose of the corporation is to provide jobs to
people so they can live their lives. If the businesses
can't do this, then there will be a violent revolution."

Such a view provides an ideology to continue to
expand a system that works for those who un-

critically mold themselves to it. It is a system that is creating privileged enclaves for careerists throughout the world.

In Mexico, Ignacio Millán has found that Mexican managers are more aware than Americans that their careers protect them from the world of the poor (and the poor of the world), but they are not aware that within their enclaves they are becoming more alienated from themselves.* Around their houses they build walls topped with broken glass or spikes; within themselves, they feel rootless and alone. Consider "A," a young executive in an important Mexican industrial company associated with a powerful foreign corporation, interviewed by Dr. Millán.

"A" was brought up in an urban middle-class family. He studied business administration at the University and then took specialized courses at corporate headquarters in Europe, learning the commercial and administrative techniques of the company. His university career was a series of successes, and after a few years in the company, he has reached a high level of middle management.

He described himself as somebody who has obtained everything he wanted: a happy family, an excellent position, and a good chance for future promotion to the very top. He also thought his job was socially important and he was sure that his activities benefitted his country by contributing to progress.

When questioned about his dreams, he said he never remembered them, or only in bits and pieces, and he seemed surprised at Dr. Millán's interest in his dreams. During the fourth of five interviews (of approximately one hour each), he said, smiling, "I haven't dreamed." During this interview, the main topic was "personal values" and he talked, fundamentally, about his relationship with his relatives, his

---

*I. T. Millán, *Mr. Mexico, Caracter e Ideologia del Ejecutivo Mexicano,* in preparation.

personal beliefs, and the history of his family.

During the last interview, "A" said he had written down a dream that he considered "absurd." He joked about it, but finally he made up his mind to read it.

Here is the dream: "I am walking on a path with my wife and with 'X,' a friend of hers. The path goes around a lake of dark and dirty water. A big dry tree with roots in the water of the lake attracts my attention. It seems as if it were planted in the water. We keep on walking. There is a deep jungle and everything is rather dark. There is a group of very poor houses, a little town of huts. Naked children with big bellies are playing on the ground. I feel bad and I walk faster with my companions. I do not know what happens, but in the following scene I am in my car driving at high speed on a highway beside the sea. My wife and her friend are with me. There is plenty of light and everything is green; the sea is a deep shade of blue. I keep on going in my car, away from the sea, climbing a mountain. When we reach the top, I see a building beside the highway. It is a porno shop. Afterward, I am in the porno shop. There is nobody there. I call out asking for somebody, but there is no answer. The floor and the pornographic magazines I see on the tables are very dusty. There are pieces of glass on the floor and I know they belong to a test tube. I do not know what happens afterward, but I remember the dream very clearly. I think I did not forget it because you asked me to pay attention to my dreams."

"A" was restless when he read his dream, which seemed completely ridiculous to him. Dr. Millán divided the dream into parts and asked him to associate to them.

In associating to the dream, "A" saw his life as a process of escaping from the world of the poor and racing to the top of society.

"The lake can look like a place my father took us for vacations when I was a little boy, near a town where some of his relatives lived. I liked that place; I do not like the one in the dream, but there was a lake there too." Why did he not like the place in the dream? "Because it was dark, the water was dirty, and then the group of slum huts with the children naked and with big bellies." Why did he feel bad? He answered, "I think I am afraid of poverty and of poor people." Was he afraid of becoming poor? "No, I know I can lose almost everything in an accident that leaves me ill, and so forth, but I would never be very poor. I do not know why, but I feel bad when I see poor people."

He went on: "The highway beside the sea is a very good one. I like to race. I feel I can control the powerful machine of the car." Who were his companions? "My wife and her friend, an older woman who might be a substitute for my wife's mother, I think. Her mother died when she was very young."

In associating to the end of the dream, he laughed. "On my last trip abroad I went to a porno shop. I saw many magazines. It is unbelievable, the sexual degeneration of foreign countries! [Pornography is officially forbidden in Mexico.] There is something for everybody; for homosexuals, for lesbians, and for everybody. I bought several magazines, but I left them in the hotel because they were too 'strong.' In the dream there is nobody. I am alone." He paused. "I feel I am alone." He said that he was upset about the dust in the porno shop. He does not like to find dust either in his house or in his office. But he had no ideas about the broken test tube on the floor of the porno shop. "That's all," he said. Before ending the interview, Dr. Millán asked him if he thought that his dream had any meaning. He said he did not know, that maybe he was impressed by his trip abroad and by the porno shop.

Suddenly "A" said, "I know what the broken test tube means! Many years ago, we had laboratory work at school, during chemistry class. I liked that very much. I used test tubes there. I loved the search for chemical elements. I still remember it, although I haven't thought about it in a long time." Why didn't he continue to study chemistry if he liked it so much? "I thought about it; I would have liked it, but as a chemist I would not have made even the sixth part of what I make now. Those careers do not produce money."

The use of the symbol of the porno shop implies a real social criticism of absolute commercialization that "A" dared to make only unconsciously. Awake, he associated the symbol with the sexual degeneration abroad. He discarded the magazines he bought in Europe because he thought they were too "strong" for his home environment. Consciously, the meaning of pornography to him seems clear, and he considered it too strong for the culture of Mexico today. Nevertheless, it is the symbol he unconsciously chose to express the experience of the social atmosphere at the top; perhaps it should be considered a new symbol of "development." The porno shop symbolizes the imported patterns of conduct, conditioned, to a certain extent, by relationships at work. Just as machines and technological assistance are imported, so are the social attitudes at this level; they are rooted neither in one's personal history nor cultural traditions.

The fragments of the test tube used in the chemistry class are the symbol that confirmed the existence of a different vital alternative. As the dream expressed quite clearly, only the broken pieces of this possibility have remained.

Suppose the careerist were to experience his full reality, undetached. How would he feel? Some of the dreams told us by careerist managers give some idea.

A repetitive dream was told by a woman who has risen near the top of a large multinational company.

In her interview with Cynthia Elliott, she continually emphasized that her job was an interesting challenge for her, one that gave her the opportunity for a great deal of independence and self-development. She said, "I really enjoy my work. I moan and groan but I've had some fantastic opportunities and challenges."

But what were the challenges she enjoyed so much? The major challenge she mentioned was the competition with other executives for top positions in the corporation. What she claimed to value—challenge and independence—appeared to be anxious struggle and lonely careerism. As she said, "The main thing is the ability to survive in this environment." Although she talked about being open and trusting and emphasized the importance of cooperation to get the work done, what she described was a suspicious and unfriendly environment. Despite her conscious enthusiasm and satisfaction with her work, on the symptom list given her to check she reported troublesome anxiety and severe headaches. She also stated that she lacks hope, feels she does not know what she wants, and that it is too often necessary for her to give in to circumstances. Her recurring dream seems to express her unconscious experience of work. She dreams that she is buried alive and all she wants is a telephone in her casket. It sounds like a joke, but such a dream is all too serious: it symbolizes the experience of emotional deadness in her work and her acceptance of her fate (as long as she can continue to stay in the executive competition). Rather than rebelling at being buried alive and fighting to become free, she asks only for a telephone so she can communicate with others, presumably in their own casket-offices. Another not inconsistent interpretation of the dream would be that it symbolizes a mechanical regression to the coffin-womb where the telephone line is an electronic umbilical cord. That interpretation implies a deeply dependent and extremely alienated individual who has transferred her mother fixation to the corporation

A disillusioned scientist-executive of great gifts dreamt he entered a large hotel on a beach (perhaps looking for an easy, protected life). The lower story is missing (everything is up in the head). There was a ladder inside and he climbed up (successful career). It was mushy with bat droppings and spiders (crazy, intrigues at the top). He finished the dream with a vision of horror: "I look out the window but the beach is no longer there. There is a stockyard. I feel death around me. I fly out of the building through the air. It is a great feeling to get out." (But this escape was only a wish; he remained in the corporation.)

Perhaps only the more conflicted managers, the ones whose hearts protest against dehumanization, have such dreams or remember them. One of the most compassionate and idealistic managers we interviewed, who experienced conflict between a gamesmanlike wish to win and a radical humanistic spirit, said, "I need love and need to give it, but I tend to cover it up in my work." This man worked in a company where paternalistic principles support a spirit that is friendlier than most companies. After visiting another corporation, where the spirit was one of cutthroat competition, he dreamt: "I went into a city of buildings. They were gleaming and slimy, all hotels. It was really a cemetery. Everybody in the rooms in the hotels was dead and embalmed. Yet they were sitting, posed as if alive. It was in Texas, where I had gone on business. A brilliant blue day and sunshine outside. The corpses were looking out of the windows."

Like the woman executive, the unconscious symbol he chose for corporate life was death, meaning killing one's feelings, molding the self into a waxen pose within ultramodern glass coffins.

When our research group discussed this man's

dream and interview, the conflict seemed so great that I felt he was headed for illness. In fact, he developed an ulcer soon after and took a leave of absence from work.

Most of the managers we interviewed did not remember their dreams. For some, remembering might be a step toward the wide-awake experience of being buried alive, and that would mean they could no longer remain in place. Of course, there are top executives who are secretly proud of their ability to adapt and survive with dignity in the dehumanized corporate world. Their Rorschach images included a polar bear moving through its habitat; a wolverine standing before an icy lake under a snow drift overhang. Yet some of the most creative top executives express self-contempt in Rorschach images of bugs, worms, rats. When I have asked them directly, they say it is because they have failed to develop their hearts and to respond to the needs of others.

Is this picture different from that of other careerist workers in the United States? Lacking comparable data, I can only speculate, although in discussions with top government bureaucrats, they quickly recognize themselves in the four types and respond to the issue of head and heart. Comparing my own experience in universities, I would say that although academics consider themselves more "humane" than businessmen, the engineers and managers we interviewed are no more competitive and a lot more cooperative with one another than most professors. If corporate managers engaged in the nitpicking and down-putting common in universities, little would be created and produced. If managers treated their subordinates with the neglect and contempt common in the attitude of professors to graduate students, no one would work for them. These days, the talented jungle fighter probably has a much better chance for advancement in the university than in the corporate psychostructure.

Many of the managers and engineers, especially those with religious concerns, were more open to issues of the heart than we had expected. They reacted as though waking up, at least for a while, to truths already half-known, and many of them asked, "What can we do about it?"

CHAPTER 8

The Psychology of "Development"

IN THE SIXTIES, certain well-known psychologists became excited about the new-technology corporations and proposed theories that managers could both succeed at work and develop themselves humanly. But these psychologists of management did not study different types of managers and workers, nor did they examine the social consequences of technology and decision-making processes. Rather than developing a critical social psychology as a tool for transforming organizations so they better fit the needs of different people, they provided an ideology to rationalize the game. In contrasting "underdeveloped" versus "developed" managers and workers, they were not referring to development of the heart. Underdevelopment meant a fearful, submissive, or "authoritarian" loser, while development signified the winning attitude of an ambitious and flexible team player, and these theorists have left an impression that careerism can be the road to development.

Douglas McGregor's book *The Human Side of Enterprise* is still one of the works most quoted by managers.* Writing at the start of the sixties, McGregor stated that by changing over from an authoritarian industrial structure to a more participative team structure, companies would become more efficient and profitable and the managers would have a better chance to become more humanly developed.

---

*Douglas McGregor, *The Human Side of Enterprise* (New York: McGraw-Hill, 1960).

This idea was supported by Abraham Maslow's new "humanistic" psychology. McGregor and Maslow became leading proponents of the idea that business could be profitable and also stimulate human development, thus appealing to a deep wish in the American psyche that it is possible to do well and do good at the same time.

As we have seen in the case of Wakefield and others, young managers and executives would like to believe this, and they often quote McGregor and Maslow to support them. They tell us that one of the main parts of their work is the "development" of those they manage. But this development is one-sided. Mainly, it means development of qualities most useful to the company, and to getting ahead in it, including ambition, self-confidence, intellectual abilities, and a cooperative but not fraternal attitude. Corporate work does not develop qualities of the heart, such as compassion, generosity, and idealism; to the contrary, it has a negative effect on this development.

In the following pages, we will explore the theories of McGregor and Maslow more closely to see in what way they considered that business organizations can further human development and to compare their theories with our own findings about what is developed and what is not developed in managers by their work.

McGregor contrasts old-style authoritarian management, which he calls Theory X, with a new style, Theory Y, based on a different view of people, which he argues fits the modern dynamic and innovative corporation and the new emerging work force. Although he does not explicitly mention either social character or social structure, McGregor's theory seems a response to changes in both. New technology had changed corporations and a new kind of manager was needed. Innovation and the integration of many management functions required highly interdependent teams that had to be flexible and responsive to new demands, and these teams had to be manned by individuals who could work cooperatively with one another.

McGregor observes that the old-style business, based on strict authority, worked well only so long as the structure of the company was relatively simple and there was not much change in the product and the marketing. The hierarchical organization manned by employees willing to take orders could produce and sell a Model-T Ford. The average manager (much less worker) could not be very innovative or independent since he had to wait for orders before he did anything. He was not likely to be a person who took risks. (The gambles were all taken by the entrepreneur-boss.) Given the modern need for managers who are controlled risk-takers, for the gamesman, the old-style authoritarian character type was fast becoming a liability to business.*

In this context, Theory Y conceptualizes the new industrial psychostructure and provides it with an ideology. Maintaining that workers were becoming less submissive to authority, McGregor claimed that Theory Y would eventually fit the needs of management and a changing national character.

According to McGregor, the old view, Theory X, was based on three assumptions, starting with the idea that the average human being has an inherent dislike of work and will avoid it if he can. This justifies trying to force people to work, and so assumption two says that most people must be coerced,

---

*A number of studies have shown that the management of technological innovation requires more teamwork and sharing of authority than old-style industry did. See, for example, T. Burns and G. M. Stalker, *The Management of Innovation* (London: Tavistock Publications, 1961), and Paul Lawrence and Jay W. Lorsch, *Organization and Environment: Managing Differentiation and Integration* (Boston: Division of Research, Harvard Business School, 1967).

controlled, directed, and threatened with punishment in order to get them to put forth adequate effort toward the achievement of organizational objectives. The third assumption says that the average human being prefers to be directed and wishes to avoid responsibility, has relatively little ambition, and wants security above all. The Theory X manager believes that the masses are mediocre and lazy and will not work unless they are forced to. McGregor maintains that many modern managers have stuck to Theory X even when it doesn't work, and some try to soften it with the "human relations approach," being nice to the worker without changing either basic attitudes or work practices. He argues that it would be better to give both managers and workers more responsibility and reward them for exercising it, but he cautions against an "industrial democracy" in which workers would be permitted to decide everything themselves, thus making it clear that the extra responsibility would be strictly limited.

The main assumptions of Theory Y are: First, the expenditure of physical and mental effort in work is as natural as play or rest; the average human being does not inherently dislike work. Rather, work can be a source of either satisfaction or punishment, depending upon the conditions. The second assumption is that external control and the threat of punishment are not the only means for bringing about effort toward organizational objectives. People will exercise self-control and self-direction in the service of objectives to which they are committed.

The third point is that commitment to objectives is a function of the rewards associated with their achievement. For McGregor, the most significant of these rewards are "ego-satisfaction" and the satisfaction of "self-actualizing needs," which can be direct products of efforts directed toward organizational objectives. (McGregor does not consider that commitment to objectives might be a function of how the objectives benefit others, including the society as a whole, and not merely whether they are personally beneficial.) The fourth assumption is that the average human being learns, under proper conditions, not only to accept but to seek responsibility. McGregor writes that "avoidance of responsibility, lack of ambition, and emphasis on security are generally consequences of experience, not inherent human characteristics."[*] Here McGregor makes a positive point that implies people can change with new experiences, that by having responsibility (authority) one becomes better able to exercise it.

The fifth principle is that the capacity to exercise a great deal of imagination, ingenuity, and creativity in the solution of organizational problems is widely, not narrowly, distributed in the population. But it is characteristic that McGregor assumes that the responsible person is invariably going to be ambitious. A constant assumption in managerial theory is that only the ambitious are responsible, hardworking, creative, an assumption contradicted by our studies of craftsmen and farmer-workers. And the sixth and final assumption is that under the conditions of modern industrial life, the intellectual potentialities of the average human being are only partially "utilized"; the implication of Theory Y is that companies could put a great deal more talent to work.

McGregor offers Theory Y as the basis from which to develop a new "realistic" approach to management, which would also be productive and profitable. It is noteworthy that McGregor does two things typical of both managerial and political polemicists. The first is to draw the extremes of a hard line (Theory X) and a soft line (compensatory human relations, or industrial democracy) so that he can put forth his own view (Theory Y) as a more reasonable middle way. The second is to claim that he could design a

---

[*]McGregor, *op. cit.*, p. 48.

system that would be both profitable and humanly developing. Such a claim is compelling, although hard to believe. One would think that he would be content to say that the new approach would be less destructive, or that at least it would stimulate the development of some positive aspects in the worker, without extravagant claims that it was the best possible road to business success and to human growth and development. But few theorists are modest. McGregor begins his book by stating that his Theory Y is built on a new view of human nature.

It is not quite clear whether McGregor is arguing that Theory Y is *necessary* for efficient management when workers are especially self-affirmative or whether in fact he goes so far as to maintain that it would *stimulate* such self-affirmation and increase productivity. The ambiguity that runs through the book is the question of whether the manager should act out of his wish to maximize profit or out of new and deeper understanding of what would be good for people. McGregor does not suggest that these two principles might conflict.

Rather, he implies that some people lack Theory Y attitudes. If it is not possible to get them motivated to be responsible for their own benefit and for the good of the organization, to fulfill the objectives of the company, then authority will have to be "the appropriate means of control." Does this imply that McGregor feels that those who are creative and intelligent but don't accept the goals of the company should be controlled by threat? The question is not raised. McGregor, together with other management theorists, seems to believe that those who reject the chance for greater responsibility must be sick Theory X people—weak, obstinate, or so damaged by their socialization that they are unable to respond to Theory Y.

McGregor believes there are effective methods of teaching willing employees to develop their Theory Y attitudes. One means for training Theory Y managers is the T-group, as developed by the National Training Laboratories. In describing how these T-groups work, McGregor admits that a skeptical reader might think that such groups are a way to control members and make them conform, but he maintains that so long as the managers share the same objectives, the groups will help them to become more creative. The argument begs the question. What if everyone does not share the same objectives? Once one signs on with the company, must one accept the objectives of continual corporate growth and profit? Yes, if one wants to be a success. In McGregor's system, there is no chance for even a top manager to change the corporate objectives, only to have some influence on how they are reached.

In the T-groups, the same principle seems to prevail. According to McGregor, the participants are not allowed to analyze one another or to talk about their personal goals or attitudes, to question the rationality of their lives. Nor do they analyze company policy and structure in terms of their human effects. Rather they are only supposed to tell one another about the subjective impact that the others' behavior has on them, without any attempt to understand objectively the reasons for this behavior. The official goal is to help people develop "skills in social interaction," not to become sensitive either to external or internal reality, including major decisions they have made in their life and work and how these decisions have affected their character and integrity, health and happiness, capacity for joy and love, compassion and concern. The participants will at best help one another become more effective and less abrasive. There is little chance to help one another to develop more rational personal goals or to improve the organization.

Implicit in McGregor's outlook is that a new kind of individual is needed to manage the exciting new businesses he has studied. The example he mentions of an advanced technological and growing segment

more likely to employ Theory Y is military industry.
McGregor writes that:

> The difference was brought home sharply to me
> recently when I spent a couple of days in each of
> two companies. The first was the division of a large
> company which is developing one of the new inter-
> continental ballistic missiles. The people who make up
> this organization are young; they are tremendously
> excited over the challenge represented by their task
> . . . I went directly from this company to the head-
> quarters of a major railroad . . . The managers with
> whom I talked there showed almost none of the ex-
> citement and challenge which had been so vividly
> demonstrated in the other organization.*

But why is it that the excitement doesn't exist in
railroading? This is the kind of question that doesn't
interest McGregor. Is it that building intercontinental
ballistic missiles more than building railroads naturally stimulates a feeling of pride and social contribution in the managers? Are there no technological
challenges in railroading? Or is it that through government funding and the lobbying power of both
the military and the trucking industry we invest
more in military R & D than in R & D for the railroads?

McGregor observed, as we have, that the new manager of a company developing new technology must
be less autocratic than the old-style entrepreneurial
jungle fighter who wanted to be the only one to command, to be alone at the top. He writes:

> The principle of divide and rule is eminently sound
> if one wants to exercise personal power over sub-
> ordinates. It is the best way to control them. But if
> the superior recognizes the existence of the intricate
> interdependent characteristic of modern industry, and
> if he is less interested in personal power than in creat-
> ing conditions such that the human resources available

*Ibid., p. 193.

to him will be utilized to achieve organizational purposes, he will seek to build a strong group. He will recognize that the highest commitment to organizational objectives, and the most successful collaboration in achieving them, require unique kinds of interactions which can only occur in a highly effective group setting. He will in fact discourage discussion or decision-making on many matters which affect his organization except in a group-setting. He will give the idea of "the team" full expression, with all the connotations it carries on the football field.*

In fact, what type of person is this new kind of manager going to be? Who will commit himself fully to the organizational objectives and put all of his energy into motivating others to work together with him? Who is it who will talk so nobly about developing people and act in terms of bringing along their skills so as to help the team? Who will enjoy the games that McGregor considers helpful to learning about new situations? We now know the answer: it is the gamesman. McGregor's book is in effect calling for the gamesman to man the psychostructure of the modern innovative company and to replace the old-style jungle-fighter boss. It is something like the plot of *The Sting*.

He makes another assumption common to many theorists who present "humanistic" alternatives to authoritarian systems. He proposes only two alternative ways of seeing human motivation, in terms of authoritarianism and in terms of his "healthier" view of man. But if we analyze his assumptions, we find that he is not describing a healthier human being, but contrasting different character types. His Theory Y assumptions describe the motivation of the ambitious gamesman, and to some extent the company man, but not that of the craftsman. His "scientific" theory can be considered an ideology to support the emergence of the gamesman into positions of leader-

*Ibid., p. 240.

ship. In my own experience, gamesmen are attracted to McGregor's theory more than other types.

Neither McGregor nor any other management theorist has suggested that we study the real character of managers and workers, what their goals are, what their psychology is. Rather they assume that they understand what motivates different types of people.

Without such study, a system that claims to be concerned with human development may in fact be designed to benefit a particular character type at the expense of others. Those who do not fit the new system are in danger of being labeled as "sick." This danger becomes clearer when we examine the motivational theory of Abraham Maslow, who constructs a "hierarchy of needs" that fits very well with the idea that those who succeed in the corporation are rewarded by richness of character as well as worldly goods.

The more liberal industrial managers, including some who are most critical of mechanization and bureaucracy, almost invariably quote Maslow, who, they say, gives them hope that once a certain level of material success is reached, corporate individuals will be more concerned with higher values of love and creativity. Maslow's psychology also supports the Theory Y viewpoint that a more human managerial system will stimulate more productive human development, or in Maslow's sense, "self-actualization."

I intend to argue that although Maslow's theory stresses humane needs and values, it is ambiguous, contradictory, and, in critical aspects, misleading about motivation and its relation to social arrangements, particularly work. The hope it offers is not rooted in the ground of understanding real needs of different kinds of people. It tends to support false optimism that will likely fade in the light of real attempts at change. At its worst, Maslow's theory can be interpreted as a rationalization of materialistic motives, presumably in the service of the future flowering of higher values, but in fact idealizing the powerful who are contemptuous of the powerless.

At his best, Maslow is an unconventional observer who describes the strengths of healthy mature people in terms of their greater attraction to "the good, the true and the beautiful."*

Unlike more mechanistic psychologists, he believes that there is a human nature, and he goes further than McGregor to maintain that if needs for love and creativity are not fulfilled, the result is "psychopathology." He writes:

> Now let me try to present briefly and at first dogmatically the essence of this newly developing conception of the psychologically healthy man. First of all and most important of all is the strong belief that man has an essential nature of his own, some skeleton of psychological structure that may be treated and discussed analogously with his physical structure, that he has some needs, capacities, and tendencies that are in part genetically based, some of which are characteristic of the whole human species, cutting across all cultural lines, and some of which are unique to the individual. These basic needs are on their face good or neutral rather than evil. Second, there is involved the conception that full health and normal and desirable development consist in actualizing this nature, in fulfilling these potentialities, and in developing into maturity along the lines that this hidden, covert, dimly seen essential nature dictates, growing from within rather than being shaped from without. Third, it is now seen clearly that most psychopathology results from the denial or the frustration or the twisting of man's essential nature. By this concept what is good? Anything that conduces to this desirable development in the direction of actualization of the inner nature of man. What is bad or abnormal? Anything that frustrates or blocks or denies the essential nature of man. What is psychopathological? Anything that disturbs or frustrates or twists the course of

---

*Abraham Maslow, *Motivation and Personality* (New York: Harper & Row, 1954), p. 201.

self-actualization. What is psychotherapy, or for
that matter any therapy or growth of any kind? Any
means of any kind that helps to restore the person to
the path of self-actualization and of development
along the lines that his inner nature dictates.*

One of Maslow's most remarkable statements is that
this is a "newly developing conception of the psychologically healthy man" when in fact it is a traditional humanistic concept shared by the early Chris-
tians, Buddhists, Aristotle, Spinoza, Marx, and many
others, including among psychologists, William James
and Erich Fromm. Maslow allows that this "new concept" has elements in common to those of the past,
but argues that "we now know a great deal more than
Aristotle and Spinoza about the true nature of the
human being."†

Maslow's theory starts to become problematic
when he constructs his well-known hierarchy of
needs. According to this theory one moves from lower-level "physiological needs" to "safety needs" to "belongingness and love needs" to "esteem needs" to the
highest-level "need for self-actualization." Brief descriptions of these levels in Maslow's words follow,
with some comments added.

The Physiological Needs

These include feeding, drinking, sexual behavior,
"with the one unqualified aim relief." Although these
are needs that everyone shares, it is worth pointing
out that Maslow did not recognize that no human
need is purely physiological. For example, the quality
of one's feeding, drinking, or sexual needs obviously differs according to one's character attitudes. If this
is understood, one realizes that to satisfy a greedy
person's appetite does not make him less greedy.

---

*Ibid., pp. 269–270.
†Ibid., p. 270.

THE SAFETY NEEDS

"If the physiological needs are relatively well-gratified, there emerges a new set of needs (security; stability; dependency; protection, freedom from fear, from anxiety and chaos; need for structure, order, law, limits; strength in the protector; and so on)."*

In lumping together freedom from fear with a need for a protector, Maslow does not distinguish the quality of different safety needs in terms of whether they lead to sacrificing one's freedom (for protection by a strong figure) or to developing a community of equals who share in protecting one another. To maintain that safety needs can in fact be satisfied is a questionable assumption. No one is fully safe. Are we not all vulnerable and mortal? The illusion that complete safety is possible can be used to justify extreme policing. Although overly fearful people (particularly the hoarding types who fear losing their property) are willing to pay any price for security, courageous and independent people prefer to live with some insecurity rather than trade it for an illusion that costs them their freedom.

THE BELONGINGNESS AND LOVE NEEDS

"If both the physiological and the safety needs are fairly well gratified, there will emerge the love and affection and belongingness needs ... Now the person will feel keenly, as never before, the absence of friends, or a sweetheart, or a wife, or children. He will hunger for affectionate relations with people in general, namely, for a place in his group or family and he will strive with great intensity to achieve this goal. He will want to forget that once, when he was hungry, he sneered at love as unreal or unneces-

Ibid., p. 39.

sary or unimportant. Now he will feel sharply the pangs of loneliness, of ostracism, of rejection, of friendlessness, of rootlessness."*

In contrast to Maslow's view, psychoanalytic study shows that the need for others may be fully as strong as the need for safety; sometimes it is even stronger. When frightened or hungry, people miss those they love at least as much as when secure and well fed. Who can stand ostracism and aloneness—unless chosen as a form of spiritual discipline—whether or not any other needs are satisfied? The totally alone person may be either a regressive psychotic (with the illusion of being in the mother's womb) or a highly disciplined mystic (feeling himself related to all of humanity). Most of us face the fact that we cannot live without others. Fromm has pointed out in *Escape from Freedom* and other works that the need for relatedness is a need for psychic survival. What Fromm goes on to explore are the different possible modes of relatedness.

THE ESTEEM NEEDS

"All people in our society (with a few pathological exceptions) have a need or desire for a stable, firmly based, usually high evaluation of themselves for self-respect, or self-esteem, and for the esteem of others. These needs may therefore be classified into two subsidiary sets. These are, first, the desire for strength, for achievement, for adequacy, for mastery and competence, for confidence in the face of the world, and for independence and freedom. Second, we have what we may call the desire for reputation or prestige (defining it as respect or esteem from other people), status, fame and glory, dominance, recognition, attention, importance, dignity, or appreciation."†

Ibid., p. 43.
†*Ibid.*, p. 45.

Although achievement, mastery, and independence can be grouped together, needs for fame and glory do not belong with needs for dignity and appreciation. The former are rooted in irrational, often unconscious strivings to transcend mortality, to gain love and adulation through power or prestige; they are much more characteristic of jungle fighters, gamesmen, and company men than craftsmen. The latter do not imply superiority over anyone else, but rather respect and recognition for one's accomplishments that have helped others or given them pleasure or enlightenment. Most people probably wouldn't want to be famous if they realized what it entailed. Even though someone may become a "household word," fame tends to isolate him from the community and subject him to envy or exploitation; he has been separated. In contrast, appreciation and dignity based on mutual respect bring one closer to the community. Maslow later states that "deserved respect" is healthier than "unwarranted adulation" (is any adulation warranted?), but he doesn't make the point strongly enough. Ambition for fame always has a driven quality, and clinical experience suggests it is rooted in the compulsive strivings of someone who doubts or has lost touch with his ability to love.

The Need for Self-actualization

"Even if all these needs are satisfied, we may still often (if not always) expect that a new discontent and restlessness will soon develop, unless the individual is doing what *he*, individually, is fitted for. A musician must make music, an artist must paint, a poet must write, if he is to be ultimately at peace with himself. What a man *can* be, he *must* be. He must be true to his own nature. This need we may call self-actualization . . .

"This term, first coined by Kurt Goldstein, is being used in this book in a much more specific and limited fashion. It refers to man's desire for self-fulfillment, namely, to the tendency for him to become actualized in what he is potentially. This tendency might be phrased as the desire to become more and more what one idiosyncratically is, to become everything that one is capable of becoming."*

Is Maslow telling us there is a mechanical progression to transcendence? It seems that way when he writes:

> It is quite true that man lives by bread alone—where there is no bread. But what happens to man's desires when there *is* plenty of bread and when his belly is chronically filled?
>
> At once other (and higher) needs emerge and these, rather than physiological hungers, dominate the organism. And when these in turn are satisfied, again new (and still higher) needs emerge, and so on. This is what we mean by saying that the basic human needs are organized into a heirarchy of relative prepotency.†

Maslow's conclusion suggests that needs for self-actualization flower in those who have "made it," and at first glance, this seems plausible. There are dramatic examples of individuals who have become rich and then sought new ways to express themselves (often to justify their wealth or, like Andrew Carnegie, to further their ideology through philanthropy and politics). Maslow's theory also seems plausible because experience tells us that most people struggling to overcome hunger and fear are not concerned with being professional poets, although we should not forget that many artists have been poor and that many struggling people express great love and courage and creativity when faced with extreme adversity.

However, while the satisfaction of basic needs may

___

*Ibid., p. 46.
†Ibid., p. 38.

improve the chances for development in those who strive toward higher goals, it obviously does not guarantee progress. Greedy people who fill their bellies regularly and well are driven to accumulate more, and they try to dominate and use others. Furthermore, the concept of "self actualization" ignores the issue of self-centeredness, egocentrism. To develop the heart, one must open it to others. Maslow considers the highest need "to become everything that one is capable of becoming," but this is naïve if it assumes that all possibilities are moral and can coexist. We are all capable of good and evil, of being lovers and murderers, wise men and women or madmen. We also may be capable of developing many talents and roles, from artist to athlete, beachcomber to manager. The point should not be that by satisfying lower needs, we automatically develop higher needs, but rather that we must choose who and what we will be and strive toward actualizing innate capacities for reason and love by overcoming greed and egocentrism, at the same time developing competencies that are socially productive and talents that are life enhancing.

What we choose depends both on the social alternatives (or class and culture), our values, and our capacity to know ourselves, to experience our strivings and emotions. For many people in modern society (especially careerists), any meaningful self-actualization requires first of all overcoming detachment and intellectualization, or in other words, opening their hearts, an experience that may be painful and humiliating as well as joyous and self-affirming. Then it is necessary to develop one's principles or guiding philosophy. But here we are talking as though individuals will find social support (or even the support of one other person) for such development, and we have seen that this is not the case in the corporation, despite satisfaction of the lower needs. If social arrangements do not support or favor either creative self-realization or concern for others, then in that social context their development becomes a task for an exceptional mystic. Few who read Maslow in the corporation are encouraged to be socially responsible, not to speak of compassionate.

Maslow's theory is misleading and inadequate as a basis for understanding the relationship between social factors and individual development for the following reasons:

By describing individuals in terms of a need hierarchy, he diverts attention from understanding real social characters with their particular needs. Instead of sensitizing people to respect different types of creative need, his theory tends to rate everyone according to a scale of development.

By this I do not mean to reject the idea of evaluating character in terms of lower or higher development. But Maslow's "new" humanistic psychology is no improvement over traditional humanism (either religious or rationalistic), with its concern for overcoming greed and egocentrism, to love one's neighbor as oneself, to practice justice rather than exploitation. Compared to traditional humanism, Maslow's highest ideal of self-actualization is curiously asocial and exclusively concerned with limitless individual expressiveness. In fact, the best of modern developmental psychology—particularly the work of Jean Piaget—demonstrates that moral development, overcoming egocentrism and gaining a sense of reciprocity with others is essential to intellectual development.*

The need hierarchy ignores internal conflict and fails to distinguish between rational and irrational, progressive and regressive needs. Maslow does not point out that love is antithetical to greed and power; real independence means that one does not desire to dominate others, etc. To understand a particular

---

*Jean Piaget, *The Moral Judgment of the Child* (London: Kegan Paul, Trench, Trubner & Co., 1965). Also see *To Understand Is to Invent: The Future of Education* (New York: Grossman Publishers, 1973).

character, we should know the creative or progressive strivings versus the regressive or irrational tendencies and how they relate to each other. Only then is it possible to trace how social factors reinforce or block creative strivings.

Maslow does not recognize the necessity of choice. He observes that psychopathology results when creative needs are blocked, but he did not ask *why* the result is psychopathological. The impression is left of mechanical cause-effect, rather than complex struggle. Thwarted in one's needs for love and creative expression, a person may become angry, despairing, vengeful, or continue to strive for such expression. Which alternative is chosen depends on many factors, for example, the individual's age, strength, and, above all, the hopeful possibilities in the environment and the support given to one's creative side. Because of deep hurts and disappointments, some may choose a destructive, cynical, or vengeful course, especially when they find no help. More likely, such people become conflicted, reason suggesting a healthy course, but irrational feelings and social forces sometimes driving the individual in another direction.

Maslow pays little attention to the conflict between rational and irrational emotional attitudes, arguing that "from our empirical studies of the healthy man we have learned that these are definitely not at odds with each other, that these sides of human nature are not necessarily antagonistic but can be cooperative and synergistic."* Although reason and passion can cooperate, such integration requires consciousness, discipline, and decision, not automatic self-actualization. "The key concepts in the newer dynamic psychology," Maslow writes, "are spontaneity, release, naturalness, self-choice, self-acceptance, impulse-awareness, gratification of basic needs."† Discipline is out, discarded with all the old, uptight

---

*Maslow, *op. cit.*, p. 271.
†*Ibid.*, p. 279.

moralism. But what use is spontaneity without technique? Through discipline, for example, a pianist or a Zen painter can express himself simply and spontaneously only after mastering technique so well that he can directly translate feeling and idea. Maslow supports the misleading impression that discipline and spontaneity are opposite when, in fact, mature spontaneity is a form of disciplined play.

From the above, it follows that Maslow will fail to analyze critically the relation between work and character. The need hierarchy sounds suspiciously like the corporate hierarchy, and the step-by-step progress to self-actualization lends itself to the impression that careerism brings happiness.

Maslow does recognize that "stupid jobs" cause pathology, but he fails to draw the inference that patterns of work need to be changed in order to satisfy the needs of different types of people. He writes:

> I have seen a few cases in which it seemed clear to me that the pathology (boredom, loss of zest in life, self-dislike, general depression of the bodily functions, steady deterioration of the intellectual life, of tastes, etc.) were produced in intelligent people leading stupid lives in stupid jobs. I have at least one case in which the appropriate cognitive therapy (resuming part-time studies, getting a position that was more intellectually demanding, insight) removed the symptoms.
>
> I have seen *many* women, intelligent, prosperous, and unoccupied, slowly develop these same symptoms of intellectual inanition. Those who followed my recommendation to immerse themselves in something worthy of them showed improvement or cure often enough to impress me with the reality of the cognitive needs.*

Here Maslow treats the problem of work in terms of cognitive enrichment without considering that in-

Ibid., p. 49.

creasingly people have to work in bureaucracies at stupid jobs and that they cannot necessarily get "more intellectually demanding" jobs because such jobs are rare. Furthermore, he sees the problem only in terms of "intelligent people," presumably those who have already had the privilege of schooling, and he pays no attention to those who are unable to develop their intelligence in part because of the type of schooling and work they had to settle for.

Nor does Maslow even consider that some intelligent people suffer exactly because they have been over-schooled and have lost their capacity for self-generated intellectual activity. These people are bored not because they lack stimuli, but because they are alienated from themselves and have become compulsive consumers who need to be "turned on" by entertainment or, as in the case of the gamesman, competition.

When Maslow's work is examined closely, one is forced to the unpleasant conclusion that he over-values the successful, educated, and ambitious and is careless of the weak losers. While he writes enthusiastically of the self-actualizing winners, he blames the victims of corporate society, rather than criticizing the system that selects the winners and losers and seduces or manipulates receptive, naïve, uneducated people. Maslow writes about the successful self-actualizers:

> They taught me to see as profoundly sick, abnormal or weak what I had always taken for granted as humanly normal; namely, that too many people do not make up their own minds, but have their minds made up for them by salesmen, advertisers, parents, propagandists, TV, newspapers, and so on. They are pawns to be moved by others rather than self-moving, self-determining individuals. Therefore they are apt to feel helpless, weak, and totally determined; they are prey for predators, flabby whiners rather than self-determining, responsible persons.*

Ibid., p. 161.

What is one to make then of Maslow's championing of love and creativity? Is self-actualization only for the rich and successful? When he began to deal directly with management theory in *Eupsychian Management*,* Maslow becomes explicit in his view that participative, democratic management (Theory Y, or participative management) would not work for inferior people, who are supposedly more rigid, "authoritarian," or dependent. Maslow's examples of evolved versus unevolved people inevitably compared Americans to people from the "underdeveloped" Third World. For example:

> Where we have fairly evolved human beings able to grow, eager to grow, then Peter Drucker's management principles seem to be fine. They will work, but only at the top of the hierarchy of human development. They assume ideally a person who has been satisfied in his basic needs in the past, while he was growing up, and who is now being satisfied in his life situation. He was and now is safety-need gratified (not anxious, not fearful). He was and is belonging-ness-need satisfied (he does not feel alienated, ostracized, orphaned, outside the group; he fits into the family, the team, the society; he is not an unwelcome intruder). He was and is love-need gratified (he has enough friends and enough good ones, a reasonable family life; he feels worthy of being loved and wanted and able to give love—this means much more than romantic love, especially in the industrial situation). He was and is respect-need gratified (he feels respect-worthy, needed, important, etc.; he feels he gets enough praise and expects to get whatever praise and reward he deserves). He was and is self-esteem-need satisfied. (As a matter of fact this doesn't happen often enough in our society; most people on unconscious levels do not have enough feelings of self-love, self-respect. But in any case, the American citizen is far better off here let's say than the Mexican citizen is.)

---

*Abraham Maslow, *Eupsychian Management, A Journal* (Homewood, Ill.: Richard D. Irwin, Inc., and The Dorsey Press, 1965).

In addition, the American citizen can feel that his curiosities, his needs for information, for knowledge, were and are satisfied or at least are capable of being satisfied, if he wants them to be. That is, he has had education, etc.*

Maslow goes on to make the ethnocentric, unsubstantiated point that in poor countries people *need* authoritarian management. He writes that:

There are many places in the world where only authoritarian management, cracking the whip over fearful people, can work. . . . Frequently it turns out that the profoundly authoritarian person has to be broken a little before he can assimilate kindness and generosity.†

In his most recent work, Peter Drucker, who is the most respected management theorist among the top executives I interviewed, all too readily accepts Maslow's criticism of his excess liberalism. He writes:

This [the organization of work in small groups and teams] demands, above all, very great self-discipline from each member of the team. Everybody has to do "the team's thing." Everybody has to take responsibility for the work of the entire team and for its performance. Indeed, Abraham Maslow's criticism of Theory Y as making inhuman demands on that large proportion of people who are weak, vulnerable, timid, impaired, applies with even greater force to free-form organization. The more flexible an organization is, the stronger do the individual members have to be and the more of the load do they have to carry.‡

"Humanistic" management theory ends up as applicable to certain character types and not others. Who are the "weak" people? They are the ones who do not adapt easily to a hierarchical corporate sys-

Ibid., p. 15.
†*Ibid.*, p. 34.
‡Peter Drucker, *Management—Tasks, Responsibilities, Practices* (New York: Harper & Row, 1974), p. 526.

tem. They may be independent farmers who are
forced off the land or craftsmen who can no longer
make a living self-employed. Their goal is not a career in the corporation, but rather more respect for
their dignity and a chance for a greater say in how
work is done and rewards are to be shared.

In our studies of both managers and workers we
have observed that there are different types of people
with different values and needs. A system that "fits"
and stimulates one character type (not to speak of
temperament and talents) may be frustrating for
another. To evolve a system that develops all but
the most hardcore jungle fighters requires democratic
processes and shared humanistic goals. Instead of
evaluating social systems in terms of how well they
help actualize the creative needs of different types
of people, Maslow's hierarchical system evaluates the
person in terms of how well he adapts to the system,
as though that were the full measure of his potential.

A majority of workers throughout the world report
they are "satisfied" with their jobs, mainly because
they feel they have no better alternatives.* They
may expresss criticism about the specific conditions
of work—safety, cleanliness, heat, cold, noise, disre-
spectful supervisors, speed of work, and lack of having a say, but they protest only when speed-ups wear
them out or unheard grievances pile up. The happiness of some is a result of their own strong love of
life. Others, less fortunate, become resigned and depressed. Instead of seeking greater health, safety, and
more humane working conditions, most workers feel
powerless to change working conditions and instead
demand more money to buy the consumer goods or
entertainment that compensates them. And to get

*For example, see George Strauss and others, eds., *Organi-
zational Behavior: Research and Issues* (Madison, Wis.: Industrial Relations Research Assn., 1974).

more money, they must agree to technological changes that sometimes, although not always, further diminish their sense of dignity, autonomy and craftsmanship.*

However, the data on alcoholism, drug taking, emotional disturbance, illness, and other symptoms of alienation from self challenge the depth of work satisfaction.†

A dream of a craftsman who had become an automobile worker in Mexico expresses his inner reality. He had told the interviewer, Dr. Alejandro Córdova, that he was satisfied with his work, which consisted of mounting the suspension of the car; this meant tightening the same screws hundreds of times a day. Although he had been a craftsman before becoming an auto worker, he even maintained that fractionating the job into two-minute cycles improved the work, and he offered no criticism of his job, at least consciously. Despite these opinions, there were other indications that he was far from happy with his work. Often he felt nervous at the factory and took it out on other workers. He got home exhausted, in a bad humor. He had lost interest in playing basketball or his guitar; now he mostly watched television and

---

*See, for example, Studs Terkel's interview with a steelworker in *Working* (New York: Pantheon Books, 1974).

†As Stanislav Kasl has written ("Mental Health and Work Environment: An Examination of the Evidence," *Journal of Occupational Medicine*, Vol. 15, No. 6, June, 1973, p. 513) in a summary of the evidence on the relationship between work and mental health:

> The point that excellent vocational adjustment, as measured by these criteria (turnover, absenteeism, and performance), can paint a misleading picture about the person's total life is dramatically illustrated in a longitudinal study of women employees of the Bell Telephone system: the women who were especially healthy, as measured by sickness, absences, company dispensary data, and psychiatrist's ratings, were those who had remained unmarried and were living a routine, dull, withdrawn existence, refusing to get involved with other people.

drank beer.* He also reported that since he began work in the factory, he had suffered constant headaches, frequent colds, and colitis. In contrast to his statement of work satisfaction, these symptoms suggested a deep conflict between what he believed, i.e., that the work was satisfying, and what he "knew," or experienced, in his body and spirit, that the work was infuriating. This conflict appeared to be the theme of a repetitive dream. "I dream that at my work there is a man who is a stranger, and we are arguing. I don't know who he is, and I don't remember what I am arguing with him about."

What a precise symbolization of alienation! The dream expresses why this worker did not connect his anger and symptoms to his experience at work. Unconsciously, he experienced himself as two people, one the conscious self, satisfied at work, the other the unconscious "stranger" with a different point of view, two aspects of the self constantly arguing with each other. What were they arguing about? He could not remember. What the evidence of the interview points to is that the unconscious stranger was telling the dreamer he had to leave the workplace, to become whole and remain sane. That this knowledge remained repressed was understandable, considering that the worker needed this job to support his family and could imagine no way of improving the quality of his work.

It might seem to psychologists of management that such a worker would not want increased responsibility. They might argue that he is the "weak" and submissive worker who is not ready for Theory Y.

But that assumes the system remains the same. What if it were to change? What if this worker, to-

---

*For an analysis of the disintegration of active leisure activities in relation to mechanized work, see Edmondo Gonzales Llaca, *Alternativas del Ocio* (Mexico: Fondo de la Cultura Economica, 1975).

gether with fellow workers, had a greater chance to control the pace of the work and to take over supervisory functions? Suppose he was stimulated to speak out and to learn more about technology and business so that he could think better about ways of working which were both economically sound and satisfying to him?

It is unlikely that an industrial work organization can ever be created to satisfy the needs of all character types. Even if all workers shared in the control of the organization, managed themselves and built products they were proud to produce, some people would still seek their major satisfactions outside of work. In the project at Harman Industries in Bolivar, Tennessee, mentioned in the next chapter, some of the workers involved would prefer to be farmers, craftsmen, nurses, beauticians, or mothers and homemakers, if they could make a go of it. These people may not want greater responsibility for the objectives of the organization, and they are not interested in a managerial career, but they have appreciated and responded to greater justice and the new hope stimulated by the chances provided by the project to learn and develop their talents. In turn, the managers have been encouraged to discard their stereotypes, to understand different types of workers, to act with respect and compassion.

Maslow's psychology and that of most management theorists have no place for the ambiguities and richness of cultural and characterological differences, or for the real experience of corporate life. Despite his conscious attempt to develop a modern humanistic psychology, Maslow ends by supporting, even celebrating, some values—hierarchy, mechanistic thought, idealization of success, careerism—that block the development of the heart.

CHAPTER 9

Leadership and the
Limits of Change

IF HE WANTS to develop his heart at work, what can
a manager do? It is all very well to advise a middle
manager to try to change the system, but even if he
takes risks, there is small chance of making a difference. Jack Wakefield, to take an exceptionally creative example, had to drop his plans for a program
that would have encouraged middle managers to
question their goals and the human effects of work.
Having puzzled over the question, the only answer
I'm sure of is simply to avoid illusions that are in the
long run always debilitating. During the past decade,
managers have been sold formulas for improving
morale, efficiency, and "self-actualization" that range
from sensitivity groups to organizational development and job enrichment. Such enthusiasms may have
led to some improvement in work, but on the whole,
they have been disappointing, largely because they
ignored the real forces that determine the corporate
psychostructure.

The chief executive officer of a company has more
power to change the organization, but even he is
limited by circumstances and by the very traits of
character that propelled him to the top. On the
whole, those whose main goal has been continued advancement leading to the executive suite are aware
of the costs of moving up in the organization and
are willing to pay the price, even to the extent of
failing as fathers or as husbands.

The new top executives of the leading technology

252

companies are flexible nonideological gamesmen. Competitive but not destructive, they are willing to play by society's rules within given boundaries, so long as they have a chance to win. It can be argued that in our economic system there is no way for such careerists to transcend role and character and stay in the race. From this point of view, the top managers might, at best, join the rest of us in protecting the environment, employees, and consumers from the excesses of business by improving the rules of the game and their enforcement.

A few of them may try to rise above career and dedicate themselves to social or ethical goals beyond themselves, either within or outside the organization. In the system, there are limits to what can be done by top managers of technology-creating corporations, even those with the best motives. Since they don't own the companies, they must answer to stockholders. Furthermore, the products they make and the structure of the organization are largely determined by factors over which they have little control: technology, the market, and human attitudes (social character).

Examining any one of these boundary factors leads quickly to the others. The very nature of technology depends on the market, and ultimately also on the attitudes of people. Companies that create new technology are responsive to what society is willing to pay for, even though this may not be in the best long-term interest of either the corporation or its employees. Many people mistakenly believe that new technology is simply the inevitable result of scientific advances, like the electric light bulb, the transistor, integrated circuits, and magnetic bubbles. According to this view, a scientific discovery eventually results in new and better ways of doing things. The new technology may be resisted because it upsets traditional ways of doing things and challenges vested interests, but gradually it prevails because it is better.

Although essential to innovation, in the companies we studied, new scientific discoveries were not the reason why new technology was being developed. Especially in the richest companies, many new technological possibilities and discoveries were buried in reports or memos from corporate scientists, never to be developed or produced, even though they might have led to better ways of doing things. And this does not even take into account the work of noncorporate scientists in universities or government.* The creation of most new technology in the United States is determined by two market demands that are, to a certain degree, interrelated but are sometimes in conflict. They are the demands of the Federal Government (the national security state) and those of the large corporations.

Above all, the modern superstate demands new weapons, strategic advantages, and internal-security systems (including spying technology and computerized control of information). The main motives that move the state to demand new technology are "security" (protection and war-making power) and prestige (or glory). These motives introduce a powerful irrational potential to the creation of new technology, and touch the most irrational strains in the corporate gamesmen. In the realm of foreign policy, there is never enough security or military superiority against powerful opponents, particularly when no state is sure about the others' capabilities. In the realm of domestic policy, even the most embryonic opposition might conceivably grow into an internal-security threat, so all sorts of spying and data-process technology can be justified, even by individuals who

---

*See Michael Maccoby, "Government, Scientists, and the Priorities of Science," *Dissent*, Winter, 1964, for a description of how a development of solar energy could get no support from either government or industry despite the fact that even then it promised to better life for many people in isolated rural areas.

personally place the highest value on privacy. Pre-occupation with internal and external security is, of course, magnified when state policies are aggressive, as has been the case with both the United States and the Soviet Union.

The desire for prestige and glory can also energize limitless hunger for new technology. Although the process is generated bureaucratically, the character of the Presidency makes a significant difference.*

John F. Kennedy, a gamesman, wanted to be "first" in the world. Lyndon B. Johnson and Richard M. Nixon were complex jungle fighters. Although he could be compassionate to the powerless, Johnson was haunted by fears of his own vulnerability and driven to prove his superiority over the powerful. Nixon was so obsessed by fear of his enemies that in trying to stamp them out he undermined himself. In contrast, company men like Dwight D. Eisenhower and Gerald Ford have been motivated to avoid making enemies by harmonizing powerful interests.

In our time, it was the innovative gamesman Kennedy who lived out the ancient fantasy—to reach the moon. His quest for glory became a high priority, supporting the development of costly new technology and setting in motion new economic interests and threats to national security. Impatient with Ike's cautious mediation which kept the adventurous in check, Kennedy set a new pace, which Johnson and Nixon were driven to try to surpass.

The excessive demands of the state for security and glory became a dictum that anything that *might* be built *should* be built. The technology-hungry state seduces or pressures industry to meet its demand for new technology, and in so doing threatens to grab the lion's share of R & D.

---

*For an analysis of these bureaucratic policies in relation to glory and prestige, see Richard Barnet, *The Roots of War* (New York: Atheneum, 1972).

The demand of the corporations, to optimize profit and growth, is subject to more constraints. If they are to prosper, corporations must sell technology to buyers who can use it. Most sales of large new technology, such as computer systems, automated machinery, new chemical processes, etc., are made to other companies and bureaucracies (federal, state or municipal governments).

Although the businessman's desire to buy technology that is glamorous, novel, and exciting (though it may be no more efficient than other products) may border on the irrational, essentially he buys new productive technologies which promise to increase efficiency and, in the case of the private sector, profits, because they promise both control and predictability over the production process and the lowering of labor costs. The need to maximize control is rooted in the character of top executives, who may experience conflict when the technology works best with a more democratic organization of work. However, for all these consumers, glamour is secondary, although it may be a consideration in buying the latest "hardware" with the "sexiest" packaging. Thus, large oligopolistic corporations specializing in research and development tend to create technology that is useful and can be sold to companies like them. (In some cases, they are their own best customers.)

Although technology developed for security and prestige has been adapted by corporations to lower labor costs or increase control over the production process—computers, airplanes, and communications satellites are examples—interests of the state and corporations do not always coincide. Symbiosis becomes parasitosis when the state demands that more and more resources be committed to specialized products like ICBM's, submarines, and nuclear weapons, threatening the growth and health of companies.

Without even considering the state's threat to individual liberty, there are at least three practical reasons why its demands may in fact damage corporations. First, because of national security, new technology for the state cannot be sold to other potential buyers. Corporations would like to sell new technology to semi-hostile states like China or the U.S.S.R. and treat other states as customer corporations rather than as rival nations, but the state emphasizes national security over corporate profits.

Second, corporations find that dependence on the state encourages bad business practices. Building whatever is technically possible is poor business for a company competing in a tight international market. Military demands for total reliability, including back-up systems in missiles and spaceships, are so costly and require such servicing that no one but the state could afford them. When a company dependent on the state tries to diversify, it must usually unlearn these uneconomical habits and fire scientists and engineers who have been ruined for business. Furthermore, financial dealings with the state are different from most other business practices, since companies often bid low and raise prices later as the state asks for changes incorporating the newest technological ideas or tactical considerations.

Third, dependency on the state is risky, since a change in national policy can suddenly upset all corporate planning. For example, Congress might cut the military budget, ending corporate projects that cannot be sold to anyone else.

Demands of the state can cramp corporate planning processes and endanger the competitive position of highly technological companies. Corporations most dependent on the state have often ended up ill equipped to compete in a world market.

From the point of view of both head and heart, the most important single goal in relation to technology should be to curb the irrationality of the state and achieve nuclear disarmament, or at least arms control that halts the weapons race, and limit technological growth that threatens human life. Everyone must obviously share the goal of survival. Although the gamesman executive may be excited by the chance to develop complex new technology, he is even more interested in the company's economic strength. Efforts to develop a more rational national security could gain allies from executives of those corporations that would benefit economically by bridling the state's technological greed. But they will not and cannot create a rational technology policy by themselves. Controlling the state requires deep-rooted political support from a public that insists on reasonable leaders who are not driven by dreams of glory. In this light, projects to change work and production technology are valuable not only in terms of making life better for the individuals involved; they may also be essential to strengthening life-loving attitudes in society.

Can we expect either managers or workers to curb the irrationality of the state if their work leads them into a world of fantasy and escapism? How can one expect them to worry about building products that undermine society if their work does not reinforce dignity and stimulate responsibility? Why should workers care about others' suffering if nothing is done to change physical and social conditions that make them angry and anxious?

The "technology of production," including both mechanical-electrical-chemical processes *and* the systems of management in factories and offices that organize this hardware, is a key factor in determining the relationships at work that reinforce certain traits and not others, and it also influences social character by selecting certain kinds of people to fit the work roles.

New technological advances—such as cheaper electronic components for mini-computers or photoengraving processes that replace hand-circuit assembly —change the types of tasks, and the types of workers

Leadership and the Limits of Change • 259

and managers required. Although the assembly line transformed craftsmen into replacable parts of the machine, automation and continuous-process technology may economically favor more democratic forms of organization.* Clearly, these production technologies, from the assembly line to the computer and continuous processing, were not designed with democratic social criteria in mind. Even though certain new technology has had progressive social consequences, the creators hardly considered the human or environmental outcomes of what they were creating.

By designing technology according to social as well as economic criteria, it will be possible to improve the quality of work, but even then exceptional leadership will be required to institute organizational principles based on values such as concern for others, increased equity, development of skills and abilities (craftsmanship), and respect for differences.

Up to now, the types of companies with the principles closest to this ideal have generally been ones run by the owner-founder or his family, where the company has a strong market position (due to creating new or high-quality products), and where the production technology allows craftsmanship. Such a structure has aspects of neofeudalism. The top managers are responsibly concerned about the worker's

---

*The research of Joan Woodward shows that while mass-production technology fits the F. W. Taylor model of hierarchical authority and fragmented tasks, the most economically successful process firms are more flexible at both the top and bottom. Workers must be willing and able to solve technical problems. If something goes wrong, workers must be able to make rapid, autonomous decisions to protect the expensive machinery. See her "Management and Technology," in Tom Burns, ed., *Industrial Man* (Baltimore: Penguin Books, 1969), pp. 196 ff. This relationship helps explain the most successful new democratic-participative projects such as General Foods in Topeka, Procter & Gamble in Lima, Hunsfos in Kristiansand, Norway, etc., in which the new organization was built to mesh with continuous-process technology.

well-being. The manager will listen sympathetically to the worker's problems (communication both ways is excellent, without the need for "human relations" experts), personally reward him for accomplishments, punish him for "misdeeds," remember weddings, the birth of children, and so on. Although the role implies a certain submissiveness and security at the expense of democratic rights, such security can be extremely comforting to all employees when in times of recession or depression paternalistic managers may even cut their own salaries to avoid layoffs.

Although many old-style paternalistic companies are disappearing, some swallowed up by larger corporations and conglomerates, there are newer ones that survive and grow. This is remarkable in itself, when we consider that for every nine or ten new businesses each year, eight others fail.* How do a few of these manage to survive and become large corporations? There are many factors involved, but leadership is essential. The builders of successful companies are often complex men who combine aspects of the jungle fighter and the craftsman. In contrast to the foxes who cunningly move up the bureaucratic hierarchy, they are lions who march boldly into new markets, conquering them through superior quality. What distinguishes them from other entrepreneurial jungle fighters is that they have adopted a working philosophy, limiting principles which define for themselves and others what they will do and what they will not do. These principles generally have to do with maximizing security, fairness in rewards, and respect for the feelings and ideas of all who are part of the corporate "family." Such principles determine management in such a way that the workers and managers develop a sense of trust because they can

---

*For a further discussion, see Michael Maccoby and Katherine A. Terzi, "Character and Work in America," in Philip Brenner and others, eds., *Exploring Contradictions: Political Economy in the Corporate State* (New York: David McKay, 1974).

count on these principles. As a result, loyalty and highly productive cooperation are gained from the workers and, naturally, these are key elements in developing a successful business.

But without the owner to embody his principles, can they be maintained? Even if he had a philosophy, the gamesman chief executive of a public corporation would not be so free to act on his personal philosophy. He plays the game and is responsive to the "needs" of the company to optimize growth and profit. Since his tenure depends on his performance, any personal relationships or trust he has built lasts only as long as he remains. Since he does not own or control the company, how can managers and workers trust him to follow any policy not easily explained in terms of profit and growth? It follows that the less trust there is, the more necessary it becomes to strengthen centralized controls.

Instead of developing an organization based on humanistic principles, the gamesman uses new behavioral-science technology to build a more exciting, highly motivated team. He hopes he can construct a more flexible organization without losing control, but unless pushed by demands of employees, and bound by firmly established limits, these experiments are likely to be partial and manipulative. The popularity of Frederick Herzberg and his followers reflects such an attempt to "enrich" work to provide managers and workers with greater opportunities for challenge and advancement. Although these games appeal to some of the more ambitious workers, by giving them a chance to move ahead rapidly, they do not change the hierarchical structure.*

---

*In *Job Power* (Baltimore: Penguin Books, 1974), David Jenkins criticizes the Herzberg position from the point of view of industrial democracy. He writes: "The way in which the job is enriched is decided, not by the employees concerned, but by the job enrichment experts. There is a fixed ceiling to the enrichment process . . . There is no provision for workers to discuss matters and propose improvements. Herzberg is against

The few businessmen I met who are dissatisfied by both paternalism and games are motivated to free themselves from their role. They do not repress or detach themselves from whatever guilt they may experience about using other people but act to alleviate it. They recognize that the way they have gotten ahead, putting the company first, has hurt themselves and others. But rather than hiding from their hearts or hardening them, they are spurred by their consciousness to try to change the boundaries and to "rectify their hearts." One corporation president described why he had been moved first to study the human effects of work and then to change his behavior. He told me, "I saw myself as a slave owner, ripping off the work of other people, and I knew I had to do something to change working conditions."

This is not a book about how to change corporations to develop the heart. Although what I have learned makes me skeptical that this is possible, there are ways to limit corporate practices which are manipulative, exploitative, humiliating, or cause needless anxiety. However, experiments in restructuring work according to humane principles must begin at the top. If relationships among executives and middle managers are not characterized by greater security, equity, respect for the individual and democracy, it will be impossible to establish these principles for other employees.*

Toward the end of the interviewing in corpora-

---

group action. Each individual is to be dealt with individually. He is also against 'participation' . . . It is easy to suspect, in fact, that Herzberg's popularity among U.S. businessmen depends to some extent on his method's very limited objectives. It satisfies somewhat employee needs for autonomy, but it is 'safe'—it does not upset anybody and it does not rock the boat . . . Above all, it does not alter the traditional stiff hierarchical structure," p. 169.

*These "principles of humanizing work" were first spelled out by Neal Q. Herrick and Michael Maccoby in L. E. Davis and A. B. Cherns, eds., *The Quality of Working Life, Volume One, Problems, Prospects, and the State of the Art* (New York: The Free Press, 1975).

tions, I met an exceptional executive, Sidney Harman, who heard me talk about the study and offered to participate. Even though he had been more socially and politically active than most managers, he still felt imprisoned by his role as president of a corporation. He asked me what he might do to liberate himself. Was he willing to create an experimental model of work and organization with the goal not of maximizing productivity and efficiency, but rather of providing opportunities for human development? That might mean a large commitment of time, energy, and money. He would have to engage his own skeptical management and workers. He enthusiastically agreed to try and asked me to help.*

One of the most interesting recent outcomes of Harman's efforts to restructure work has been to attract creative high technology managers to his company. Two of these are company men who left higher positions doing technically more interesting work with larger organizations precisely because they were dissatisfied with heartless games and wanted to commit themselves to a company with principles they shared.

Another such businessman is James P. Gibbons, president of Consumers United Group, an insurance

---

*Harman International Industries includes a number of factories in the U.S. and abroad making different kinds of products, including hi-fidelity components and automobile parts. Some of the plants are unionized; others are not. The plant we chose for a model project is a factory in Bolivar, Tennessee, that makes outside mirrors for cars, and where most workers are members of the United Automobile Workers International. We reasoned that a joint union-management project might be more socially generative because it could become a laboratory for the union to learn methods of work humanization. We were able to gain the support and cooperation of Irving Bluestone, a UAW vice-president and visionary labor leader who also shared the goal of creating a democratic workplace.

See Michael Maccoby, "Changing Work: The Bolivar Project," *Working Papers,* Summer, 1975, Vol. III, No. 2. For another account of the Bolivar Project, see Paul Dickson, *The Future of the Workplace* (New York: Weybright & Talley, 1975).

company in Washington, D.C. After he had spent ten years establishing a $50 million company, Gibbons, who owned all the stock, gave it to the employees in a trust and dedicated himself to developing an economically viable model for a democratically run company based on the principle of "maximizing the humanness of every employee."*

Like the most creative gamesmen, both Gibbons and Harman are boyish, supersalesmen, and inspirational managers. But unlike the typical gamesman, they are compassionate, idealistic, and courageous entrepreneurs who stimulate loyalty by their concern for others and their constant effort to understand and strengthen what is creative in others and their organizations. I see them as a kind of managerial mutant, a new corporate type, the gamesman who develops his heart as well as his head, and who could become examples for leadership in a changing society where the goal is economic democracy and the humanization of technology. The results of their idealism and generosity are not yet clear, since no one can give others their freedom if they are unwilling to work for it. If they can create new practical models, it will not be long before workers in other companies demand these benefits. Then gamesman executives can deal with real pressures rather than vague ideals, and pioneers like Harman and Gibbons will then have had an effect on changing the boundaries. Their personal liberation, which has already improved life for employees in their companies, will then become a contribution to society as a whole.

Harman and Gibbons and a few others are the exceptions both because of their gifts and their power. As things stand in most companies, just as in leading universities and bureaucracies, the more successful managers live as servants to their careers and stran-

---

*I plan to write a separate account of my work with the Bolivar and CUG projects and the attempts to change structure and spirit in these organizations.

gers to themselves and others. There are some who do not wish to pay that price. They do their work and prefer to detach themselves from the contest rather than from the self. Until work is changed, many of the most gifted individuals will have to make that choice.

The Interpretive Questionnaire

A. DESCRIPTION OF WORK

NAME _____ TITLE _____ ORGANIZATION _____

Some of these questions may not exactly fit your circumstances; modify or qualify whenever useful.

1. Age___

2. Where did you grow up? _____

3. How many brothers and sisters do you have? ___

4. What is your position in the family (eldest, youngest)? _____

5. Education (high school, college, university; degrees received and field of study).

6. Married? ___ Single? ___ Ever divorced? ___

7. Children (sex and age)?

8. Father's education and occupation.

9. Mother's education and occupation.

10. Occupation and national background of father's father.

11. Occupation and national background of mother's father.

12. Give your work history (or attach vitae).

13. How many hours a week do you usually work? ___

14. Does your work ever require an environment for thought where you will not be interrupted? ___

15. About how much time do you need each day for uninterrupted analytical work (design, programming, planning, etc.)? _____

16. Do you have any problems in finding this time at work? Yes___ No___

17. Do you find at least part of this time at home? Yes___ No___

18. If so, how many hours a week do you generally work by yourself at home? ___

19. Do you feel there are too many demands at work to be responsive? ___

20. Are you responsible for expenditures? Yes___ No___

21. If so, how much money are you responsible for:
    a. by yourself? _____
    b. in consultation with others? _____

22. If you are responsible for the work of others, how many people do you supervise? ___

23. What kinds of people do you supervise directly?
    a. ___other managers   d. ___technicians
    b. ___staff   e. ___inventors
    c. ___scientists   f. ___other

24. Describe in a few sentences what you do at work:

25. Check one or more of the following that best describe your work. If several are appropriate, give approximate percentages. Cross out words or phrases that do not apply. Space is provided for modification or comment that might help us understand what you do.
    a. ___You are the manager of a project where you meet frequently with the whole project staff. You also spend time representing the project to higher management.
    b. ___You are the manager of a line. You mainly spend your time with those reporting to you. They in turn report on their subordinates. You in turn meet with your superior.
    c. ___You manage a group and primarily meet with its members individually. Regardless of their position, you spend time with your subordinates, directly informing yourself of their work, even though they may have a manager who reports directly to you.
    d. ___You are a manager who spends much of his time with others in the corporation who are on your level, working on coordination and planning.
    e. ___You are a manager who delegates much of the management to subordinates, while you spend much of your time planning and consulting with those higher in the corporation.

f. ___You are a manager who works mostly by yourself. You find that your co-managers and subordinates carry out their tasks without constant checking.

g. ___You have a staff position in which you primarily support the work of one other person for whom you work on specific assignments.

h. ___You are an independent contributor and you work primarily by yourself. Your rank is equivalent to managerial rank, though you have no administrative responsibilities.

i. ___You work individually under the supervision of another and have no managerial responsibility.

j. ___You work primarily as a member of a team and have no administrative managerial responsibility.

k. ___If the above descriptions seem generally inapplicable, can you give a brief description of what your work is:

26. Check the phrases which are descriptive of the work you do.

1. ___Determining goals, policies, courses of action

2. ___Having responsibility for a project or product

3. ___Having responsibility for others' work

4. ___Developing new products

5. ___Long-range economic planning

6. ___Being a sounding board for the ideas of others

7. ___Talking with others to maintain a good emotional atmosphere

8. ___Talking with others to help them organize their work

9. ___Attending meetings

10. ___Talking to subordinates

11. ___Talking to superiors

12. ___Talking to peers

13. ___Giving directions to others

14. ___Maintaining an exchange of information with people in other areas

15. ___Building support for ideas and projects

16. ___Sensing potential (personnel) problems

17. ___Interviewing prospective employees

18. ___Making presentations to the public

19. ___Making presentations within the company

20. ___Making presentations to customers

21. ___Keeping up with social trends in general, current events, etc.

22. ___Coordinating different aspects of work
23. ___Promoting employees

24. ___Keeping up with what is happening in the business world

25. ___Product testing
26. ___Preparing agendas
27. ___Scheduling work
28. ___Setting up procedures
29. ___Budgeting
30. ___Maintaining the work force of one or more units
31. ___Placing employees
32. ___Judging other people's work

33. ___Preparing financial statements
34. ___Inventorying
35. ___Job analysis and description
36. ___Arranging meetings
37. ___Evaluating financial reports
38. ___Handling complaints from subordinates
39. ___Disciplining
40. ___Recruiting
41. ___Transferring employees

42. ___Facility maintenance
43. ___Computer data analysis

44. ___Measuring output
45. ___Monitoring machines

46. ___Writing reports
47. ___Assembling technological subunits
48. ___Analyzing competitors' products or potential
49. ___Uninterrupted analytical work
50. ___Computer programming
51. ___Representing the company at conferences, conventions, trade fairs

52. ___Writing for house publications
53. ___Writing up new ideas or discoveries for publication
54. ___Studying the state of the art
55. ___Reading technical or scientific literature
56. ___Communicating with the press

27. Circle the numbers of the items which are most important.

28. Does your work require keeping up with new technical literature? Yes___ No___

29. If so, what journals do you regularly read?

30. Does your work require knowledge of current events, social change, etc.? Yes___ No___

31. If so, how do you do this? (What magazines do you regularly read?)

32. In what circumstances do you get your best ideas? Check (and if appropriate, underline choice in parentheses).
    a. ___While working alone in your office (writing, calculating, designing, relaxing).
    b. ___In conversation with one other person (equal, subordinate, superior); (formal conversation, informal conversation).
    c. ___In meetings with a number of people (problem-solving sessions, general work meetings, brainstorming sessions, presentations, _____).
    d. ___While working with equipment.
    e. ___While working with salespeople.
    f. ___While reading (technical journals, operating manuals, about competitors).
    g. ___While driving.
    h. ___During sports events (spectator, participant).
    i. ___While eating.
    j. ___In bed (during the night, napping, dreaming).
    k. ___While watching TV.
    l. ___While listening to music.   m. ___Other _____

33. Check which of the following types of situation has been an effective incentive for your best ideas.
    a. ___When there is a problem and somebody has to come up with a solution.
    b. ___In a situation in which there is no problem but you know that one must have new ideas to get ahead.
    c. ___When there is no specific problem but you see how to do something new or better.

34. On the basis of what criteria is your work judged by your superiors?

35. How are you doing, in general, in attaining these criteria?

36. Which of these criteria are the most meaningful to you?

37. (FOR MANAGERS) What are the criteria by which you judge the work of subordinates?

38. What is the relationship of your work to the development of new technology?

39. Does your work require innovation? If so, describe. (For example, developing new techniques of organizing information, new designs, new systems, new components, etc.?)

40. Does your work require using existing technology in new ways? If so, describe. (For example, for a particular customer?) What aspects of your work are most creative?

41. How might your work be changed to make it more satisfying for you?

42. Do you consider that changes in knowledge, technology, or ways of doing things have made your training or past experience inadequate for your current work?

43. Does your organization provide the opportunity for retraining?

44. Do you consider that some of the people whom you work with need such retraining? Why?

B. INTELLECTUAL AND PSYCHOLOGICAL FACTORS IN WORK

1. To start out, how would you describe your character in your own words?

2. Indicate the extent to which the following kinds of intellectual capabilities are important in your work.

	Very Important	Somewhat Important	Not Important
1. Concern for practical details	1. ___	___	___
2. Integrating or synthesizing ideas into an overall plan	2. ___	___	___
3. Inventing new ideas	3. ___	___	___
4. Awareness of others' feelings	4. ___	___	___
5. Attention to small details	5. ___	___	___
6. Working facts into a logical order	6. ___	___	___
7. Good memory for facts	7. ___	___	___
8. Speed	8. ___	___	___
9. Ability to dramatize (and sell) one's ideas	9. ___	___	___
10. Ability to create an environment in which others work better	10. ___	___	___
11. Ability to listen carefully to others	11. ___	___	___

		Very Important	Somewhat Important	Not Important
12.	Mathematical ability	12. ___	___	___
13.	Ability to stimulate or activate others	13. ___	___	___
14.	Ability to sell oneself	14. ___	___	___
15.	Extensive English vocabulary	15. ___	___	___
16.	Extensive technical vocabulary	16. ___	___	___
17.	Ability to communicate verbally	17. ___	___	___
18.	Ability to communicate in writing	18. ___	___	___
19.	Ability to reach conclusions with a minimum of information	19. ___	___	___
20.	Critical thinking, questioning methods and techniques that others take for granted	20. ___	___	___
21.	Ability to size up another's character	21. ___	___	___
22.	Ability to concentrate by oneself	22. ___	___	___
23.	Systems thinking	23. ___	___	___
24.	Ability to recognize good ideas	24. ___	___	___
25.	Ability to be critical of bad ideas	25. ___	___	___
26.	Imagination	26. ___	___	___
27.	Ability to see the whole, not merely the parts	27. ___	___	___
28.	Perspective or vision	28. ___	___	___

CIRCLE THE NUMBERS of those abilities which you consider have been stimulated and developed by your work.

3. Which do you consider your strongest intellectual abilities?

4. Which of your intellectual abilities do you feel need improvement?

5. Indicate the extent to which the following traits of character are important in your work.

	Very Important	Somewhat Important	Not Important
1. Cooperativeness	1. ___		
2. Orderliness	2. ___	___	___
3. Openness, spontaneity	3. ___	___	___
4. Independence (vs. dependence)	4. ___	___	___
5. Loyalty to the company	5. ___		
6. Loyalty to subordinates	6. ___		
7. Loyalty to fellow workers	7. ___		___
8. Loyalty to superiors	8. ___	___	___
9. Drive to be the best	9. ___	___	___
10. Drive for power over others	10. ___	___	___
11. Satisfaction in creating something new	11. ___	___	___
12. Pleasure in learning something new	12. ___	___	___
13. Critical and questioning attitude toward authority	13. ___	___	___
14. Sense of humor	14. ___	___	___
15. Toughness, lack of sentimentality	15. ___	___	___
16. Modesty	16. ___	___	___
17. Personal charm	17. ___	___	___
18. Idealism	18. ___	___	___
19. Ability to take orders	19. ___	___	___
20. Considerateness to subordinates	20. ___	___	___
21. Ability to take the initiative	21. ___	___	___
22. Self-confidence	22. ___	___	___
23. Patience	23. ___	___	___
24. Tenacity	24. ___	___	___
25. Coolness under stress	25. ___	___	___
26. Stubbornness	26. ___	___	___
27. Fairness	27. ___	___	___
28. Generosity	28. ___	___	___
29. Flexibility	29. ___	___	___
30. Open-mindedness	30. ___	___	___
31. Compassion	31. ___	___	___
32. Need for achievement	32. ___	___	___
33. Need to win	33. ___	___	___
34. Detachment	34. ___	___	___
35. Aggressiveness	35. ___	___	___
36. Pride in performance	36. ___	___	___
37. Self-actualizing drive	37. ___	___	___
38. Efficiency	38. ___	___	___

	Very Important	Somewhat Important	Not Important
39. Honesty	39. ___	___	___
40. Self-control	40. ___	___	___
41. Decisiveness	41. ___	___	___
42. Friendliness	42. ___	___	___
43. Energy	43. ___	___	___

CIRCLE THE NUMBERS of those traits which you consider have been stimulated or reinforced by your work.

6. Do you have any traits which get in the way of your work (for example, any of the ones on the above list)? If so, which ones?

7. We are interested in how you describe the personality of people for whom you work now.

8. We are interested in how you describe the personality of people whom you manage now.

9. Describe briefly the kinds of people you most like to work with, for, and for you.

10. Describe briefly the kinds of people you least like to work with, for, and for you.

11. Do you earn enough to satisfy your needs? Yes___ No___

12. How much do you earn per year now? _____

13. How much would you ideally like to earn per year? _____

14. Besides the need to earn money, how important a place would you say your work occupies in your life?
   1. ___the single most important thing
   2. ___extremely important
   3. ___quite important
   4. ___fairly important
   5. ___of little importance
   6. ___of no importance

15. Which of the following describes your feelings about your present job? Check the ones that express your feelings.
   1. ___This job is an interesting technical challenge for me.
   2. ___My assignment is below my technical ability.
   3. ___The work allows me to be creative.
   4. ___I feel like a part in the machine.
   5. ___I feel I have the opportunity for a great deal of independence in my work.
   6. ___The work is oversupervised.
   7. ___My individual contribution is visible to my supervisors.
   8. ___My individual contribution is important to the success of the project.

16. What do you most like about your work?

17. What do you like least about your work?

18. Why did you go into science or engineering?

19. Why did you go into industry?

20. If you had the opportunity, what would you like to do or study?

21. Have you ever had a dream related to work? Yes___ No___ If yes, can you recall and describe it?

22. If not, can you recall and describe any dream that you have had?

23. In getting ahead in this organization, what is the relative importance of the following factors?

	Very Important	Somewhat Important	Of Relatively Little Importance	Negative Factor
1. Technical ability	1. ___	___	___	___
2. Managerial ability	2. ___	___	___	___
3. Friendships and connections with superiors	3. ___	___	___	___
4. Building a power base in the organization	4. ___	___	___	___
5. Talking down others in order to get ahead	5. ___	___	___	___
6. Survival skills, being able to protect oneself from others	6. ___	___	___	___
7. Not causing trouble, not being noticed	7. ___	___	___	___
8. Successful work with customers	8. ___	___	___	___
9. Ability to sell ideas to the organization	9. ___	___	___	___
10. Ability to think in terms of what is good for the organization and not just oneself	10. ___	___	___	___

	Very Important	Somewhat Important	Of Relatively Little Importance	Negative Factor
11. Ability to sell oneself	11. ——	——	——	——

24. Are you ever bothered by not knowing what opportunities for advancement or promotion exist? Yes—— No——

25. Do you feel that you have been classified by management as someone who cannot handle broader responsibilities? Yes—— No——

26. Looking ahead a few years, what do you have to look forward to in terms of your work? What position in the organization would you like to reach?

27. Do you expect new technological developments to influence your work, either by making it easier, more interesting, or altogether replaceable by a machine?

28. Have you ever seriously considered doing totally different work? Yes—— No—— If so, what kind of work and how seriously have you considered it?

29. What is the most productive age for your kind of work?

30. At what age do you think that managers of advanced technology begin to slow down?

31. Besides your work in the organization, do you do any other work? Yes—— No——

32. Did you ever have the idea of building or creating or doing something that you then shelved away? If so, could you describe it?

33. When you started out, did you have an idea of what you wanted to achieve? If so, could you describe it?

34. How does your present work compare with that original idea?

35. As a teen-ager, what kind of work did you most want to do when you grew up?

36. If you could freely choose, what job or profession would you most like for yourself? Why?

37. Would you rather work in a small company or in a large company? Why?

38. Would you rather work in a small company of your own or on a high level in a large organization?
    ___Small company of my own
    ___High level in a large organization

39. What size organizations have you worked in?

    a. ___Under 20   d. ___Under 10,000
    b. ___Under 100   e. ___Under 100,000
    c. ___Under 1,000   f. ___100,000 or more

40. What kinds of material and personal rewards can be gained from your work (for example, financial, respect, recognition, influence, power, esteem, etc.)?

41. To what extent are you, in general, attaining these?

42. Which of these rewards is most meaningful to you and why?

43. When have you felt most successful?

44. What does the concept of self-actualization mean to you?

45. Do you have any say in decisions made by your organization? Yes___ No___

46. Do you consider that you should have more say in the policies of the organization?
    a. In terms of work policies? Yes___ No___
    b. In terms of products to be developed? Yes___ No___
    c. Other _____

47. Explain any way in which you consider that employees might participate more in making organizational decisions.

48. Indicate the extent to which you experience the following kinds of difficulties:

	Not a Difficulty	A Minor Difficulty	A Major Difficulty
1. Depression	1. ___	___	___
2. Sleep badly	2. ___	___	___
3. Have obsessive thoughts	3. ___	___	___
4. Tend to blame yourself too much	4. ___	___	___
5. Give in easily to others	5. ___	___	___
6. Often restless	6. ___	___	___
7. Overeat	7. ___	___	___
8. Tend to physical illness	8. ___	___	___
9. Keep your feelings to yourself	9. ___	___	___
10. Avoid people	10. ___	___	___

	Not a Difficulty	A Minor Difficulty	A Major Difficulty
11. Have unwarranted fears	11. ___	___	___
12. Overly neat	12. ___	___	___
13. Plan too carefully	13. ___	___	___
14. Vague feelings of misfortune coming	14. ___	___	___
15. Daydream excessively	15. ___	___	___
16. Unable to stick to plans	16. ___	___	___
17. Lack hope	17. ___	___	___
18. Anxious	18. ___	___	___
19. Severe headaches	19. ___	___	___
20. Feel you are slowing down too much	20. ___	___	___
21. Have had thoughts of suicide	21. ___	___	___
22. Difficulty in making decisions	22. ___	___	___
23. At times misperceive important events	23. ___	___	___
24. Have thoughts of acting destructively	24. ___	___	___
25. Difficulty saying what you mean	25. ___	___	___
26. Violate rules without good reason	26. ___	___	___
27. Uncooperative	27. ___	___	___
28. Difficulty with your wife	28. ___	___	___
29. Sexual difficulties	29. ___	___	___
30. Difficulties with your children	30. ___	___	___
31. Difficulties with your friends	31. ___	___	___
32. Difficulties with your parents	32. ___	___	___
33. Difficulties with those you work for	33. ___	___	___
34. Difficulties with those who work for you	34. ___	___	___
35. Difficulty working with women	35. ___	___	___
36. Difficulty working with men	36. ___	___	___
37. Difficulty paying bills	37. ___	___	___
38. Difficulties being by yourself	38. ___	___	___

	Not a Difficulty	A Minor Difficulty	A Major Difficulty
39. Don't know what you want	39. ___	___	___
40. Feel it's too necessary to give in to circumstances	40. ___	___	___
41. Lack sufficient energy to do what you want	41. ___	___	___
42. Too easily influenced by others	42. ___	___	___
43. Gastrointestinal problems (ulcers, colitis, etc.)	43. ___	___	___
44. Frequent back troubles	44. ___	___	___

49. Check the following items if they describe goals that are important to you:
    1. ___Receiving higher than average salary
    2. ___Receiving higher than average increases in salary
    3. ___Making a lot of money
    4. ___Acquiring ownership of stocks in your company
    5. ___Acquiring ownership of stocks in other companies
    6. ___Working on a high technological level
    7. ___Exploring new technologies
    8. ___Working with people of high technical achievements
    9. ___Having prestige as an authority in your technological field
    10. ___Contributing to scientific advances
    11. ___Being part of a scientific community
    12. ___Being a winner
    13. ___Being the originator of the project you work on
    14. ___Having an impact on the corporation in terms of policies
    15. ___Helping your people develop themselves
    16. ___Having knowledge of the company's plans and practices
    17. ___Getting ahead rapidly
    18. ___Getting ahead steadily
    19. ___Having power over others
    20. ___Having direct personal influence over others
    21. ___Having a well-ordered work situation where you can be creative
    22. ___Having an unstructured work situation where you can be creative
    23. ___Working in a cooperative friendly atmosphere
    24. ___Working in an atmosphere free of pressures
    25. ___Working under the challenge of competitive pressures
    26. ___Working with an efficient high-powered team

27. ____Working with people you can be friends with
28. ____Working with people who don't make personal demands on you
29. ____Having time to talk freely to people at work
30. ____Having the opportunity to explore and develop ideas
31. ____Having intellectually interesting work
32. ____Seeing the concrete results of your work as a product
33. ____Earning awards
34. ____Getting promotions
35. ____Seeing an increase in profits
36. ____Building things
37. ____Having the esteem of your co-workers
38. ____Being an effective manager
39. ____To become self-actualized
40. ____Having work that is important to human welfare
41. ____Having the esteem of your superiors
42. ____Having the esteem of your subordinates
43. ____Freedom to choose personal relations, independent of the company hierarchy or implicit norms
44. ____The respect of your wife, children, parents for your position and work
45. ____Having time to spend with your family
46. ____Living in an area which you like
47. ____Living in an area which your wife likes
48. ____Living in an area which your children like

CIRCLE THE NUMBERS of the most important goals.

C. SOCIAL IMPLICATION OF WORK

1. Are you working in an advanced area of technology? Yes____ No____ If so, do you prefer
   a. ____To develop a new type of technology that will perform a similar task or the same task better?
   b. ____To find new, wider uses for present types of technology?

2. Have you given any thought to the social value of the product you are making? If so, what have you thought?

3. Is this an important consideration in your choice of job?

4. What kinds of products do you consider of social value?

5. What kinds of products do you consider socially harmful?

6. Do you think that the project you are working on is technically important? Yes____ No____

7. Do you feel that it is socially important? Yes___ No___

8. Do you feel that it is important for the company? Yes___ No___

9. Do you feel that it is important for the national economy? Yes___ No___

10. What social effects, if any, do you think it will have?

11. Do you feel proud to work on this project? Yes___ No___

12. Have you ever worked with the consumers (users) of your product? Yes___ No___ If so, did you find that satisfying and why?

13. Have you ever worked closely with people other than your fellow scientists and engineers? If so, with what types of people?

14. Did you find that experience satisfying? Why?

15. Have you worked or would you be prepared to work with local city governments or citizens groups on projects of importance to them? If you have done this, describe the project.

16. Is there other work that you have done with others in your community?

17. Is there anything you would like to achieve or do in terms of the community in which you live?

18. Are there any kinds of projects you would not work on for moral reasons? If so, which ones?

19. Do you believe that advanced technology of the type developed for military weapons systems can play an important role in solving the ills of our domestic society? Yes___ No___
If yes, how? If no, why not?

20. Would you be interested personally in working on the application of this technology to solving the ills of our domestic society?
   1. ___Very interested
   2. ___Somewhat interested
   3. ___Not particularly interested

21. Does your current project depend (directly or indirectly) on government funds?

22. If so, have you considered what you would do if the government decided to terminate this type of research or engineering project? If yes, what would your alternative be?

23. If this were to happen, would you try to find employment in the same field you are now working in, or would you explore opportunities in other fields? If in other fields, which ones?

24. Do you feel that advanced technology will have an important role in solving any of the following social problems? If so, state in your opinion how this might happen. Be as speculative as you wish.

    a. Poverty
    b. Air and water pollution
    c. Overpopulation
    d. Mental illness
    e. Food supply
    f. International tensions
    g. Political dissent
    h. Political participation
    i. World government
    j. Drug use
    k. Crime
    l. Education
    m. The quality of life
    n. Aging
    o. Generation gap

25. Are there any social problems that you feel cannot be solved by advanced technology? Yes__ No__ If so, which ones and why?

26. Do you think that if a new development is technically possible, it should be built? Yes__ No__ If so, why? If not, why not?

27. In matters of the use of advanced technology, which of the following statements best expresses your opinion?
    a. __Decisions should be made through maximum participation of all citizens who are affected.
    b. __Decisions should be made mainly by experts.

28. Do you think the SST should be built? Yes__ No__ Why?

29. Does advanced technology contribute in any way to dehumanization? If you think so, explain.

30. Does advanced technology contribute in any way to overcompetitiveness? If you think so, explain.

31. How would you define progress for America? (For example, does it necessarily include a growing GNP; does it imply a change in quality of life, etc.?)

32. Check the issues you feel are the most important for Americans to face and resolve:

1. ____Bureaucracy
2. ____Ending the Vietnam war
3. ____Winning the Vietnam war
4. ____Strengthening the police
5. ____Humanizing the police
6. ____Tightening the enforcement of anti-drug laws
7. ____Legalizing marijuana
8. ____Reducing taxes
9. ____Guaranteed income for all Americans
10. ____Controlling inflation
11. ____White racism
12. ____Controlling rebellious youth
13. ____Improving black/white relations
14. ____Pollution of air and water
15. ____Fighting Communism
16. ____Guaranteed job opportunities
17. ____Developing low-cost housing
18. ____Better public transportation
19. ____Overinvestment in military expenditures
20. ____Strengthening national defense
21. ____Rebuilding cities
22. ____Militarism
23. ____Consumer mentality
24. ____Crime
25. ____Gun control
26. ____Parking shortages
27. ____Traffic
28. ____Overpopulation
29. ____Better care for old people
30. ____Ending big-government interference in local issues
31. ____Need for community control
32. ____Bringing the country together

33. Have you personally worked to solve any of these problems? If so, how?

34. Describe briefly the main changes you consider are needed in America.

35. Do you consider that professional politicians are, in general, qualified to resolve today's social problems?

36. If not, what kinds of people would be better qualified to do so?

a. ____Natural scientists
b. ____Social scientists
c. ____Bankers
d. ____Industrial managers
e. ____Lawyers
f. ____Military leaders
g. ____Religious leaders
h. ____Economists
i. ____Others: explain

37. What kinds of emphases, if any, do you consider are lacking in primary and secondary education? What changes, if any, would you suggest?

38. Describe your political philosophy, if any.

39. Check the statements that best express what you think:
   1. ___The company should take moral and political stands.
   2. ___The company should stay out of issues that don't concern it directly.
   3. ___The company should encourage and set up ways for employees to learn about, discuss, and take positions on social and political issues.
   4. ___Employees should not mix work with politics.

40. Do you think there are social and political issues on which your organization should take a stand? If yes, which ones? If no, why not?

41. How should the organization's position on political and social questions be decided? For example, essentially by the top management? By the top management in consultation with employees and stockholders? Through formal participation of employees? Etc.?

42. Do you think it would be a good idea for managers and engineers to belong to
   1. A strong professional association? Yes___ No___
   2. A union? Yes___ No___

D. PERSONAL VALUES

1. Name three persons, either living or historical figures, whom you most admire and briefly state why.
In the following questions we are particularly interested in your spontaneous emotional response. Therefore, give the answer that first occurs to you.

2. Which of the following are the 4 most important qualities or virtues for a man to have?

a. ___discipline	f. ___joy of life	k. ___honesty
b. ___love	g. ___cleanliness	l. ___sincerity
c. ___obedience	h. ___punctuality	m. ___intelligence
d. ___defense of honor	i. ___charity	n. ___moderation
e. ___patriotism	j. ___consideration of others	o. ___respect

3. Which of the above are the 4 most important qualities or virtues for a woman?

4. Which of the following are the 4 worst evils?

a. ___murder for gain   f. ___rape   k. ___greediness

b. ___murder out of passion   g. ___malicious gossip   l. ___dope selling

c. ___betrayal of a friend   h. ___drunkenness   m. ___taking drugs

d. ___robbery   i. ___adultery   n. ___cruelty to children

e. ___homosexuality   j. ___dirtiness

5. Which is a better quality for a wife to have? Cook well___ Keep a house neat___

6. What annoys you most? Too messy person___ Too neat person___

7. Are you in favor of capital punishment (death penalty)? Yes___ No___

8. How important do you feel it is for those who break the law to pay for their crimes?
Very important___ Somewhat important___ Not important___

9. Assume you saw a burglar running away from your house with some of your valuables. Would you
a. ___shoot to kill or wound him
b. ___shoot to scare him
c. ___let him go and call the police
d. ___do nothing

10. If you were to buy a new car and soon after found a scratch on the door, how upset would you be?
a. ___very upset
b. ___somewhat upset but not for long
c. ___a little upset
d. ___not upset

11. Is it irresponsible for a person to spend most of his income on food, pleasure, and travel and not save any money except for life insurance?
Yes___ No___

12. Do you think about how you want to be buried?
Often___ Sometimes___ No___

13. How many times a year should one visit the cemetery where loved ones are buried? ___

14. Do you agree that everyone has a right to live? Agree___ Disagree___

15. Do you agree that the fittest should survive? Agree___ Disagree___

16. Should everyone be provided with the minimal necessities of life, whether or not they work?
Yes, they should___ No, they should not___

17. Should men and women have the same rights? Yes___ No___

18. What should a man do if his wife is unfaithful?

19. What should a woman do if her husband is unfaithful?

20. What is your idea of a happy marriage?

The following questions concern your spiritual views and goals in life:

21. Do you believe in God? Yes___ No___

22. Do you have a religious affiliation? If so, which one? How often do you attend religious ceremonies?

23. Describe your basic religious or philosophical beliefs.

24. Has any religious or philosophic person—teacher, thinker, or writer—significantly influenced your life? Explain.

25. Has any other person—as teacher, coach, or superior at work—significantly influenced you or stimulated your development? Explain.

26. What is your concept of a good friend? What relationship in your life has come closest to this ideal?

27. What do you believe love is? (What is your concept of love?)

28. What is your goal in life?

E. OUTSIDE OF WORK

The following questions are about your family:

1. Describe briefly your wife and children.

2. How are your children doing at school?

3. Do you help them with homework? Yes___ No___

4. What stories, if any, do you tell your children?

5. What games, if any, do you play with your children?

6. Do you think learning to play a musical instrument is an important part of a child's development?

7. Do your children play any musical instruments?

8. Do you play a musical instrument? If yes, which one?

9. What cultural activities do you engage in with your family?

a. ___go to movies
b. ___play musical instruments together
c. ___sing together
d. ___visit museums
e. ___take trips
f. ___read together
g. ___discuss current events together
h. ___other _____

10. Do you think Little League sports are good for boys? Yes___ No___

11. Do you think Scouting is good for children? Yes___ No___

12. When was the last time that your children made you lose your temper and why?

13. What are the best ways of punishing children if they misbehave?

14. Do you ever threaten your children? If so, how? (For example, God will punish you; withholding privileges; money; not loving them; with the police, etc.)

15. Who is stricter with the children, you or your wife (husband)?

16. What bad habits, if any, do your children have?

17. If any of your children have bad habits, how do you explain them? (Do you think they were born with them? Did they inherit them from a relative? Is it the result of their education, etc.?)

18. How do you try to correct them?

19. What attitudes or behavior on the part of young people do you most disapprove of?

20. Do your children make you suffer? If so, how?

21. On what occasion do you feel happiest with your children?

22. Do you spend enough time with your family? Explain.

23. Is it necessary to sacrifice one's family for success in business.

24. Describe the qualities of a good mother.

25. Describe the qualities of a good father.

26. In what way, if any, are your children different from you in their attitudes toward life? (If your children are young, in what way do you expect them to have attitudes toward life that are different from yours?)

27. What profession or occupation would you most wish for your children?

Now some questions about your childhood:

28. Describe briefly what your parents (or substitutes) were like when you were a child:
Mother:
Father:

29. Describe your family situation as you were growing up. (In terms of family income, whether you lived in a city or a town, kind of neighborhood, religious background, any special national cultural background, whether family moved a great deal, etc.)

30. How are your present circumstances similar to or different from your family situation as you were growing up?

31. Which parent did you feel closer to and why?

32. Which parent did you fear the most and why?

33. Whose approval did you value the most and why?

34. Did you ever act against your mother's wishes in an important matter? If so, describe.

35. Did you ever act against your father's wishes in an important matter? If so, describe.

36. Were your parents divorced? Yes___ No___

37. Did one or more of your parents die before you grew up? If so, which parent and what was your age?

The following questions are about your leisure activities:

38. What do you do with your free time—your main satisfactions outside of work? Do you seek social activities outside of work that are useful for your career?

39. At what age do you plan to retire? ____ What are your thoughts about retirement?

40. Of the people you see socially outside of work, can you estimate what percentage are from your company and what percentage are not? ____From the company ____Not from the company

41. Do you know and meet managers from other organizations? ____Frequently ____Seldom ____Never

42. What books have you read recently?

43. What science fiction, if any, do you read?

44. Name a movie or play you enjoyed particularly and briefly state why. Was there a character in the movie or play with whom you sympathized most?

45. Which sports do you like best?_____
Which have you played and where (high school, college, etc.)?_____
Which do you watch on TV?

46. In general, how many hours of TV do you watch a week?

47. What kinds of TV programs do you like best? List examples:

48. Are you interested in good food?
Very much so (gourmet food)____ Moderately so____ Not particularly____

49. Do you take an interest in wines? Yes____ No____

50. What is (are) the make(s) and year(s) of your car(s)?

51. In what circumstances, if any, do you drink alcoholic drinks?
a. ____before dinner
b. ____after lunch
c. ____at meals
d. ____at parties
e. ____at social occasions in
f. ____general
g. ____when alone
____never

52. How many drinks do you usually have?

53. What kind of drink do you usually have?
    a. ___ beer   d. ___ martinis
    b. ___ wine   e. ___ other ___
    c. ___ whiskey

54. What effect does drinking have on you?
    a. ___ become more cheer-   d. ___ less inhibited
       ful   e. ___ more effective
    b. ___ get sad   f. ___ less effective
    c. ___ go to sleep

55. In what circumstances, if any, does your wife (husband) drink?
    a. ___ before dinner   e. ___ at social occasions in
    b. ___ after lunch   general
    c. ___ at meals   f. ___ when alone
    d. ___ at parties   g. ___ never

56. Are her (his) drinking habits different from yours? Yes ___ No ___ If so, in what way?

57. Do you smoke? Yes ___ No ___ If yes, how much?

58. Would you say that you have a problem about buying things that you don't really need?

59. Does your wife (husband) have a problem about buying things she (he) doesn't need?

60. Have you ever been in a Sensitivity Group or T-Group? Yes ___ No ___
    a. If so, was it arranged by your company? Yes ___ No ___
    b. If not at business, was your wife (husband) also at it? Yes ___ No ___
    c. Was it personally helpful to you? Yes ___ No ___
    d. Would you go again? Yes ___ No ___
    e. Do you feel, in general, that such groups are or would be helpful to the company in improving work relationships? Yes ___ No ___
    f. Do you feel they are dangerous? Yes ___ No ___

61. What is the earliest memory you have?

62. What was the saddest situation you have experienced?

63. What was the most embarrassing situation you can remember?

64. What experience in your life has been the happiest?

65. What have you felt most a failure?

66. Have you ever suffered an emotional disturbance? If so, what kind and what were the circumstances?

67. Is there any aspect of your personality and your work which you feel is not touched on in this questionnaire? If so, please describe.

Index

ABOUT THE AUTHOR

MICHAEL MACCOBY was born in 1933, and received a B.A. and Ph.D. from Harvard in social and clinical psychology before completing psychoanalytic training at the Mexican Institute of Psychoanalysis. Since 1969, he has been a fellow of the Institute for Policy Studies and Director of the Harvard Project on Technology, Work, and Character. He practices psychoanalysis in Washington, D.C., and is on the faculty of the Washington School of Psychiatry. He is a fellow of the American Anthropological Association and a member of the International Council for the Quality of Working Life. He is married and the father of four children.

MONEY TALKS!

How to get it and How to keep it!

Bantam Book Catalog

Here's your up-to-the-minute listing of every book currently available from Bantam.

This easy-to-use catalog is divided into categories and contains over 1400 titles by your favorite authors.

So don't delay—take advantage of this special opportunity to increase your reading pleasure.

Just send us your name and address and 25¢ (to help defray postage and handling costs).